NEW YORKER PROFILES 1925-1992

A Bibliography

Compiled by

Gail Shivel

University Press of America, ® Inc.
Lanham • New York • Oxford

University Press of America, ® Inc.
4720 Boston Way
Lanham, Maryland 20706

12 Hid's Copse Rd.
Cumnor Hill, Oxford OX2 9JJ

Library of Congress Cataloging-in-Publication Data

Shivel, Gail.
New Yorker Profiles, 1925-1992 : a bibliography / compiled by
Gail Shivel.
p.cm.
Includes index.
1.   United States—Biography—Bibliography. 2. Biography—20th
Century—Bibliography. 3. New Yorker (New York, N.Y.: 1925)
—Bibliography. I. Title.
Z5305.U5 S55   016 .920073—dc21   00-036417 CIP
(CT220)

ISBN 0-7618-1714-X (cloth: alk. ppr)

∞[TM] The paper used in this publication meets the minimum
requirements of American National Standard for Information
Sciences—Permanence of Paper for Printed Library Materials,
ANSI Z39.48—1984

Contents

Acknowledgments

I wish to thank Charles Elkins of Florida International University for his encouragement from the beginning of this project. I received many helpful comments from Maneck Daruwala and Phillip Marcus, also of Florida International University.

Many thanks are due, as always, to S.L. Harrison for his valuable ideas and advice, and for reading the manuscript.

Thanks also to Andy Grof of the Florida International University Library (University Park), Gail Gutten of the Otto G. Richter Library at the University of Miami, and Sonia Moss of the New York Public Library.

Introduction

The New Yorker 1925-1992

New Yorker Profiles and other biographical articles in the magazine combine journalism and biography, and often have the strengths and weaknesses of both disciplines. Journalism is of the moment, fleeting, and magazines themselves are ostensibly designed to be read and discarded; they are a vehicle for public taste and for timely advertising, and their messages must change. But *The New Yorker* long ago joined a select group of periodicals blessed with permanent relevance.

Advertising in the *New Yorker*, from 1925 on, reflects what a reader could expect in a periodical aimed at an elite audience: jewelry, automobiles, insurance and banking services, expensive clothing, cruises, real estate and posh hotels. Among the tony ads, one humble item occupied its page, for an obvious reason: the ubiquitous Fleischmann's yeast ad. Raoul Fleischmann bankrolled the *New Yorker*, and full-page ads for his company's yeast cakes appeared in virtually every issue for years; but those ads was never aimed at a reader who bakes. The *New Yorker* yeast ads are testimonials from smartly-dressed young people who improve complexion and digestion by eating raw cakes of Fleischmann's thrice daily.

In addition to being the targets of sophisticated advertising, readers of *The New Yorker* were "in the know" on subjects that were not fodder for the general press. In the 1930s, most people in the United States did not know Franklin Delano Roosevelt couldn't walk, and Roosevelt maintained carefully the illusion of relatively unimpaired mobility in all public appearances. In 1933, the second *New Yorker* Profile on Roosevelt contained, not merely a discreet reference to his disability, but several inches of extremely candid discussion of his polio-ravaged physical condition, including a graphic description of how the President had to be lifted from his wheelchair into his chair. In these trifling facts lies a wealth of information about who *The New Yorker* reader was.

The historical and cultural significance of *New Yorker* Profiles and other biographical articles lies not only in the interest of the people they describe, but in the evocation of the times in which they were written. Most of the Profiles were by professionally and socially active writers, describing people they had met and spoken with and sometimes knew well. A few were close friends of their subjects. Heywood Broun, Edmund Wilson and poet John Betjeman wrote Profiles on themselves; Hannah Arendt and Bertolt Brecht wrote each other's. *New Yorker* biographies, while many later ones exceed 6,000 words, began as brief essays that filled a page or two of the magazine. Many of the best were written before the publication had become conscious of itself as a literary and cultural influence. Barring a few Profiles that were "composites," and a few that were parody or outright fiction, *The New Yorker* maintained standards of journalistic integrity—not an oxymoron.

In July 1928 Ring Lardner wrote a spoof on playwright George S. Kaufman's wife, Beatrice, in which he made up a false maiden name for Mrs. Kaufman and otherwise had fun with his subject: not out of spite—Lardner and Kaufman were friends and occasional collaborators. The piece drew scorn, however, from Alexander Woollcott, who complained in a later issue that the occasion was the first time the "Spirit of Whimsy" had entered the Profiles. The fake Profile of Mrs. Kaufman failed to meet a standard that the magazine was already taking quite seriously; the only other whimsical materialization was in E.B. White's "Profile" in verse of Elinor Wylie.

Profiles of later years are much more than mere sketches and often contain a wealth of biographical material on their subjects. Many books, of course, appeared first in the pages of *The New Yorker,* either as saplings or in their full growth. All *New Yorker* biographical articles are included in this bibliography:

non-biographical Profiles are not. In the 1970s and 80s, more than forty articles appeared under the Profiles heading on non-human subjects–bananas, oil tankers, whales–well-written and sometimes great fun, but not germane to this bibliography. Biographical pieces that appeared under other headings, such as A Reporter at Large and Our Far-Flung Correspondents, are included because many of them are important; among them Lillian Ross' 1978 article on Sir Charles Chaplin; 1975 and 1979 treatments of Senator Edward Kennedy, and Robert A. Caro's three-part series on city planner Robert Moses, the initial appearance of his book on Moses.

Some background on the editorial history of *The New Yorker* is useful for understanding how the Profiles and other biographical pieces developed conceptually over time. The editorial history of *The New Yorker* is well-known, compared to that of other magazines, to the reading public. Harold Ross, its legendary founding editor, set the tone for the magazine, and his early conversations with yeast magnate Fleischmann brought *The New Yorker* to life. Thomas Kunkel's *Genius in Disguise: Harold Ross of The New Yorker* shows how under Ross, the Profiles were an integral part of the magazine, appearing in practically every issue for the first four years. In later years their frequency tapered off, but under Ross' editorship, the typical *New Yorker* Profiles were always concise, informative, often witty, sometimes sparkling.

After Ross' death in 1952, William Shawn succeeded Ross as editor. Shawn has been both praised and condemned diligently preserving–some would say embalming–what he found most important about the character of *The New Yorker*– its status as a cultural and intellectual presence. It was still not what it had originally been; nothing created in 1925 could have remained the same in 1955 and still have been relevant. Under Shawn's vigilance *New Yorker* pieces, including the Profiles, reached a solid and rather weighty maturity, increasing in scholarship and therefore in length. Still insightful, less often amusing, the Profiles gained in length and perhaps lost some of their former vivacity. The original *New Yorker* had occasionally been flippant, and sometimes even vicious; under Shawn there could be no "Spirit of Whimsy."

The story of how S.I. Newhouse took over *The New Yorker*

in the 1980s is well known; Peter Fleischmann, son of founding publisher Raoul Fleischmann, let the magazine go because, as editors and top managers had often through the years been given stock as bonuses, the Fleischmann family no longer held a controlling interest. Newhouse's father had expressed interest in buying *The New Yorker* some years before to the elder Fleischmann, who dismissed the offer. The desire to own the magazine amounted to a minor obsession for Newhouse, who saw the venerable publication as a status symbol that would presumably bring with it some intellectual aura that his newspapers and his other magazines, including *Vanity Fair* and *Vogue,* could never have.

As new owner, Newhouse abruptly dismissed Shawn, who had been editor for more than thirty years, replacing him with Robert Gottlieb, an editor at Alfred A. Knopf, another of Newhouse's acquisitions. Several members of a distressed *New Yorker* editorial staff wrote a futile letter of protest, rejecting Gottlieb's appointment. Gottlieb entered his new position in the worst possible atmosphere thanks to Newhouse's bungling of Shawn's "retirement," and after decades of an insulated existence, the *New Yorker* staff was at odds with its editor.

Under its third editor, a disgruntled and dismayed *New Yorker* staff continued to produce good journalism, but editorial direction was unsure. Gottlieb's influence on the Profiles, as on other portions of the magazine, was limited to a reining-in of the tremendous multi-issue length characteristic of Shawn's tenure. Thomas Maier notes for example in *Newhouse* that Ved Mehta's "Daddyji," commissioned during Shawn's editorship and completed during Gottlieb's, was envisioned as a long series but wound up considerably shortened to appear in one issue instead of three. The staff's loyalty to Shawn and the egregious way his replacement was handled continued to be a problem. Also, Gottlieb was essentially a book editor, not a journalist. Gottlieb wrote of his predecessor: "Perhaps his most significant contribution to journalism lay in the triumph of his passionate and un-cynical view of what a publication and its readers can mean to each other–a view unique in our time."

In 1992, Newhouse removed Gottlieb and replaced him with Tina Brown, former editor of his *Vanity Fair.* Maier reports that Brown said of Gottlieb: "He was not a journalist, and I think you need to be. Shawn was a great journalist. You have to be a great journalist to organize it." Both Gottlieb and Brown knew what a strong editor can mean to a magazine. However well or ill either provided that direction, both were aware, as Newhouse was not, that a coherent, confident editorial vision coupled with journalistic excellence had made *The New Yorker* different from other magazines. The resulting homogenization of *The New Yorker* attests to what happens when the publisher, who after all is usually in the business to make money, has too much influence over the decisions that are best left to editors. Under Ross the magazine had blossomed and under Shawn had held a steady if staid course; under Gottlieb and especially Brown, the editor belonged to the publisher and the change was noticeable.

In March 1998, newspaper columnist William Pfaff, a *New Yorker* contributor from 1971 to 1985, wrote in the Baltimore *Sun:* "Ms. Brown, who is undoubtedly the most brilliant tabloid editor of her day, took the magazine downmarket, making it a brilliant and vulgar celebrity, gossip and insider-dope politics magazine." Pfaff, one of the several *New Yorker* staff members who left after Gottlieb replaced Shawn, concluded: "Since Mr. Newhouse and Ms. Brown have been in charge, when the only reason for publishing the magazine has been to make money, it has lost $100 million. The old *New Yorker* has its revenge." Brown left *The New Yorker* in 1999 and was replaced as editor by David Remnick, formerly with the *Washington Post*.

My aim has been to make *New Yorker* biographical articles more accessible for researchers. The author index that follows the list of subjects includes for most of the writers a short list of their works; for major writers who contributed few Profiles, including James Thurber and E.B. White, this information, readily available elsewhere, is omitted. Viewing this assembly of citations of biographical articles under the magazine's first three editors, seeing it all in one place, must lead to all sorts of observations and ruminations, the seeds of scholarly endeavor. *The New Yorker* is a seminal text in American literature and culture, and with time will increase in importance as a key to understanding some portion of twentieth century intellectual life.

Gail Shivel

New Yorker Profiles 1925-1992

Subjects are arranged alphabetically by name, followed by a brief description of the subject's profession or other identification. An asterisk (*) indicates that the article was not a Profile proper but appeared under another heading.

Abrams, Charles
City planner
"A Lover of Cities"
Feb. 4, 1967 (39-91)
Feb. 11, 1967 (45-115)
Vol. 42 Nos. 50-51
Bernard Taper

Ace, Goodman
Radio/TV comedy writer
"Goody"
April 4, 1977 (41-80)
Vol. 53 No. 7
Mark Singer

Achelis, Elisabeth
Permanent-calendar
advocate
"Lady With a Cause"
Dec. 30, 1939 (21-25)
Vol. 15 No. 46
Geoffrey T. Hellman

Acheson, Dean Gooderham
U.S. Secretary of State
"Mr. Secretary"
Nov. 12, 1949 (38-53)
Nov. 19, 1949 (40-61)
Vol. 25 Nos. 38-39
Philip Hamburger

Ackerman, Robert Allen
Theater director
"Moment"
July 7, 1980 (39-57)
Vol. 56 No. 20
James Stevenson

Acord, James L. Jr.
Sculptor
"Moving to Richland"
Oct. 14, 1991 (59-96)
Oct. 21, 1991 (62-107)
Vol. 67 Nos. 34-35
Philip Schuyler

Adams, Charles Francis
Lawyer, politician,
yachtsman
"The Scholarly Skipper"
Sept. 4, 1926 (17-18)
Vol. 2 No. 29
James Robbins

Adams, Evangeline Smith
Astrologer
"Lady of the Stars"
October 27, 1928 (28-32)
Vol. 4 No. 36
Alva Johnston

Adams, Gridley
Chairman, National Flag
Code Committee
"Three Cheers For the
Blue, White, and Red"
July 5, 1952 (29-44)
Vol. 28 No. 20
E. J. Kahn, Jr.

Adams, Ted
Cockney flower-seller
"Dashin' About"
Feb. 25, 1974 (42-81)
Vol. 50 No. 1
Thomas Whiteside

Adler, Dr. Alfred
Psychiatrist, translator
of Freud
"Viennese Visitor"
May 5, 1928 (29-31)
Vol. 4 No. 11
Lola Jean Simpson

Adler, Larry
Harmonica player
"Big-Time Urchin"
July 18, 1942 (19-28)
Vol. 18 No. 22
Margaret Case Harriman

Aldrich, Richard S.
Summer theater producer
"The Level Head"
July 30, 1955 (31-43)
August 6, 1955 (27-47)
Vol. 31 Nos. 24-25
Robert Lewis Taylor

Allen, Kelcey
Drama critic, *Women's
Wear Daily*
"How to Be a Critic"
March 11, 1944 (30-47)
Vol. 20 No. 4
Wolcott Gibbs

Allen, Henry "Red"
Jazz trumpet player
"The Blues is a Slow
Story"
June 25, 1966 (33-52)
Vol. 42 No. 18
Whitney Balliett

Allen, Terry de la Mesa
Major General, U.S. Army
"Find 'em, Fix 'em, and
Fight 'em"
April 24, 1943 (22-26)
May 1, 1943 (24-30)
Vol. 19 Nos.10-11
A.J. Liebling

Allen, Woody
Film director, writer, actor
"Guilty, With an
Explanation"
February 4, 1974 (39-44)
Vol. 49 No. 50
Penelope Gilliatt

Allers, Franz
Conductor
"Four Hundred and Forty
Vibrations"
April 2, 1960 (47-80)
Vol. 36 No. 7
Joseph Wechsberg

Ames, Winthrop
Theater producer
"Bostonian Through the
Looking-Glass"
October 19, 1929 (30-33)
Vol. 5 No. 35
Niven Busch, Jr.

Ammann, Othmar Hermann
Bridge engineer
"Poet in Steel"
June 2, 1934 (23-27)
Vol. 10 No. 16
Milton MacKaye

Amsden, Sherman Culver
Head of telephone
answering service
"The Man Who Answers
Telephones"
April 22, 1939 (21-27)
Vol. 15 No. 10
Jack Alexander

Anastos, Peter
Choreographer
"The Tiresias Factor"
May 28, 1990 (41-64)
Vol. 66 No. 15
Arlene Croce

Anderson, Margaret
Publisher; serialized
Joyce's *Ulysses* in *The
Little Review*
"A Life on a Cloud"
June 3, 1974 (44-67)
Vol. 50 No. 15
Janet Flanner

Andreas, Dwayne Orville
CEO, Archer Daniels
Midland
"The Absolute Beginning"
Feb. 16, 1987 (41-68)
Vol. 62 No. 52
E.J. Kahn, Jr.

Andrews, Roy Chapman
Explorer; scientist
"Hunter of the Snark"
June 29, 1929 (22-25)
Vol. 5 No. 19
Helena Huntington Smith

Anthoine, Mo
Mountain climber
"Feeding the Rat"
April 18, 1988 (89-115)
Vol. 64 No. 9
A. Alvarez

Arader, W. Graham III
Art dealer
"Wall Power"
Nov. 30, 1987 (44-97)
Vol. 63 No. 41
Mark Singer

Arcaro, Edward
Jockey
"One Jump to Four Miles"
July 30, 1938 (16-21)
Vol. 14 No. 24
A.J. Liebling

Arendt, Hannah
Author; philosopher
Nov. 5, 1966 (68-122)
Vol. 42 No. 37
Bertolt Brecht

Arikha, Avigdor
Artist
"Painting Dervish"
June 1, 1987 (37-56)
Vol. 63 No. 15
Dan Hofstadter

Armajani, Siah
   Artist; designer of the
   Whitney Bridge
   "Open, Available, Useful"
   March 19, 1990 (48-72)
   Vol. 66 No. 5
   Calvin Tomkins

Arnold, Paul Dean
   Bakery owner
   "The Restless Baker"
   Dec. 14, 1957 (49-80)
   Vol. 33 No. 43
   Robert Lewis Taylor

Arnold, Stanley N.
   Marketing consultant
   "They Bought It!"
   October 29, 1960 (51-85)
   Vol. 36 No. 37
   Geoffrey T. Hellman

Arnstein, Daniel G.
   U.S. Ambassador to
   China; expert on the
   Burma Road
   "Hu Shih's Musketeer"
   January 10, 1942 (22-27)
   January 17, 1942 (23-32)
   Vol. 17 Nos. 48-49
   John Bainbridge

Ashe, Arthur
   Tennis player
   "Levels of the Game"
   June 7, 1969 (45-111)
   June 14, 1969 (45-81)
   Vol. 45 Nos. 16-17
   John McPhee

Astor, (William) Vincent
   Real estate investor
   "The Golden Spoon"
   March 5, 1938 (22-27)
   March 12, 1938 (25-29)
   Vol. 14 Nos. 3-4
   Jack Alexander

Atlas, Charles
   Body-builder
   "I Was Once a 97-Pound
   Weakling"
   January 3, 1942 (21-27)
   Vol. 17 No. 47
   Robert Lewis Taylor

Auden, W.H.
   Poet
   * Reflections
   "Remembering Wystan H.
   Auden, Who Died in the
   Night of the Twenty-
   Eighth of September,
   1973"
   January 20, 1975 (39-46)
   Vol. 50 No. 48
   Hannah Arendt

Auer, Leopold
   Violin professor, teacher
   of Zimbalist, Heifetz,
   Elman
   "Master of Masters"
   April 27, 1929 (24-27)
   Vol. 5 No. 10
   Helena Huntington Smith

Avedon, Richard
Fashion photographer
"A Woman Entering a
Taxi in the Rain"
Nov. 8, 1958 (49-84)
Vol. 34 No. 38
Winthrop Sargeant

Avinoff, Andrey
Lepidopterist; painter
"Black Tie and
Cyanide Jar"
August 21, 1948 (32-47)
Vol. 24 No. 26
Geoffrey T. Hellman

Babson, Roger W.
Businessman, predicted
the October 1929 crash
"Prophet of Doom"
Feb. 15, 1930 (23-25)
Vol. 5 No. 52
Henry F. Pringle

Bach, Jean
Author; radio producer
"City Voices"
July 18, 1983 (39-48)
Vol. 59 No. 22
Whitney Balliett

Bach, Richard F.
Industrial arts specialist,
Metropolitan Museum
"A Man, a Museum—and
Their Secret Vice"
Sept. 12, 1925 (22)
Vol. 1 No. 30
Murdock Pemberton

Baedeker, Karl Friedrich
Publisher, Baedeker travel
guides; great-grandson of
founder
"The House of Baedeker"
Sept. 22, 1975 (42-93)
Vol. 51 No. 31
Herbert Warren Wind

Baer, Max Adalbert
Heavyweight boxer
"Prizefighter to
Gentleman—En Route"
June 9, 1934 (20-24)
Vol. 10 No. 17
Paul Gallico

Bagby, Albert Morris
Arts patron; socialite
"Musical Mornings"
Dec. 31, 1938 (21-27)
Vol. 14 No. 46
Mary Van Rensselear
Thayer

Baker, George "Father Divine"
Minister
"Who is this King of
Glory?"
June 13, 1936 (21-28)
June 20, 1936 (22-28)
June 27, 1936 (22-36)
Vol. 12 Nos. 17-19
St. Clair McKelway and
A.J. Liebling

Baker, James
    Secretary of State, Bush
    Administration
    May 7, 1990 (50-82)
    Vol. 66 No. 12
    John Newhouse

Balanchine, George
    Choreographer, New York
    City Ballet
    "Choreographer"
    April 16, 1960 (49-131)
    April 23, 1960 (51-115)
    Vol. 36 Nos. 9-10
    Bernard Taper

    "An Eternal Present"
    October 22, 1973 (48-90)
    Vol. 49 No. 35
    Bernard Taper

Baldwin, Joseph Clark III
    U.S. Congressman,
    New York County
    "The Festive Touch"
    Feb. 27, 1943 (22-32)
    March 6, 1943 (26-39)
    Vol. 19 Nos. 2-3
    Geoffrey T. Hellman

Baldwin, Roger Nash
    Founder, American Civil
    Liberties Union
    "The Defense of
    Everybody"
    July 11, 1953 (31-55)
    July 18, 1953 (29-59)
    Vol. 29 Nos. 21-22
    Dwight Macdonald

Bamberger, J. David
    Rancher, conservationist
    "A Place and an Attitude"
    January 21, 1991 (64-76)
    Vol. 66 No. 49
    Emily Hahn

Bankhead, Tallulah
    Actress
    "Making a Noise in the
    World"
    Oct. 7, 1972 (45-99)
    Oct. 14, 1972 (50-122)
    Vol. 48 Nos. 33-34
    Brendan Gill

Barnard, George Grey
    Sculptor
    "Sculpture, Not
    Machinery"
    January 17, 1931 (26-29)
    Vol. 6 No. 48
    Babette Deutsch

Barnell, Jane
    "Bearded lady,"
    circus sideshow
    "Lady Olga"
    August 3, 1940 (20-28)
    Vol. 16 No. 25
    Joseph Mitchell

Barnes, Dr. Albert C.
    Art collector, Barnes
    Foundation (Philadelphia)
    "De Medici in Merion"
    Sept. 22, 1928 (29-34)
    Vol. 4 No. 31
    A.H. Shaw

Barr, Alfred H., Jr.
Director of Collections,
Museum of Modern Art
"Action of West Fifty-
Third Street"
Dec. 12, 1953 (49-82)
Dec. 19, 1953 (35-72)
Vol. 29 No. 43-44
Dwight Macdonald

Barry, Philip
Playwright
"The Dark Advantage"
Sept. 15, 1975 (42-92)
Vol. 51 No. 30
Brendan Gill

Barstow, Richard
Director and choreogra-
pher, Ringling Brothers &
Barnum & Bailey Circus
"Evolution of an Iron-
Toed Boy"
April 20, 1957 (41-76)
April 27, 1957 (39-65)
Vol. 33 No. 9-10
Robert Lewis Taylor

Bartlett, Frederic Huntington
Pediatrician; author
"Emergencies, Advice for"
July 15, 1944 (26-32)
Vol. 20 No. 22
Brendan Gill

Bartlett, Jennifer
Artist
"Getting Everything In"
April 15, 1985 (50-68)
Vol. 61 No. 8
Calvin Tomkins

Barton, Bruce
Author; advertising
executive
"It Pays to Preach"
Nov. 1, 1930 (21-24)
Vol. 6 No. 37
Richard Fay Warner

Baruch, Bernard Mannes
Financier
"Ulysses Ashore–For a
While"
August 7, 1926 (15-16)
Vol. 2 No. 25
Arthur Krock

"The Old Man"
January 3, 1948 (28-37)
January 10, 1948 (30-40)
January 17, 1948 (30-41)
Vol. 23 Nos. 46-48
John Hersey

Basquette, Lina
Motion picture actress
"Godless Girl"
Feb. 13, 1989 (54-73)
Vol. 64 No. 52
Barry Paris

Bates, B.L.M.
Owner, Murray Hill Hotel
"Plush and Gaslight"
June 15, 1929 (23-26)
Vol. 5 No. 17
Joseph Gollomb

Battle, George Gordon
Lawyer; philanthropist;
chairman of many fund-
raising committees
"Mr. Chairman"
March 11, 1933 (21-25)
Vol. 9 No. 4
Geoffrey T. Hellman

Beard, Daniel Carter
National Commissioner,
Boy Scouts of America;
illustrator
"Vanishing American"
July 23, 1932 (17-20)
Vol. 8 No. 23
Joel Sayre

Bearden, Romare
Painter
"Putting Something Over
Something Else"
Nov. 28, 1977 (53-77)
Vol. 53 No. 41
Calvin Tomkins

Beebe, Lucius
Society newspaper
columnist
"The Diamond Gardenia"
Nov. 20, 1937 (24-29)
Nov. 27, 1937 (25-29)
Vol. 13 No. 40-41
Wolcott Gibbs

Beerbohm, Sir (Max) Henry
Maximilian
Writer, caricaturist, critic
"Conversations
With Max"
Feb. 6, 1960 (45-80)
Feb. 13, 1960 (40-82)
Feb. 20, 1960 (50-90)
Feb. 27, 1960 (43-91)
March 5, 1960 (47-111)
March 12, 1960 (59-104)
March 19, 1960 (50-104)
Vol. 35 Nos. 51-52 and
Vol 36 Nos. 1-5
S.N. Behrman

Beery, Wallace
Motion picture actor;
comedian
"Jumbo"
Nov. 9, 1935 (22-27)
Vol. 11 No. 39
Alva Johnston

Belasco, David
   Theatrical producer
   "The Great
   Impersonation"
   October 18, 1930 (30-33)
   October 25, 1930 (30-33)
   Vol. 6 No. 35-36
   Niven Busch, Jr.

Bellanca, Giuseppe Mario
   Aviator
   "Wings Over America"
   March 30, 1929 (22-25)
   Vol. 5 No. 6
   William Weimar

Bellet, Robert
   Chief purser, S.S. *Liberté*
   "Creating an
   Atmosphere"
   August 17, 1957 (35-78)
   Vol. 33 No. 26
   Joseph Wechsberg

Benetton, Luciano
   Head, Maglificio di
   Ponzano Veneto deo
   Fratelli Benetton
   "Being Everywhere"
   Nov. 10, 1986 (53-74)
   Vol. 62 No. 38
   Andrea Lee

Benford, Tommy
   Drummer
   "New York Drummers"
   Nov. 5, 1979 (52-76)
   Vol. 55 No. 38
   Whitney Balliett

Benjamin, Mary A.
   Autograph dealer
   "What a Moment! What
   a Feeling!"
   Dec. 5, 1959 (57-92)
   Vol. 35 No. 42
   Morton M. Hunt

Bennet, Robert Russell
   Musical comedy
   orchestrator
   "Another Opening,
   Another Show"
   Nov. 17, 1951 (46-73)
   Vol. 27 No. 39
   Herbert Warren Wind

Bennett, Tony
   Popular singer
   "A Quality That Lets
   You In"
   January 7, 1974 (33-43)
   Vol. 49 No. 46
   Whitney Balliett

Benson, Richard
   Photographer;
   MacArthur Fellow
   "A Single Person Making a
   Single Thing"
   Dec. 17, 1990 (48-71)
   Vol. 66 No. 44
   Calvin Tomkins

Bergman, Ingrid
    Motion picture actor
    "The Player"
    Oct. 21, 1961 (100-103)
    Vol. 37 No. 36
    Lillian Ross

Berle, Adolf Augustus, Jr.
    U.S. Assistant Secretary
    of State
    "Atlas With Ideas"
    January 16, 1943 (22-30)
    January 23, 1943 (22-23)
    Vol. 18 Nos. 48-49
    John McCarten

Bernier, Rosamond
    Lecturer on Fine Arts
    "Stage Pictures"
    January 19, 1987 (38-51)
    Vol. 62 No. 48
    Calvin Tomkins
Bernstein, Leonard
    Conductor, New York
    Philharmonic; composer
    "The Pervasive Musician"
    January 11, 1958 (37-63)
    January 18, 1958 (35-65)
    Vol. 33 Nos. 47-48
    Robert Rice

Bethe, Hans Albrecht
    Theoretical physicist
    "Master of the Trade"
    Dec. 3, 1979 (50-107)
    Dec. 10, 1979 (52-108)
    Dec. 17, 1979 (48-99)
    Vol. 55 Nos. 42-44
    Jeremy Bernstein

Betjeman, John
    Poet
    "Summoned by Bells"
    August 27, 1960 (31-42)
    Vol. 36 No. 28
    John Betjeman

Biddle, Anthony Joseph
Dexter Jr.
    U.S. Ambassador to
    foreign governments
    in London
    "The Omnibus Diplomat"
    June 6, 1942 (22-30)
    June 13, 1942 (23-35)
    June 20, 1942 (23-32)
    Vol. 18 Nos. 16-18
    A.J. Liebling

Biddle, George
    Painter
    "Groton, Harvard, and
    Tahiti"
    May 30, 1936 (20-25)
    Vol. 12 No. 15
    Geoffrey T. Hellman

Bimstein, Morris
    Prizefight second
    "The Man in the Corner"
    March 20, 1937 (30-35)
    Vol. 13 No. 5
    A.J. Liebling

Bing, Rudolph
  General manager,
  Metropolitan Opera
  Company
  "The General Manager"
  Sept. 17, 1966 (65-124)
  Vol. 42 No. 30
  Joseph Wechsberg

Birdwell, Russell (Juarez)
  Press agent
  "Public Relations"
  August 19, 1944 (22-28)
  August 26, 1944 (26-34)
  Sept. 2, 1944 (24-28)
  Sept. 9, 1944 (30-38)
  Vol. 20 Nos. 27-30
  Alva Johnston

Birkhead, Leon Milton
  National Director, Friends
  of Democracy, Inc.
  "Democracy's Friend"
  July 26, 1947 (28-39)
  August 2, 1947 (28-39)
  August 9, 1947 (27-38)
  Vol. 23 No. 23-25
  Ely Jaques Kahn

Bishop, Howard Berkey
  Anti-tobacco crusader
  "On the Formula"
  Sept. 1, 1945 (25-35)
  Vol. 21 No. 29
  Andy Logan

Blackburn, Harold Fredric
  Pilot, Trans World
  Airlines
  "You Come and Go"
  May 5, 1956 (38-78)
  Vol. 32 No. 11
  John Bainbridge

  "Like a Homesick Angel"
  Nov. 10, 1962 (61-145)
  Vol. 38 No. 38
  John Bainbridge

Blair, Bruce
  Veterinarian
  "Dog's Best Friend"
  Dec. 3, 1938 (27-33)
  Vol. 14 No. 42
  Geoffrey T. Hellman

Blanton, Henry
  Ranch foreman
  "Cowboy"
  May 30, 1977 (44-83)
  June 6, 1977 (40-91)
  Vol. 53 Nos. 15-16
  Jane Kramer

Bloch, Ernest
  Composer
  "Madness and Music"
  Sept. 11, 1926 (25-26)
  Vol. 2 No. 30
  "Searchlight"
  (Waldo Frank)

Block, Martin
    Radio disc jockey
    "Socko!"
    July 29, 1944 (27-37)
    Vol. 20 No. 24
    Philip Hamburger

Bloom, Sol
    U.S. Congressman (N.Y.)
    "I Know My Washington"
    Feb. 20, 1932 (24-27)
    Vol. 8 No. 1
    Robert Sharon Allen

Blumenthal, Alfred Cleveland
    Real estate, theater
    promoter
    "Blumey"
    Feb. 4, 1933 (19-23)
    Feb. 11, 1933 (21-24)
    Vol. 8 Nos. 51-52
    Alva Johnston

Bob and Ray *see* Elliott,
Robert Brackett and
Goulding, Raymond Walter

Bob, Charles V.
    Promoter, financier
    "South Pole Charlie"
    July 4, 1931 (22-25)
    Vol. 7 No. 20
    Alva Johnston

Bocher, Main
    Fashion designer
    "Pioneer"
    January 13, 1940 (24-28)
    Vol. 15 No. 48
    Janet Flanner

Bodanzky, Arthur
    Conductor (retired),
    Metropolitan Opera
    "Alt Wien"
    March 15, 1930 (23-26)
    Vol. 6 No. 4
    Hollister Noble

Bogdanov, Peter Alexyevitch
    Chairman, Amtorg Group,
    U.S.S.R.
    "Bolshevik Businessman"
    July 15, 1933 (16-20)
    Vol. 9 No. 22
    William C. White

Boomer, Lucius
    President, hotel and
    restaurant chain
    "Front Boy"
    Sept. 24, 1927 (22-24)
    Vol. 3 No. 32
    Niven Busch, Jr.

Booth, Evangeline
    Commander, Salvation
    Army; daughter of
    founder
    "The Commander"
    June 21, 1930 (22-25)
    Vol. 6 No. 18
    Virgilia Peterson Ross

Boothe, Clare
Playwright; actress; U.S.
Ambassador to Italy
"The Candor Kid"
January 4, 1941 (21-29)
January 11, 1941 (24-32)
Vol. 16 Nos. 47-48
Margaret Case Harriman

Borge, Victor
Pianist; comedian;
poultry breeder
"Birds in the Hand"
May 7, 1955 (51-87)
Vol. 31 No. 12
Geoffrey T. Hellman

Borotra, Jean
Tennis player
"D'Artagnan of the
Courts"
Sept. 6, 1930 (24-27)
Vol. 6 No. 29
J.R. Tunis

Bostwick, (Pete) George H.
Polo player
"Polo's Little Man"
Sept. 3, 1938 (18-22)
Vol. 14 No. 29
Meyer Berger

Boulez, Pierre
Composer, conductor
"Taking Leave of
Predecessors "
March 24, 1973 (45-71)
March 31, 1973 (45-75)
Vol. 49 Nos. 5-6
Peter Heyworth

Bowie, Walter Russell
Pastor, Grace Episcopal
Church
"The Gentleman in the
Pulpit"
October 22, 1938 (27-33)
Vol. 14 No. 36
Richard Owen Boyer

Bowlby, Dr. Harry Laity
General secretary, Lord's
Day Alliance of the U.S.
(Sunday blue laws)
"Red, White, and Blue"
Sept. 28, 1929 (30-33)
Vol. 5 No. 32
Henry F. Pringle

Bowman, John McEntee
Director, Bowman
Biltmore Hotels
Corporation
"The Amiable Innkeeper"
Nov. 12, 1927 (25-27)
Vol. 3 No. 39
William Weimar

Boyden, Frank Learoyd
  Headmaster, Deerfield
  Academy
  "The Headmaster"
  March 19, 1966 (57-159)
  Vol. 42 No. 4
  John McPhee

Braddell, Maurice
  Actor
  "Taking it All In"
  January 13, 1986 (33-49)
  Vol. 61 No. 47
  James Lardner

Bradley, Edward Riley
  Horse breeder;
  casino owner
  "Idle Hour Man"
  January 19, 1935 (21-26)
  Vol. 10 No. 49
  David B. Campbell

Bradley, General Omar
Nelson
  General, U.S. Army;
  Chairman, Joint Chiefs
  of Staff
  "Five-Star Schoolmaster"
  March 3, 1951 (38-75)
  March 10, 1951 (40-77)
  Vol. 27 Nos. 3-4
  A.J. Liebling

Bradley, William Warren
  Basketball player
  "A Sense of Where
  You Are"
  January 23, 1965 (40-91)
  Vol. 40 No. 49
  John McPhee

Brady, James Buchanan
  ("Diamond Jim")
  Celebrity
  "That Was New York"
  October 17, 1931 (21-24)
  Vol. 7 No. 35
  Gilbert Seldes

Braff, Ruby
  Jazz trumpeter
  "The Center of the Note"
  July 8, 1974 (41-47)
  Vol. 50 No. 20
  Whitney Balliett

Brando, Marlon
  Motion picture actor
  "The Duke in His
  Domain"
  Nov. 9, 1957 (53-100)
  Vol. 33 No. 38
  Truman Capote

Brandt, Willy
  West German Chancellor
  "The Outsider"
  January 14, 1974 (35-57)
  Vol. 49 No. 47
  Joseph Wechsberg

Braque, Georges
  Painter
  "Master"
  October 6, 1956 (49-83)
  October 13, 1956 (50-97)
  Vol. 32 Nos. 33-34
  Janet Flanner

Brathwaite, Fred ("Fab Five
Freddy")
  Rapper; painter; host,
  "Yo! MTV Raps"
  "Living Large"
  June 17, 1991 (41-55)
  Vol. 67 No. 17
  Susan Orlean

Brealey, John M.
  Chairman, Department of
  Paintings Conservation,
  Metropolitan Museum of
  Fine Arts
  "Colored Muds in a Sticky
  Substance"
  March 16, 1987 (44-70)
  Vol. 63 No. 4
  Calvin Tomkins

Brecht, Bertolt
  Playwright
  "What is Permitted
  to Jove"
  Nov. 5, 1966 (68-122)
  Vol. 42 No. 37
  Hannah Arendt

Brecker, Lewis J.
  Owner, Roseland
  dance hall
  "Home of Refined
  Dancing"
  June 27, 1942 (22-29)
  Vol. 18 No. 19
  John Kobler

Breder, Charles M., Jr.
  Icthyologist; director of
  New York City aquarium
  "Behind the Tanks"
  February 5, 1938 (18-23)
  Vol. 13 No. 51
  A.J. Liebling

Brennan, William
  U.S. Supreme Court Justice
  "The Constitutionalist"
  March 12, 1990 (45-70)
  Vol. 66 No. 4
  Nat Hentoff

Brewster, Kingman
  U.S. Ambassador
  * Our Far-Flung
  Correspondents
  "Excellency"
  Dec. 12, 1977 (141-152)
  Vol. 53 No. 43
  John Bainbridge

Brice, Fanny
  Entertainer
  "Fire Sign"
  April 20, 1929 (25-27)
  Vol. 5 No. 9
  Niven Busch, Jr.

Brill, Dr. Abraham Arden
  Psychiatrist, translator of
  Freud's works
  "Joyful Wisdom"
  October 17, 1925 (11-12)
  Vol. 1 No. 35
  "Search-light"
  (Waldo Frank)

Brinkley, David
  Television news
  correspondent
  "An Accident of Casting"
  August 3, 1968 (34-60)
  Vol. 44 No. 24
  William Whitworth

Broderick, John J.
  Detective, N.Y.C. Police
  "Wham! Pow! Zowie!"
  Dec. 26, 1931 (18-21)
  Vol. 7 No. 45
  Joel Sayre

Brooks, Louise
  Motion picture actress
  "The Girl in the Black
  Helmet"
  June 11, 1979 (45-78)
  Vol. 55 No. 17
  Kenneth Tynan

Brooks, Mel
  Filmmaker, comedian
  "Frolics and Detours of a
  Short Hebrew Man"
  Oct. 30, 1978 (46-130)
  Vol. 54 No. 37
  Kenneth Tynan

Brophy, Thomas Patrick
  N.Y.C. Chief Fire Marshall
  "Firebug-Catcher"
  January 18, 1936 (18-23)
  January 25, 1936 (20-24)
  Vol. 11 Nos. 49-50
  St. Clair McKelway

Broun, Heywood
  Newspaper columnist
  "The Rabbit That Bit the
  Bulldog"
  October 1, 1927 (18-22)
  Vol. 3 No. 33
  "R.A."
  (Heywood Broun)

Browder, Earl Russell
  General Secretary, U.S.
  Communist Party
  "Party Linesman"
  Sept. 24, 1938 (22-26)
  October 1, 1938 (24-29)
  Vol. 14 Nos. 32-33
  John McCarten

Brower, David
  Conservationist
  "Encounters With the
  Archdruid"
  March 20, 1971 (42-91)
  March 27, 1971 (42-80)
  April 3, 1971 (41-93)
  Vol. 47 Nos. 5-7
  John McPhee

Brown, Bill
Health farm owner;
member, N.Y. State
Athletic Commission
"Farm and Ringside"
May 18, 1935 (23-28)
Vol. 11 No. 14
Earl Sparling

Brown, J. Carter
Director, National Gallery
of Art (Washington, D.C.)
"For the Nation"
Sept. 3, 1990 (48-90)
Vol. 66 No. 29
Calvin Tomkins

Brown, Joe E.
Comedian; actor
"Comedy"
July 7, 1945 (26-33)
Vol. 21 No. 21
Alva Johnston

Brown, John Mason
Critic,author, lecturer
"Circuit Rider"
October 18, 1952 (44-81)
October 25, 1952 (39-73)
Vol. 28 No. 35-36
Herbert Warren Wind

Brown, William Montgomery
Communist, former
Bishop of Arkansas
"Benign Heretic"
January 23, 1926 (17-18)
Vol. 1 No. 49
Charles W. Wood

Brubeck, David Warren
Jazz pianist; orchestra
leader
"The Cleanup Man"
June 3, 1961 (41-89)
Vol. 37 No. 16
Robert Rice

Bruce, Arthur Loring *see*
Crowninshield, Frank

Brundage, Avery
President, International
Olympic Committee
"Amateur"
July 23, 1960 (28-70)
Vol. 36 No. 23
Robert Shaplen

Brunet, Pierre
New York Skating Club
"Philosophy and Figure
Eights"
Dec. 25, 1954 (28-41)
Vol. 30 No. 45
Robert Lewis Taylor

Bryan, William Jennings
Orator, politician, real
estate speculator
"Silver-Tongue"
June 13, 1925 (9-10)
Vol. 1 No. 17
Charles Willis Thompson

Brzezinski, Zbigniew
National security advisor
to President Carter
* A Reporter at Large
"Brzezinski"
May 1, 1978 (90-130)
Vol. 54 No. 11
Elizabeth Drew

Buchanan, Edna
Crime reporter
"Covering the Cops"
Feb. 17, 1986 (39-57)
Vol. 61 No. 52
Calvin Trillin

Buchman, Frank Nathan
Daniel
Evangelistic minister
"Soul Surgeon"
April 23, 1932 (22-25)
Vol. 8 No. 10
Alva Johnston

Buchter, Jacob
Chief electrician,
Metropolitan Opera
Company
"The Whole Thing is All
With Lights"
Nov. 15, 1947 (38-53)
Vol. 23 No. 39
John Kobler

Buck, Eugene Edward (Gene)
Songwriter; producer;
ASCAP president
"Czar of Song"
Dec. 17, 1932 (22-25)
Dec. 24, 1932 (19-22)
Vol. 8 No. 44-45
Alva Johnston

Buckner, Emory Roy
Lawyer
"Courtroom Warrior"
March 12, 1932 (21-23)
March 19, 1932 (24-27)
Vol. 8 Nos. 4-5
Alva Johnston

Buffet, Bernard
Painter
"Le Gamin"
Nov. 21, 1959 (57-108)
Vol. 35 No. 40
Janet Flanner

Bulger, William
President, Massachusetts
State Senate
"Dancing With the Girl
that Brung Him"
October 28, 1991 (44-84)
Vol. 67 No. 36
Richard Brookhiser

Bullins, Ed
Playwright
"Dramatist"
June 16, 1973 (40-79)
Vol. 49 No. 17
Jervis Anderson

Bullitt, William Christian
U.S. Ambassador to
France
"Mr. Ambassador"
Dec. 10, 1938 (30-33)
Dec. 17, 1938 (22-27)
Vol. 14 Nos. 43-44
Janet Flanner

Bullock, Hugh
Investment manager
"The Happy Venture"
March 8, 1958 (47-83)
Vol. 34 No. 3
John Brooks

Bunting, Garland
Alcoholic beverage
control officer
"Moonshine"
August 19, 1985 (35-73)
Vol. 61 No. 26
Alec Wilkinson

Buñuel, Louis
Surrealist filmmaker
"Long Live the Living!"
Dec. 5, 1977 (53-72)
Vol. 53 No. 42
Penelope Gilliatt

Burgess, W. Starling
Racing yacht designer
"Man of Ideas"
July 31, 1937 (20-26)
Vol. 13 No. 24
H.K. Rigg

Burke, Randolph Forrest
(Randy)
Socialite
"Glamour Boy"
April 6, 1940 (23-27)
Vol. 16 No. 8
E.J. Kahn, Jr.

Burrows, Abe
Comedian; playwright
"The Easygoing Method"
May 11, 1957 (51-81)
May 18, 1957 (41-67)
Vol. 33 Nos. 12-13
E.J. Kahn, Jr.

Bush, Irving T.
Builder of the Bush
Terminal Brooklyn
Warehouse district;
business journalist
"Over Babel"
April 2, 1927 (26-28)
Vol. 3 No. 7
Niven Busch, Jr.

Butler, James
Chain grocery and
racetrack owner
"Green Front"
July 9, 1932 (20-23)
Vol. 8 No. 21
Stanley Walker

Butler, Nicholas Murray
   Author; president,
   Columbia University
   "Cosmos"
   Nov. 8, 1930 (28-32)
   Nov. 15, 1930 (33-41)
   Vol. 6 Nos. 38-39
   Alva Johnston

Butler, Roland
   Publicity director,
   Ringling Brothers &
   Barnum & Bailey Circus
   "Fiendish"
   April 18, 1953 (38-66)
   April 25, 1953 (37-67)
   Vol. 29 Nos. 9-10
   Robert Lewis Taylor

Butterworth, Charles
   Comedian
   "The Mad Hatter of
   Hollywood"
   July 27, 1935 (20-26)
   Vol. 11 No. 24
   Alva Johnston

Cabot, John Moors
   U.S. Ambassador to Brazil
   "Ambassador"
   March 4, 1961 (39-90)
   Vol. 37 No. 3
   Robert Shaplen

Cage, John M., Jr.
   Composer
   "Figure in an Imaginary
   Landscape"
   Nov. 28, 1964 (64-128)
   Vol. 40 No. 41
   Calvin Tomkins

Calder, Alexander
   Mobile maker and seller
   "Everything is Mobile"
   October 4, 1941 (25-33)
   Vol. 17 No. 34
   Geoffrey T. Hellman

Caldwell, Sarah
   Stage director, Opera
   Company of Boston
   "Infinite Pains"
   Dec. 24, 1973 (43-49)
   Vol. 49 No. 44
   Winthrop Sargeant

Campbell, Frank E.
   Mortician
   "Come, Ye Disconsolate"
   Nov. 20, 1926 (25-28)
   Vol. 2 No. 40
   Charles Gordon MacArthur

Campion, Daniel J.
   Detective, New York
   City Police
   "The Beautiful Flower"
   June 4, 1955 (39-89)
   Vol. 31 No. 16
   Joseph Mitchell

Caniff, Milton (Arthur)
Comic strip cartoonist
"Significant Sig and the
Funnies"
January 8, 1944 (25-37)
Vol. 19 No. 47
John Bainbridge

Cantor, Eddie
Comedian; actor
"Chutspo"
Dec. 10, 1932 (23-27)
Vol. 8 No. 43
S.N. Behrman

Capp, Al
Comic strip cartoonist
"Ooff! (sob!) eep!! (gulp!)
zowie!!!"
Nov. 29, 1947 (45-57)
Dec. 6, 1947 (46-61)
Vol. 23 Nos. 41-42
E.J. Kahn, Jr.

Capra, Frank R.
Film director
"Thinker in Hollywood"
Feb. 24, 1940 (23-28)
Vol. 16 No. 2
Geoffrey T. Hellman

Cardozo, Benjamin Nathan
Chief Judge, New York
Supreme Court
"The Cloister and the
Bench"
March 22, 1930 (25-28)
Vol. 6 No. 5
Babette Deutsch

Carey, William F.
President, Madison
Square Garden Corp.
"Spread Eagle"
July 13, 1929 (21-24)
Vol. 5 No. 21
Niven Busch, Jr.

Carlsen, Henrik Kurt
Merchant ship captain
"A Powerful Sense of
His Duty"
Dec. 13, 1958 (49-99)
Vol. 34 No. 43
Thomas Whiteside

Carnegie, Hattie
Clothing designer
"Luxury, Inc."
March 31, 1934 (23-27)
Vol. 10 No. 7
"L.H." (Lois Long)

Carney, Don
Radio personality
"Uncle Don"
Dec. 16, 1933 (24-29)
Vol. 9 No. 44
Margaret Case Harriman

Carpenter, John
Filmmaker
"People Start Running"
January 28, 1980 (41-58)
Vol. 55 No. 50
James Stevenson

Carr, John Dickson
Mystery writer
"Two Authors in an Attic"
Sept. 8, 1951 (39-48)
Sept. 15, 1951 (36-51)
Vol. 27 Nos. 30-31
Robert Lewis Taylor

Lord Carrington
Member, British House
of Lords
"A Sense of Duty"
Feb. 14, 1983 (47-83)
Vol. 58 No. 52
John Newhouse

Carson, Johnny
Host, *The Tonight Show*
"Fifteen Years of the
Salto Mortale"
Feb. 20, 1978 (47-98)
Vol. 54 No. 1
Kenneth Tynan

Casals, Pablo
Concert cellist
"A Cellist in Exile"
Feb. 24, 1962 (38-98)
Vol. 38 No. 1
Bernard Taper

Casey, James E.
President, United Parcel
Service
"Ah, Packages!"
May 10, 1947 (34-49)
Vol. 23 No. 12
Philip Hamburger

Cashin, William E.
Chaplain, New York
State Prison
"Father Bill"
January 7, 1928 (19-21)
Vol. 3 No. 47
Henry F. Pringle

Castelli, Leo
Art dealer
"A Good Eye and a
Good Ear"
May 26, 1980 (40-72)
Vol. 56 No. 14
Calvin Tomkins

Cather, Willa Sibert
Author
"American Classic"
August 8, 1931 (19-22)
Vol. 7 No. 25
Louise Bogan

Cavallero, Gene
Waiter, Colony Restaurant
"Two Waiters and a Chef"
June 1, 1935 (20-24)
June 8, 1935 (22-26)
Vol. 11 Nos. 16-17
Margaret Case Harriman

Cavett, Dick
Television personality
"Work, For the Night
is Coming"
May 6, 1972 (42-52)
Vol. 48 No. 11
L.E. Sissman

Cecchi, Mario
  Italian communist
  "The San Vincenzo Cell"
  Sept. 24, 1979 (47-131)
  Vol. 55 No. 32
  Jane Kramer

Cerf, Bennett
  President,
  Random House
  "Publisher"
  May 9, 1959 (48-88)
  May 16, 1959 (49-84)
  Vol. 35 Nos. 12-13
  Geoffrey T. Hellman

Cerutti, Ernest
  Waiter, Colony Restaurant
  "Two Waiters and a Chef"
  June 1, 1935 (20-24)
  June 8, 1935 (22-26)
  Vol. 11 Nos. 16-17
  Margaret Case Harriman

Cesoli, Leo
  European train conductor
  "Nagelmacker's Way"
  August 11, 1956 (29-49)
  Vol. 32 No. 25
  Joseph Wechsberg

Chaliapin, Feodor
  Bass, Metropolitan Opera
  "Artist of the People"
  April 7, 1928 (29-31)
  Vol. 4 No. 7
  Sulamith Ish-Kishor

Chanel, Gabrielle
  Fashion designer
  "31, Rue Cambon"
  March 14, 1931 (25-28)
  Vol. 7 No. 4
  Janet Flanner

Chanin, Irwin Salmon
  Realtor; architectural
  engineer
  "Skybinder"
  January 26,1929 (20-24)
  Vol. 4 No. 49
  Niven Busch, Jr.

Chaplin, Charlie (Sir Charles
Spencer)
  Filmmaker, comedian
  May 23, 1925 (9-10)
  Vol. 1 No. 14
  "Searchlight"
  (Waldo Frank)

  * A Reporter at Large
  "Moments From Chaplin"
  May 22, 1978 (94-109)
  Vol. 54 No. 14
  Lillian Ross

Chapman, Frank Mitchler
  Curator of Ornithology,
  American Museum of
  Natural History
  "Boy Meets Bullfinch"
  March 4, 1939 (22-27)
  Vol. 15 No. 3
  Geoffrey T. Hellman

Charney, Steve
  Radio personality
  "Illusionist"
  February 4, 1985 (48-59)
  Vol. 60 No. 51
  C.P. Crow

Chavez, Cesar
  Farm labor advocate
  "Organizer"
  June 21, 1969 (42-85)
  June 28, 1969 (43-71)
  Vol. 45 Nos. 18-19
  Peter Matthiessen

Cheatham, Doc
  Trumpet player
  "Light Everywhere"
  January 25, 1982 (42-52)
  Vol. 57 No. 49
  Whitney Balliett

Cherne, Leo M.
  Executive Secretary,
  Research Institute of
  America
  "Cassandra, Inc."
  October 5, 1940 (23-32)
  Vol. 16 No. 34
  George R. Leighton

Child, Julia
  Celebrity chef, author,
  television personality
  "Good Cooking"
  Dec. 23, 1974 (36-52)
  Vol. 50 No. 44
  Calvin Tomkins

Childers, Erskine Hamilton
  Late President of Ireland
  "Son and Father"
  January 27, 1975 (44-67)
  Vol. 50 No. 49
  Anthony Bailey

Childers, Robert Erskine
  Irish political leader
  "Son and Father"
  January 27, 1975 (44-67)
  Vol. 50 No. 49
  Anthony Bailey

Childs, William
  Owner, Childs restau-
  rants; vegetarian
  "The Hand That
  Feeds You"
  April 9, 1927 (25-28)
  Vol. 3 No. 8
  Brock Pemberton and
  Foster Ware

Chouinard, Yvon
  Mountain climber
  "Ascending"
  January 31, 1977 (36-52)
  Vol. 52 No. 50
  Jeremy Bernstein

Chrysler, Walter P.
  Founder, Chrysler
  auto company
  "Type Model"
  January 8, 1927 (21-24)
  Vol. 2 No. 47
  Lurton Blassingame

Chudnovsky, David and
George
Supercomputer designers
"The Mountains of Pi"
March 2, 1992 (36-67)
Vol. 68 No. 2
Richard Preston

Cierplikowski, Antoine
Hairdresser
"Coiffeur pour Dames"
Nov. 21, 1931 (23 26)
Vol. 7 No. 40
Bessie Breuer

Cipriani, Giuseppe
Proprietor, Harry's Bar
"Veronese in Venice"
July 22, 1972 (34-39)
Vol. 48 No. 22
Winthrop Sargeant

Clark, Bobby (Robert Edwin)
Comedian
"Comedian"
Sept. 13, 1947 (35-43)
Sept. 20, 1947 (32-41)
Sept. 27, 1947 (36-46)
Vol. 23 Nos. 30-32
Robert Lewis Taylor

Clark, F. Ambrose
Horse breeder, trainer;
president, United Hunts
"Stirrup and Leather"
Sept. 29, 1934 (20-24)
Vol. 10 No. 33
Margaret Case Harriman

Clark, Dr. Kenneth Bancroft
Psychology professor,
City College of N.Y.
"The Integrationist"
August 23, 1982 (37-73)
Vol. 58 No. 27
Nat Hentoff

Clark, Walter L.
Director, Grand Central
Gallery of Art
"A Genius Who Made Art
Into Big Business"
August 1, 1925 (9-10)
Vol. 1 No. 24
"Van Gogh"
(Murdock Pemberton)

Clarke, Arthur C.
Science fiction writer
"Out of the Ego
Chamber"
August 9, 1969 (40-65)
Vol. 45 No. 25
Jeremy Bernstein

Clay, Lucius Du Bignon
General, U.S. Army;
Director, Office of
Defense Mobilization
"Soldier in Mufti"
January 13, 1951 (29-41)
Vol. 26 No. 47
E.J. Kahn, Jr.

Cleese, John
  Actor, comedian
  "Height's Delight"
  May 2, 1988 (41-56)
  Vol. 64 No. 11
  Penelope Gilliatt

Clooney, Rosemary
  Popular singer
  "The Heart, the Head,
  and the Pipes"
  August 3, 1992 (37-42)
  Vol. 68 No. 24
  Whitney Balliett

Clutterbuck, Richard Lewis
  Author; expert on
  terrorism
  "How Do We Explain
  Them?"
  June 12, 1978 (37-62)
  Vol. 54 No. 17
  E.J. Kahn, J

Cochet, Henri
  Tennis professional
  "Lucky Cochet"
  Sept. 15, 1928 (28-30)
  Vol. 4 No. 30
  J.R. Tunis

Cochran, Philip
  Major, U.S. Army
  Air Force
  "Guerilla From Erie, Pa."
  Feb. 13, 1943 (22-29)
  Vol. 18 No. 52
  A.J. Liebling

Cohan, George M.
  Playwright, songwriter
  "Song and Dance Man"
  March 17, 1934 (27-31)
  March 24, 1934 (22-27)
  Vol. 10 Nos. 5-6
  Gilbert Seldes

Cohn, Sam
  Talent agent
  "Dealmaker"
  January 11, 1982 (40-84)
  Vol. 57 No. 47
  Mark Singer

Coleman, Emil
  Orchestra leader
  "Music With Meals"
  October 19, 1935 (26-30)
  Vol. 11 No. 36
  Gilbert Seldes

Collett, Glenna
  Golfer
  "Sports Model, Misses"
  Sept. 17, 1927 (26-28)
  Vol. 3 No. 31
  Niven Busch, Jr.

Conant, James Bryant
  President, Harvard U.
  "Mr. President "
  Sept. 12, 1936 (20-24)
  Sept. 19, 1936 (23-27)
  Vol. 12 Nos. 30-31
  Henry F. Pringle

Concello, Antoinette and
Arthur
    Trapeze artists
    "Family Under Canvas"
    April 23, 1949 (31-45)
    April 30, 1949 (36-51)
    Vol. 25 Nos. 9-10
    Robert Lewis Taylor

Condon, (Eddie) Albert Edwin
    Jazz guitarist
    "Spokesman With a
    Temperature"
    April 28, 1945 (28-37)
    May 5, 1945 (28-41)
    Vol. 21 Nos. 11-12
    Rogers E.M. Whitaker

Condon, John Francis
    Public school teacher
    "Goodbye, Mr. Jafsie"
    Dec. 29, 1934 (20-26)
    Vol. 10 No. 46
    St. Clair McKelway

Connelly, Marc
    Playwright
    "Two-Eyed Connelly"
    April 12, 1930 (29-32)
    Vol. 6 No. 8
    Alexander Woollcott

Content, Harry C.
    Stockbroker
    "Fifty Years of
    Wall Street"
    October 1, 1932 (22-26)
    Vol. 8 No. 33
    Matthew Josephson

Cook, Joe
    Entertainer
    "A Boy in a Barn"
    March 31, 1928 (29-31)
    Vol. 4 No. 6
    Marc Connelly

Coolidge, Grace (Mrs. Calvin)
    Wife of President
    Calvin Coolidge
    "The First Lady"
    May 15, 1926 (17-18)
    Vol. 2 No. 13
    Paul A. Burns

Cooper, Merian C.
    Motion picture
    photographer
    "Man With Camera"
    May 30, 1931 (21-25)
    Vol. 7 No. 15
    Gilbert Seldes

Copeland, Charles Townsend
    Rhetoric professor,
    Harvard University
    "The Passionate
    Professor"
    January 21, 1928 (20-22)
    Vol. 3 No. 49
    Heywood Broun

Copeland, Royal S.
    U.S. Senator (R-N.Y.)
    "Master Hinter"
    August 18, 1928 (21-24)
    Vol. 4 No. 26
    Alva Johnston

Cordes, John
    Detective, New York
    City Police
    "With the Meat in
    Their Mouth"
    Sept. 5, 1953 (37-61)
    Sept. 12, 1953 (39-59)
    Vol. 29 Nos. 29-30
    Joel Sayre

Cornell, Katharine
    Actress
    "Actress-Manager"
    Feb. 14, 1931 (23-25)
    Vol. 6 No. 52
    Gilbert Seldes

    "The Player - II"
    October 28, 1961 (82-90)
    Vol. 37 No. 37
    Lillian Ross

Corrigan, Joseph E.
    Judge, New York City
    Criminal Courts
    "Good Morning, Judge"
    August 30, 1930 (22-25)
    Vol. 6 No. 28
    Milton MacKaye

Corsi, Edward
    Director, Emergency
    Home Relief Bureau;
    immigration commissioner
    "Hands Across the Sea"
    March 9, 1935 (20-24)
    March 16, 1935 (28-33)
    Vol. 11 Nos. 4-5
    Milton MacKaye

Corwin, Norman
    Radio writer and director
    "The Odyssey of the
    Oblong Blur"
    April 5, 1947 (36-49)
    Vol. 23 No. 7
    Philip Hamburger

Cosey, Joseph (pseud.)
    Autograph forger
    "Yrs. Truly, A. Lincoln"
    Feb. 25, 1956 (38-85)
    Vol. 32 No. 1
    John Kobler

Cosgrave, Jessica Garretson
    (Mrs. John O'Hara)
    Educator; founder of
    Finch Junior College
    "Recurrent and
    Irreducible"
    April 13, 1946 (35-51)
    Vol. 22 No. 9
    Angelica Gibbs

Coty, François
    Perfumer, journalist,
    politician
    "Perfume and Politics"
    May 3, 1930 (22-25)
    Vol. 6 No. 11
    "Hippolyta"
    (Janet Flanner)

Coughlin, John D.
  Police inspector
  "The Cop in the
  Silk Shirt"
  Sept. 25, 1926 (22-24)
  Vol. 2 No. 32
  Niven Busch, Jr. and
  A. Barr Gray

Couney, Martin A.
  Obstetrician
  "Patron of the Preemies"
  June 3, 1939 (20-24)
  Vol. 15 No. 16
  A.J. Liebling

Cousy, Robert Joseph
  Basketball player
  "A Victim of *Noblesse
  Oblige*"
  February 4, 1961 (38-60)
  Vol. 36 No. 51
  Robert Rice

Coward, Noel
  Playwright, actor
  "Heureux Noel"
  January 19, 1929 (21-25)
  Vol. 4 No. 48
  Alexander Woollcott

Cowen, Joshua Lionel
  Chairman, Lionel Lines
  toy electric trains
  "High Railers and
  Full Scalers"
  Dec. 13, 1947 (38-49)
  Vol. 23 No. 43
  Robert Lewis Taylor

Cox, Walter
  Trotting horse trainer
  "Yankee Horse Trader"
  August 10, 1935 (19-24)
  Vol. 11 No. 26
  Arthur C. Bartlett

Craig, John C.
  Fireworks consultant,
  New York World's Fair
  "The Human Firecracker"
  June 17, 1939 (23-28)
  Vol. 15 No. 18
  Geoffrey T. Hellman

Craige, Captain John H.
  Publicity officer, U.S.M.C.
  "A Gentleman With Two
  Cauliflower Ears"
  April 4, 1925 (9-10)
  Vol. 1 No. 7
  "Quid"
  (Marquis James)

Cram, Ralph Adams
  Architect, expert on
  Gothic revival
  "Seven Centuries Late"
  March 13, 1926 (15-16)
  Vol. 2 No. 4
  Helena Huntington Smith

Crane, Joe
  National champion
  skydiver
  "Parachute Jumper"
  Dec. 31, 1932 (16-19)
  Vol. 8 No. 46
  Geoffrey T. Hellman

Cravath, Paul Drennan
    Lawyer; corporation
    director
    "Public Man"
    January 2, 1932 (21-24)
    Vol. 7 No. 46
    Milton MacKaye

Crawford, Cheryl
    Musical comedy producer
    "A Woman in the House"
    May 8, 1948 (34-51)
    Vol. 24 No. 11
    Janet Flanner

Creel, George
    Chairman, Committee of
    Public Information;
    humorist
    "Incredible Mr. Creel"
    July 4, 1925 (7-8)
    Vol. 1 No. 20
    Harvey O'Higgins

Cripps, Sir Stafford
    British statesman
    "No. 11 Downing Street"
    August 8, 1942 (19-29)
    Vol. 18 No. 25
    Mollie Panter-Downes

Cronin, John
    Conservationist
    "Riverkeeper"
    May 11, 1987 (49-78)
    Vol. 63 No. 12
    Alec Wilkinson

Cronyn, Hume
    Actor
    "The Player - I"
    Oct. 21, 1961 (103-111)
    Vol. 37 No. 36
    Lillian Ross

Crosby, John
    Impresario, Santa Fe
    Opera
    "A Miracle in the Desert"
    August 4, 1975 (35-50)
    Vol. 51 No. 24
    Winthrop Sargeant

Crowninshield, (Frank)
Francis Welsh
    Editor, *Vanity Fair*
    "Last of the Species"
    Sept. 19, 1942 (22-33)
    Sept. 26, 1942 (24-31)
    Vol. 18 Nos. 31-32
    Geoffrey T. Hellman

Crumbine, Samuel J.
    Physician, public
    health worker
    "Swat the Fly!"
    July 17, 1948 (31-38)
    July 24, 1948 (28-36)
    Vol. 24 Nos. 21-22
    Robert Lewis Taylor

Cuda, Tony
    Mayor of Futani, Italy
    "Mayor of Futani"
    May 27, 1944 (32-39)
    Vol. 20 No. 15
    John Lardner

Cullman, Howard S. ("Stix")
Partner, Cullman Brothers
(tobacco); president,
Beekman Hospital;
theatrical investor
"Tobacco, Tunnels,
Arsenic and Old Lace"
Feb. 9, 1946 (28-38)
Feb. 16, 1946 (36-44)
Vol. 21 No. 51 and
Vol. 22 No. 1
Geoffrey T. Hellman

Culver, John C.
U.S. Senator (D-Iowa)
* A Reporter at Large
"Senator"
Sept. 11, 1978 (40-125)
Sept. 18, 1978 (45-134)
Vol. 54 Nos. 30-31
Elizabeth Drew

Cunningham, Bradley
Restaurant proprietor
"City Voices"
October 11, 1982 (52-72)
Vol. 58 No. 34
Whitney Balliett

Cunningham, Merce
Choreographer
"An Appetite for Motion"
May 4, 1968 (52-126)
Vol. 44 No. 11
Calvin Tomkins

Cuomo, Mario
Governor, State of
New York
"Governor "
April 9, 1984 (50-113)
April 16, 1984 (53-126)
Vol. 60 Nos. 8-9
Ken Auletta

Curley, Jack
Fight promoter
"Cauliflowers and
Pachyderms "
July 14, 1934 (21-25)
July 21, 1934 (20-25)
July 28, 1934 (20-24)
Vol. 10 Nos. 22-24
Alva Johnston

Curran, Henry Hastings
Member, N.Y. Board of
Estimate; president,
American Association
Against the Prohibition
Amendment
"Wet Hope"
June 14, 1930 (22-25)
Vol. 6 No. 17
Henry F. Pringle

Curran, Joseph
President, National
Maritime Union
"Union President"
July 6, 1946 (24-33)
July 13, 1946 (30-40)
July 20, 1946 (26-47)
Vol. 22 Nos. 21-23
Richard Owen Boyer

Curry, John Francis
Leader, New York County
Democratic Party
"Local Boy Makes Good"
August 3, 1929 (21-24)
Vol. 5 No. 24
Henry F. Pringle

Daché, Lilly (Mme. Jean
Despres)
Milliner
"Hats Will Be Worn"
April 4, 1942 (20-27)
Vol. 18 No. 7
Margaret Case Harriman

D'Agostino, Pasquale "Patsy"
Grocer
"If Trouble Can Be
Avoided"
May 15, 1943 (25-35)
Vol. 19 No. 13
Mark Murphy

Dale, Chester
President, National
Gallery of Art
"Custodian"
October 25, 1958 (49-84)
Vol. 34 No. 36
Geoffrey T. Hellman

Dali, Salvador
Surrealist painter
"A Dream Walking"
July 1, 1939 (22-27)
Vol. 15 No. 20
Margaret Case Harriman

Dalley, John
Second violin,
Guarneri Quartet
"String Quartet"
Oct. 23, 1978 (45-131)
Vol. 54 No. 36
Helen Drees Ruttencutter

"Dame Edna" *see* Humphries,
Barry

Damita, Lily
Motion picture actress
"Little Narcissus"
October 26, 1929 (30-33)
Vol. 5 No. 36
Henry F. Pringle

Damrosch, Walter
Conductor (retired), New
York Philharmonic;
founder, National
Symphony
"Godfather to Polymnia"
Nov. 2, 1929 (28-31)
Vol. 5 No. 37
Deems Taylor

Darlington, Thomas
Physician, New York City
Commission of Health;
author; Grand Sachem,
Society of Tammany
"Grand Sachem"
August 6, 1932 (19-23)
Vol. 8 No. 25
Milton MacKaye

Davenport, Marcia
  Writer
  "Unconquerable"
  April 22, 1991 (42-88)
  Vol. 67 No. 9
  Barry Paris

Davidson, Jo
  Sculptor
  "Sculptors Are Different"
  March 26, 1927 (27-29)
  Vol. 3 No. 6
  "F.T."
  (Ferdinand Tuohy)

Davies, J. Clarence
  Real estate developer
  "King of the Bronx"
  Dec. 7, 1929 (33-35)
  Vol. 5 No. 42
  Robert M. Coates

Davies, Marjorie Post
  Socialite; wife of U.S.
  Ambassador to Russia
  "Lady Bountiful"
  Feb. 4, 1939 (23-28)
  Feb. 11, 1939 (23-27)
  Feb. 18, 1939 (24-27)
  Vol. 14 Nos. 51-52 and
  Vol. 15 No. 1
  Arthur C. Bartlett

Davis, Bette
  Motion picture actress
  "Cotton-dress Girl"
  Feb. 20, 1943 (19-29)
  Vol. 19 No. 1
  Janet Flanner

Davis, Meyer
  Orchestra leader
  "Me"
  March 11, 1939 (26-32)
  Vol. 15 No. 4
  Richard Owen Boyer

Day, Dorothy
  Author; founder, Catholic
  Worker movement
  "The Foolish Things of
  the World"
  October 4, 1952 (37-60)
  October 11, 1952 (37-58
  Vol. 28 Nos. 33-34
  Dwight Macdonald

Day, Joseph P.
  Real estate auctioneer
  "Prometheus Bound"
  May 27, 1933 (18-22)
  Vol. 9 No. 15
  Geoffrey T. Hellman

Deane, Martha *see* Mary
Margaret McBride

Dearie, Blossom
  Singer
  "Hanging Out With
  Blossom Dearie"
  May 26, 1973 (46-52)
  Vol. 49 No. 14
  Whitney Balliett

de Florez, Luis
Captain, U.S. Naval
Reserve; inventor of
synthetic training devices
"Captain Among the
Synthetics"
Nov. 11, 1944 (34-43)
Nov. 18, 1944 (32-43)
Vol. 20 Nos. 39-40
Robert Lewis Taylor

Delacour, Jean
Aviculturalist; operator,
Bronx Zoo
"The Great Aviculturalist"
August 10, 1946 (24-34)
August 17, 1946 (26-39)
Vol. 22 Nos. 26-27
Geoffrey T. Hellman

Delehanty, Michael Joseph
President, Civil
Service School
"Prexy"
May 24, 1941 (24-30)
Vol. 17 No. 15
Robert Lewis Taylor

Delaunay, Charles
Jazz critic
"Panassié, Delaunay
et cie"
Feb. 14, 1977 (43-52)
Vol. 52 No. 52
Whitney Balliett

deMarco, Renee and Tony
Dancers
"Dance Team"
January 6, 1940 (22-27)
Vol. 15 No. 47
Margaret Case Harriman

deMille, Agnes
Choreographer
"Choreographer"
Sept. 14, 1946 (32-45)
Vol. 22 No. 31
Angelica Gibbs

DeMille, Cecil B.
Film director
"The Hollywood Zeus"
Nov. 28, 1925 (11-12)
Vol. 1 No. 40
Robert Sherwood

Dempsey, Jack
Pugilist
"A Symbol in Pugilism"
March 14, 1925 (15-16)
Vol. 1 No. 4
James Kevin McGuinness

Dengel, Veronica McKenna
Beautician
"One Sweet Little
Business"
July 31, 1948 (26-37)
Vol. 24 No. 23
Angelica Gibbs

Denison, Frank Emerson
  Tea grader and blender
  "Challenge and Delight"
  January 15, 1947 (33-47)
  Berton Roueché

Deren, Jim
  Fishing-tackle shop
  proprietor
  "Angler at Heart"
  April 19, 1982 (53-82)
  Vol. 58 No. 9
  Ian Frazier

De Sica, Vittorio
  Film director; actor
  "Bread, Love, and
  Neo-Realismo"
  June 29, 1957 (35-58)
  July 6, 1957 (35-53)
  Vol. 33 Nos. 19-20
  Winthrop Sargeant

Deskey, Donald
  Furniture designer
  "Long Road to Roxy"
  Feb. 25, 1933 (22-26)
  Vol. 9 No. 2
  Gilbert Seldes

de Valois, Ninette
  Director, Sadler's
  Wells Ballet
  "Madam"
  Sept. 16, 1950 (32-54)
  Vol. 26 No. 30
  Mollie Panter-Downes

Dewey, Edward Russell
  Director, Foundation for
  the Study of Cycles
  "Something Out There"
  February 3, 1962 (37-69)
  Vol. 37 No. 51
  John Brooks

Dewey, John
  Essayist; educator
  "The Man Who Made
  Us What We Are"
  May 22, 1926 (15-16)
  Vol. 2 No. 14
  "Search-Light"
  (Waldo Frank)

Dewey, Thomas Edmund
  District Attorney,
  Governor of New York;
  Presidential candidate
  "St. George and
  the Dragnet"
  May 25, 1940 (24-38)
  Vol. 16 No. 15
  Wolcott Gibbs and
  John Bainbridge

de Wolfe, Elsie ("Lady Mendl")
  Actress
  "Handsprings Across
  the Sea"
  January 15, 1938 (25-29)
  Vol. 13 No. 48
  Janet Flanner

De Zembler, Charles
Barber shop owner
"Barber's Progress"
Nov. 16, 1946 (37-56)
Vol. 22 No. 40
Richard Owen Boyer

d'Harnoncourt, Rene
Director, Museum of
Modern Art
"Imperturbable Noble"
May 7, 1960 (49-112)
Vol. 36 No. 12
Geoffrey T. Hellman

Diamond, John ("Jack Legs")
Gambler; racketeer
"Big Shot-at"
June 13, 1931 (24-27)
Vol. 7 No. 17
Joel Sayre

Dickenson, Vic
Trombonist
"Three Tones"
Sept. 7, 1981 (39-49)
Vol. 57 No. 29
Whitney Balliett

Diebenkorn, Richard
Artist
"Almost Free of
the Mirror"
Sept. 7, 1987 (54-73)
Vol. 63 No. 29
Dan Hofstadter

Dilley, Arthur Urbane
Oriental rug dealer;
author
"No. 1 Picaroon"
Sept. 2, 1939 (24-31)
Vol. 15 No. 29
Richard Owen Boyer

Dilling, Mildred
Concert harpist
"The Harp Lady"
February 3, 1940 (25-29)
Vol. 15 No. 51
E.J. Kahn, Jr.

Dillon, Clarence
Pres., Dillon, Read & Co.
"A Billion-Dollar Banker"
October 20, 1928 (29-36)
Vol. 4 No. 35
John K. Winkler

Dillon, John J.
Publisher, the *Rural
New-Yorker*
"Rural New Yorker"
May 21, 1938 (25-29)
Vol. 14 No. 14
Arthur Charles Bartlett

Disney, Walt (Walter E.)
Motion picture cartoonist;
founder of Disney
entertainment empire
"Mickey-Mouse Maker"
Dec. 19, 1931 (23-27)
Vol. 7 No. 44
Gilbert Seldes

Ditmars, Raymond
Supervisor, Bronx Zoo
snake house
"A Specialist in Snakes"
July 14, 1928 (24-27)
Vol. 4 No. 21
Cameron Rogers

Dominy, Floyd
Rancher
"Encounters With the
Archdruid III"
April 3, 1971 (41-93)
Vol. 47 No. 7
John McPhee

Donegan, Dorothy
Concert pianist
"Wonder Woman"
Feb. 18, 1991 (37-41)
Vol. 66 No. 53
Whitney Balliett

Donon, Joseph
Private chef
"The Best of the Best"
March 10, 1962 (47-78)
Vol. 38 No. 3
Geoffrey T. Hellman

Doubleday, Nelson
Publisher
"Grown in Garden City"
Feb. 18, 1928 (21-23)
Vol. 3 No. 53
Foster Ware

Dowling, Robert Whittle
Architect; head of arts
committee for National
Cultural Center
"Useful on the
Grand Scale"
Nov. 5, 1960 (61-113)
Vol. 36 No. 38
Robert Shaplen

Doxiadis, Constantinos
City planner
"The Ekistic World"
May 11, 1963 (49-87)
Vol. 39 No. 12
Christopher Rand

Draper, Paul
Tap dancer
"Dancing Hamlet"
January 7, 1939 (24-29)
Vol. 14 No. 47
Russell Maloney

Drebin, Sam (Samuel)
Soldier
"Sam Drebin"
May 2, 1925 (13-14)
Vol. 1 No. 11
William Slavens McNutt

Dreiser, Theodore
Author
"The Colossus of
Children"
August 15, 1925 (6-7)
Vol. 1 No. 26
"Search-light"
(Waldo Frank)

Dreyfus, Max
  Music publisher
  "Accocheur"
  February 6, 1932 (20-40)
  Vol. 7 No. 51
  S.N. Behrman

Dreyfuss, Henry
  Theatrical designer
  "Artist in a Factory"
  August 29, 1931 (22-24)
  Vol. 7 No. 28
  Gilbert Seldes

Dublin, Louis I.
  Statistician
  "Friend of the
  Average Man"
  May 23, 1942 (20-26)
  Vol. 18 No. 14
  Joseph Gollomb

Duchamp, Marcel
  Artist
  "Not Seen and/or
  Less Seen"
  February 6, 1965 (37-93)
  Vol. 40 No. 51
  Calvin Tomkins

Dufour, Lew
  Midway concessionaire,
  New York World's Fair
  "Masters of the Midway"
  August 12, 1939 (22-25)
  August 19, 1939 (23-27)
  Vol. 15 Nos. 26-27
  A.J. Liebling

Duke, Angier Biddle
  U.S. Chief of Protocol
  "Good Manners and
  Common Sense"
  August 15, 1964 (34-83)
  Vol. 40 No. 26
  E.J. Kahn, Jr.

Dumaine, Alexandre
  Chef
  "Tempest in a Kitchen"
  June 18, 1955 (32-64)
  Vol. 31 No. 18
  Joseph Wechsberg

Dumas, Roland
  Foreign Minister
  of France
  "Air of Mystery"
  Dec. 30, 1985 (33-57)
  Vol. 61 No. 45
  John Newhouse

DuMont, Allen Balcom
  Inventor; television
  pioneer
  "The Prudent Pioneer"
  January 27, 1951 (35-53)
  Vol. 26 No. 49
  Robert Rice

Duncan, Isadora
  Dancer
  "Isadora"
  January 1, 1927 (17-19)
  Vol. 2 No. 46
  "Hippolyta"
  (Janet Flanner)

Dunninger, Joseph
Magician
"Nothing Up His Sleeve"
Nov. 29, 1941 (26-36)
Vol. 17 No. 42
E.J. Kahn, Jr.

Duveen, Sir Joseph
Department store owner;
art dealer
"Noble Merchandise"
April 21, 1928 (29-31)
Vol. 4 No. 9
Alva Johnston

"The Days of Duveen"
Sept. 29, 1951 (33-61)
October 6, 1951 (41-62)
October 13, 1951 (41-80)
October 20, 1951 (36-59)
October 27, 1951 (38-63)
Nov. 3, 1951 (40-88)
Vol. 27 Nos. 33-38
S.N. Behrman

Dylan, Bob
Musician
"The Crackin', Shakin',
Breakin' Sounds"
October 24, 1964 (64-90)
Vol. 40 No. 36
Nat Hentoff

Eagle, Nate
Sideshow manager,
Ringling Brothers &
Barnum & Bailey Circus
"Talker"
April 19, 1958 (47-71)
April 26, 1958 (39-73)
Vol. 34 Nos. 9-10
Robert Lewis Taylor

Eastman, George
Inventor of the
Kodak camera
"Camera Shy"
Nov. 3, 1928 (27-30)
Vol. 4 No. 37
Terry Ramsaye

Eaton, Cyrus
Capitalist
"Communists' Capitalist"
October 10, 1977 (50-86)
October 17, 1977 (54-87)
Vol. 53 Nos. 34-35
E.J. Kahn, Jr.

Edel, Leon
Writer; English professor
"Chairman of the Board"
March 13, 1971 (43-86)
Vol. 47 No. 4
Geoffrey T. Hellman

Eden, Robert Anthony
British Foreign Minister,
Prime Minister
"Foreign Secretary"
Dec. 2, 1944 (35-43)
Dec. 9, 1944 (36-43)
Vol. 20 Nos. 42-43
Mollie Panter-Downes

Ederle, Gertrude
Swimmer
"The Girl of the Channel"
August 28, 1926 (15-16)
Vol. 2 No. 28
Lurton Blassingame

Edge, Rosalie Barrow
Chairman, Emergency
Conservation Committee
"Oh, Hawk of Mercy!"
April 17, 1948 (31-45)
Vol. 24 No. 8
Robert Lewis Taylor

Edison, Thomas Alva
Inventor
"The Wizard"
Dec. 28, 1929 (21-24)
January 4, 1930 (24-26)
January 11, 1930 (22-25)
Vol. 5 Nos. 45-47
Alva Johnston

Edward, Prince of Wales
Later Edward VIII of
England; abdicated 1936
"Edward's Grandson"
October 3, 1931 (27-30)
October 10, 1931 (26-29)
Vol. 7 Nos. 33-34
Anthony Gibbs

Edwards, Everett Joshua
Shore whaler
"Shore Whaler"
Sept. 24, 1949 (37-49)
Vol. 25 No. 31
Berton Roueche

Eilschemius, Louis Michael
Artist
"The Mahatma"
Sept. 14, 1935 (24-28)
Vol. 11 No. 31
Milton MacKaye

Einstein, Albert
Scientist
"Scientist and Mob Idol "
Dec. 2, 1933 (23-26)
Dec. 9, 1933 (29-32)
Vol. 9 Nos. 42-43
Alva Johnston

"Secrets of the Old One"
March 10, 1973 (44-101)
March 17, 1973 (44-91)
Vol. 49 Nos. 3-4
Jeremy Bernstein

Eisenhardt, Roy
  President, Oakland A's
  "Being Green"
  August 15, 1983 (40-69)
  Vol. 59 No. 26
  Roger Angell

Eliot, George Fielding
  Military analyst; author
  "Business Behind
  the Lines"
  Sept. 5, 1942 (20-28)
  Sept. 12, 1942 (22-29)
  Vol. 18 Nos. 29-30
  John Bainbridge

Elizabeth II
  Queen of England
  "The Elder Daughter"
  April 11, 1977 (42-83)
  April 18, 1977 (51-101)
  Vol. 53 Nos. 8-9
  Anthony Bailey

Ellington, Duke (Edward)
  Band leader, composer
  "The Hot Bach"
  June 24, 1944 (30-44)
  July 1, 1944 (26-34)
  July 8, 1944 (26-31)
  Vol. 20 Nos. 19-21
  Richard Owen Boyer

Elliott, James W.
  Sales promoter
  "Coloratura
  Salesmanship"
  Sept. 17, 1932 (21-25)
  Vol. 8 No. 31
  Alva Johnston

Elliott, Robert Brackett
  Bob of "Bob and Ray"
  comedy team
  "Their Own Gravity"
  Sept. 24, 1973 (42-65)
  Vol. 49 No. 31
  Whitney Balliett

Ellis, Abraham
  Hat check concessionaire
  "The Almighty Buck"
  May 26, 1951 (30-47)
  Vol. 27 No. 15
  Lillian Ross

Ellis, Anita
  Singer
  "Coming Out Again"
  July 31, 1978 (35-45)
  Vol. 54 No. 24
  Whitney Balliett

Ellison, Ralph
  Author
  "Going to the Territory"
  Nov. 22, 1976 (55-108)
  Vol. 52 No. 40
  Jervis Anderson

Erdmann, Dr. John Frederick
Surgeon
"Pandora and the Doctor"
Dec. 4, 1926 (32-34)
Vol. 2 No. 42
Niven Busch, Jr.

Erickson, Arthur
Architect
"Seven Stones"
June 4, 1979 (42-86)
Vol. 55 No. 16
Edith Iglauer

Erikson, Erik H.
Psychoanalyst
"The Measure of a Man"
Nov. 7, 1970 (51-131)
Nov. 14, 1970 (59-138)
Vol. 46 Nos. 38-39
Robert Coles

Erskine, John
Author
"Professor's Progress"
Dec. 10, 1927 (27-29)
Vol. 3 No. 43
Helena Huntington Smith

Ertegun, Ahmet
President, Atlantic Records
"Eclectic, Reminiscent,
Amused, Fickle, Perverse"
May 29, 1978 (37-83)
June 5, 1978 (45-81)
Vol. 54 Nos. 15-16
George W.S. Trow, Jr.

Evans, Merle
Band leader, Ringling
Brothers & Barnum &
Bailey Circus
"One Beat to the Bar"
April 16, 1955 (47-73)
April 23, 1955 (39-64)
Vol. 31 No. 9
Robert Lewis Taylor

Evans, Ponce Cruse
Syndicated columnist
"Nobody Better, Better
Than Nobody"
Feb. 21, 1983 (50-83)
Vol. 59 No. 1
Ian Frazier

Ewing, Maurice
Deep-sea geologist
"Explorer"
Nov. 4, 1974 (54-118)
Nov. 11, 1974 (52-100)
Nov. 18, 1974 (60-110)
Vol. 50 Nos. 37-39
William Wertenbaker

Fairchild, Sherman Mills
Airplane manufacturer;
authority on aerial
photography
"Airman-About-Town"
Dec. 27, 1941 (22-29)
Vol. 17 No. 46
Geoffrey T. Hellman

Falcaro, Joe (Joseph)
  Bowler
  "Man With a Thumb"
  April 5, 1941 (23-32)
  Vol. 17 No. 8
  Robert Lewis Taylor

Farley, James A.
  U.S. Postmaster General
  "Big Jim"
  Nov. 28, 1931 (23-27)
  Vol. 7 No. 41
  Alva Johnston

Farmer, Art
  Flugelhornist
  "Here and Abroad"
  Sept. 23, 1985 (43-55)
  Vol. 61 No. 31
  Whitney Balliett

Farrell, Eileen
  Singer
  "Home Sweet Home"
  May 23, 1959 (47-67)
  Vol. 35 No. 14
  Winthrop Sargeant

Feder, Abe H.
  Lighting designer
  "The Right Light"
  October 22, 1960 (49-84)
  Vol. 36 No. 36
  Joseph Wechsberg

Feldman, Sam
  Public defender, defense
  attorney
  "Enfant Terrible"
  August 25, 1928 (22-25)
  Vol. 4 No. 27
  Newman Levy

Fellini, Federico
  Film director
  "10 1/2"
  Oct. 30, 1965 (63-107)
  Vol. 41 No. 37
  Lillian Ross

Ferrari, Enzo
  Automobile designer,
  manufacturer
  "The Terrible Joys"
  January 15, 1966 (40-66)
  Vol. 41 No. 48
  Winthrop Sargeant

Feuer, Cy
  Theatrical producer
  "The Hit's the Thing"
  January 7, 1956 (29-53)
  January 14, 1956 (33-59)
  Vol. 31 Nos. 47-48
  E.J. Kahn, Jr.

Fielding, Temple Hornaday
  Guidebook author
  "Templex"
  January 6, 1968 (32-67)
  Vol. 43 No. 46
  John McPhee

Fields, W.C.
Actor; entertainer
"Legitimate Nonchalance"
Feb. 2, 1935 (23-26)
Feb. 9, 1935 (25-28)
Feb. 16, 1935 (22-26)
Vol. 10 Nos. 51-52 and
Vol. 11 No. 1
Alva Johnston

Finn, William Joseph
Roman Catholic priest;
leader of Paulist
choristers
"Sixteenth-century Style"
Dec. 20, 1930 (26-28)
Vol. 6 No. 44
Helena Huntington Smith

Finney, Benjamin Ficklin, Jr.
(and his German shepherd,
Egon)
Senior Regent, University
of the South (Sewannee,
Tenn.)
"The Owner of Ben
Finney"
May 12, 1928 (25-28)
Vol. 4 No. 12
Alexander Woollcott

Finucane, Brendane
Flight Lieutenant,
Royal Air Force
"Paddy of the R.A.F."
Dec. 6, 1941 (37-49)
Vol. 17 No. 43
A.J. Liebling

Fischer, Clifford C.
Producer of
musical revues
"La, La, Inc."
May 15, 1937 (27-32)
Vol. 13 No. 13
A.J. Liebling

Fish, Hamilton, Jr.
U.S. Congressman
"The Gentleman
in Politics"
October 7, 1933 (23-26)
Vol. 9 No. 34
Geoffrey T. Hellman

Fishberg, Isaac
Flautist
"The Five Generations"
October 29, 1949 (32-51)
Vol. 25 No. 36
Andy Logan

Fisher, Clyde
Curator-in-Chief,
Hayden Planetarium
"The Moon's Best Friend"
Dec. 28, 1940 (23-28)
Vol. 16 No. 46
E.J. Kahn, Jr.

Fisher, (Bud) Harry Conway
Cartoonist ("Mutt and
Jeff")
"Me–Mutt!"
Nov. 26, 1927 (27-29)
Vol. 3 No. 41
Kelly Coombs

Fisk, Eliot
Classical guitarist
"Figuring It Out"
March 30, 1992 (56-65)
Vol. 68 No. 6
Kennedy Fraser

Fitzgerald, F. Scott
Author
"That Sad Young Man"
April 17, 1926 (20-21)
Vol. 2 No. 9
John Chapin Mosher

Flaherty, Robert J.
Documentary film
producer
"Moviemaker"
June 11, 1949 (30-45)
June 18, 1949 (28-41)
Vol. 25 Nos. 16-17
Robert Lewis Taylor

Flexner, Abraham
Educator; Rockefeller
Foundation executive
"Robin Hood, 1930"
Nov. 22, 1930 (29-32)
Vol. 6 No. 40
Samuel Chotzinoff

Flood, Hugh G.
House-wrecking
contractor
"The Mayor of the
Fish Market"
January 1, 1944 (25-34)
Vol. 19 No. 46
Joseph Mitchell

Flynn, Edward Joseph
Lawyer; chairman,
Democratic National
Committee
"Nothing Much to It"
Sept. 8, 1945 (28-41)
Vol. 21 No. 30
Richard H. Rovere

Fokker, Anthony Herman
Gerald
Airplane designer,
manufacturer
"Flying Dutchman"
February 7, 1931 (20-24)
Vol. 6 No. 51
Doree Smedley and
Hollister Noble

Fonda, Henry
Motion picture actor
"The Player - II"
October 28, 1961 (61-72)
Vol. 37 No. 37
Lillian Ross

Ford, Henry
Owner, Ford Automobile
Company
"Model T"
March 3, 1928 (29-31)
March 10, 1928 (29-31)
March 17, 1928 (33-36)
March 24, 1928 (26-28)
Vol. 4 Nos. 2-5
Niven Busch, Jr.

Forster, E.M. (Edward Morgan)
Author
"Kingsman"
Sept. 19, 1959 (51-80)
Vol. 35 No. 31
Mollie Panter-Downes

Fosdick, (Harry) Emerson
Minister
"A Twentieth-century
Puritan"
June 18, 1927 (18-20)
Vol. 3 No. 18
Lurton Blassingame

Foster, William Zebulon
Communist; imprisoned
at Hart's Island
"Our Own Lenin"
June 28, 1930 (19-22)
Vol. 6 No. 19
Alva Johnston

Fraad, Daniel, Jr.
President, Allied
Maintenance Corp.
"Holy Smokestacks,
What a Mess!"
March 24, 1956 (39-73)
Vol. 32 No. 5
Thomas Whiteside

Frankfurter, Felix
U.S. S.C. Justice
"Jurist"
Nov. 30, 1940 (24-32)
Dec. 7, 1940 (34-44)
Dec. 14, 1940 (24-34)
Vol. 16 Nos. 42-44
Matthew Josephson

Franklin, Joe
Television personality
"Broadway Joe"
May 22, 1971 (44-55)
Vol. 47 No. 14
William Whitworth

Franklin, Marty
Confidence man
"Broadway Chiseller"
April 20, 1935 (22-26)
Vol. 11 No. 10
Meyer Berger

Franklin, Sidney
Matador
"El Unico Matador"
March 12, 1949 (34-47)
March 19, 1949 (34-51)
March 26, 1949 (32-56)
Vol. 25 Nos. 3-5
Lillian Ross

Fraser, Charles
Developer
"Encounters With the
Archdruid - II"
March 27, 1971 (42-80)
Vol. 47 No. 6
John McPhee

Fraser, Leon
  Bank president
  "The Hat on the
  Roll-Top Desk"
  Feb. 14, 1942 (22-26)
  Feb. 21, 1942 (21-28)
  Vol. 17 No. 53 and
  Vol. 18 No. 1
  Matthew Josephson

Frazier, Brenda Diana Duff
  Socialite; débutante
  "Just a Débutante"
  June 10, 1939 (23-28)
  Vol. 15 No. 17
  E.J. Kahn, Jr.

Freeman, Bud
  Jazz musician
  * Our Far-Flung
  Correspondents
  April 2, 1979 (98-108)
  Vol. 55 No. 7
  John Bainbridge

Freitas, Robert
  Western field representa
  tive, National Association
  of Professional Baseball
  Leagues
  "Down in the Minors"
  October 6, 1975 (46-96)
  Vol. 51 No. 33
  Hendrik Hertzberg

French, Fred F.
  Real estate investor;
  building contractor
  "Realtor"
  June 1, 1929 (22-25)
  Vol. 5 No. 15
  Robert M. Coates

Frey, Fritz
  Swiss hotelier
  "The Impeccable Glass"
  August 13, 1955 (29-47)
  Vol. 31 No. 26
  Joseph Wechsberg

Frick, Helen Clay
  Director, Frick Art
  Reference Library;
  philanthropist
  "Daughter of Her Father"
  July 15, 1939 (21-25)
  July 22, 1939 (23-26)
  Vol. 15 Nos. 22-23
  John McCarten

Friendly, Fred W.
  Television producer
  "The One-Ton Pencil"
  Feb. 17, 1962 (41-88)
  Vol. 37 No. 53
  Thomas Whiteside

Frohman, Daniel
  Theater agent
  "Dean of the Theatre"
  October 28, 1933 (21-23)
  Nov. 4, 1933 (21-24)
  Vol. 9 Nos. 36-37
  Alva Johnston

Frost, Robert
    Poet
    "North of Boston"
    June 6, 1931 (24-27)
    Vol. 7 No. 16
    Raymond Holden

Fugard, Athol
    Playwright, director
    "Witness"
    Dec. 20, 1982 (47-94)
    Vol. 58 No. 44
    Mel Gussow

Fuller, Alfred Carl
    President, Fuller
    Brush Company
    "May I Just Step Inside?"
    Nov. 13, 1948 (36-59)
    Vol. 24 No. 38
    John Bainbridge

Fuller, Richard Buckminster
    Architect; designer;
    inventor; engineer
    "In the Outlaw Area"
    January 8, 1966 (35-97)
    Vol. 41 No. 47
    Calvin Tomkins

Funt, Allen
    Cameraman; host,
    "Candid Camera"
    television show
    "Student of the
    Spontaneous"
    Dec. 10, 1960 (59-92)
    Vol. 36 No. 43
    J.M. Flagler

Furman, Max
    Burlesque comedian
    "Takes"
    August 31, 1981 (42-59)
    Vol. 57 No. 28
    James Stevenson

Furst, Bruno
    Hypnotist; graphologist
    "Mnemonist"
    Feb. 23, 1946 (32-43)
    Vol. 22 No. 2
    Richard H. Rovere

Gabler, Milton
    Owner, Commodore
    Music Shop
    "For Kicks"
    March 9, 1946 (30-37)
    March 16, 1946 (34-43)
    Vol. 22 Nos. 4-5
    Gilbert Millstein

Gadd, May
    Authority on folk dancing
    "Lilt"
    February 7, 1953 (36-55)
    Vol. 28 No. 51
    Angelica Gibbs

Gallatin, Albert Eugene
    Founder, manager,
    Museum of Living Art
    "The Medici on
    Washington Square"
    January 18, 1941 (25-32)
    Vol. 16 No. 49
    Geoffrey T. Hellman

Gallup, George Horace
Opinion poll taker
"Black Beans and
White Beans"
March 2, 1940 (20-24)
Vol. 16 No. 3
J.J. O'Malley

Gambon, Michael
Actor
"The Complete Actor"
Jan. 28, 1991 (60-77)
Vol. 66 No. 50
Mel Gussow

Gamelin, Maurice-Gustave
Commander, Allied
Armies in France
"Generalissimo"
May 11, 1940 (24-27)
May 18, 1940 (22-26)
Vol. 16 Nos. 13-14
A.J. Liebling

Gandhi, Mohandas
Karamchand
Pacifist leader, India
"Mahatma Gandhi and
His Apostles"
May 10, 1976 (43-102)
May 17, 1976 (38-123)
May 24, 1976 (41-102)
Vol. 52 Nos. 12-14
Ved Mehta

Ganger, I. Arthur
Director, bar
equipment business
"Second-Hand Hot Spots"
Sept. 21, 1940 (24-31)
Vol. 16 No. 32
Joseph Mitchell

Garand, John C.
Inventor, semi-automatic
rifle
"The Man Behind
the Gun"
February 6, 1943 (22-28)
Vol. 18 No. 51
John McCarten

Garbo, Greta
Motion picture actress
"American Pro Tem"
March 7, 1931 (28-31)
Vol. 7 No. 3
"Virgilia Saphiea"
(Virgilia Peterson Ross)

Garcia, Dolores
Native American (N.M.)
"Una Anciana"
Nov. 5, 1973 (54-86)
Vol. 49 No. 37
Robert Coles

Garden, Mary
Soprano
"Salome Redivivus"
Dec. 11, 1926 (31-33)
Vol. 2 No. 43
John K. Winkler

Gardner, John
  Republican politician
  * A Reporter at Large
  "Conversation With a
  Citizen"
  July 23, 1973 (35-55)
  Vol. 49 No. 22
  Elizabeth Drew

Garroway, Dave
  Television personality
  "The Time is Twenty-One
  After"
  Sept. 5, 1959 (39-71)
  Vol. 35 No. 29
  Thomas Whiteside

Gaston, Raymond D. (pseud.)
  Monte Carlo croupier
  "Rouge, Impair, et
  Manque"
  July 9, 1949 (25-36)
  Vol. 25 No. 20
  Joseph Wechsberg

Gatti-Casazza, Giulio
  Impresario, Metropolitan
  Opera Company
  "Maestrissimo!"
  February 22, 1925 (9-10)
  Vol. 1 No. 1
  "Golly-Wogg"
  (Gilbert W. Gabriel)

Geer, Alpheus
  Leader of the Marshall
  Stillman Movement,
  anti-crime reform
  "The M-S-M"
  May 11, 1929 (23-26)
  Vol. 5 No. 12
  Alva Johnston

Gehrig, Lou
  New York Yankees
  "The Little Heinie"
  August 10, 1929 (22-25)
  Vol. 5 No. 25
  Niven Busch, Jr.

Geisel, Theodore Seuss
  Author, illustrator
  "Children's Friend"
  Dec. 17, 1960 (47-93)
  Vol. 36 No. 44
  E.J. Kahn, Jr.

Geldzahler, Henry
  Curator
  "Moving With the Flow"
  Nov. 6, 1971 (58-113)
  Vol. 47 No. 38
  Calvin Tomkins

Gerguson, Harry F. ("Prince
Dmitri Michl Obolenski-
Romanoff")
  Restaurateur, impostor
  "The Education of
  a Prince"
  October 29, 1932 (19-23)
  Nov. 5, 1932 (28-32)
  Nov. 12, 1932 (24-28)
  Nov. 19, 1932 (24-28)
  Nov. 26, 1932 (24-29)
  Vol. 8 Nos. 37-41
  Alva Johnston

Gershwin, George
  Composer
  "Troubadour"
  May 25, 1929 (27-29)
  Vol. 5 No. 14
  S.N. Behrman

Gest, Morris
  Theatrical producer
  "The Black Hat"
  June 27, 1925 (7-8)
  Vol. 1 No. 19
  Gilbert W. Gabriel

Gheen, Celeste
  Model
  "Powers Model"
  Sept. 14, 1940 (26-33)
  Vol. 16 No. 31
  E.J. Kahn, Jr.

Gibbons, Euell Theophilus
  Author of books on
  wild food
  "A Forager"
  April 6, 1968 (45-104)
  Vol. 44 No. 7
  John McPhee

Gibbs, William Francis
  Naval architect
  "The Best I Know How"
  June 6, 1964 (49-84)
  Vol. 40 No. 16
  Winthrop Sargeant

Giegengack, Augustus E.
  Head, U.S. Government
  Printing Office
  "Mr. Public Printer"
  June 12, 1943 (24-33)
  June 19, 1943 (28-39)
  June 26, 1943 (24-30)
  Vol. 19 Nos. 17-19
  Geoffrey T. Hellman

Gielgud, Sir John
  Actor
  "The Player - III"
  Nov. 4, 1961 (110-125)
  Vol. 37 No. 38
  Lillian Ross

Gifford, Walter Sherman
President, American
Telephone and Telegraph
Company
"Chief Operator"
June 5, 1937 (22-27)
June 12, 1937 (22-27)
June 19, 1937 (22-28)
Vol. 13 Nos. 16-18
Jack Alexander

Gilbert, Alfred Carlton
Founder, A.C. Gilbert
toy company
"American Boy"
Dec. 20, 1952 (36-55)
Vol. 28 No. 44
John Bainbridge

Gilbert, Eugene
Author; advertising
researcher
"A Caste, a Culture,
A Market"
Nov. 22, 1958 (57-94)
Nov. 29, 1958 (57-107)
Vol. 34 Nos. 40-41
Dwight Macdonald

Gilbert, Louis Dusenbery
Minority stockholder
"The Talking
Stockbroker"
Dec. 11, 1948 (40-54)
Dec. 18, 1948 (33-47)
Vol. 24 Nos. 42-43
John Bainbridge

Gillespie, Dizzy (John Berks)
Orchestra leader;
trumpet player
"Bop"
July 3, 1948 (28-37)
Vol. 24 No. 19
Richard Owen Boyer

"Dizzy"
Sept. 17, 1990 (48-58)
Vol. 66 No. 31
Whitney Balliett

Gillhaus, John
Trolley operator, Sixth
Avenue line
"Ex-Motorman"
Nov. 7, 1936 (23-27)
Vol. 12 No. 38
Ik Shuman

Gingold, Josef
Violinist
"A Gold Coin"
February 4, 1991 (34-57)
Vol. 66 No. 51
David Blum

Ginsberg, Allen
Poet
"Paterfamilias"
August 17, 1968 (32-73)
August 24, 1968 (38-91)
Vol. 44 Nos. 26-27
Jane Kramer

Glendon, Richard A. and
Richard J.
    U.S. Naval Academy
    rowing coaches
    "Old Dick and
    Young Dick"
    June 16, 1928 (25-27)
    Vol. 4 No. 17
    Robert F. Kelley

Glow, Bernie
    Trumpet player
    "Lead Player"
    Dec. 20, 1969 (43-54)
    Vol. 45 No. 44
    William Whitworth

Gmeiner, Hermann
    Organizer, SOS Children's
    Villages
    "A House Called Peace"
    Dec. 22, 1962 (39-65)
    Vol. 38 No. 43
    Joseph Wechsberg

Godard, Jean-Luc
    Film director
    "The Urgent Whisper"
    October 25, 1976 (47-58)
    Vol. 52 No. 36
    Penelope Gilliatt

Godowsky, Leopold
    Co-inventor, Kodachrome
    film developing process
    "Whistling in the
    Darkroom"
    Nov. 10, 1956 (61-109)
    Vol. 32 No. 38
    Joseph Wechsberg

Goelet, Robert G.
    President, American
    Museum of Natural
    History (N.Y.)
    "You've Simply Got to Go
    Out and Raise the
    Scratch"
    October 18, 1976 (45-69)
    Vol. 52 No. 35
    Geoffrey T. Hellman

Goldberg, Arthur Joseph
    U.S. Secretary of Labor;
    Justice, U.S. Supreme
    Court
    "Peacemaker"
    April 7, 1962 (49-112)
    April 14, 1962 (49-105)
    Vol. 38 Nos. 7-8
    Robert Shaplen

Goldrick, Joseph D.
    N.Y.C. Comptroller
    "Professor in Politics"
    August 11, 1934 (19-22)
    Vol. 10 No. 26
    Milton MacKaye

Goldwater, Barry
    U.S. Senator (retired)
    "AuH2O"
    April 25, 1988 (43-73)
    Vol. 64 No. 10
    Burton Bernstein

Goldwyn, Samuel
    Motion picture producer
    "The Celluloid Prince"
    April 25, 1925 (13-14)
    Vol. 1 No. 10
    Carl Brandt (no byline)

Goode, Richard
    Concert pianist
    "Going to the Core"
    June 29, 1992 (39-62)
    Vol. 68 No. 19
    David Blum

Goodman, Benny
    Band leader, clarinetist
    "Alligators' Idol"
    April 17, 1937 (31-38)
    Vol. 13 No. 9
    Anton Steig

    * Our Local
    Correspondents
    "S.R.O."
    Dec. 26, 1977 (33-41)
    Vol. 53 No. 45
    Whitney Balliett

Goodman, Edwin
    Owner, Bergdorf
    Goodman
    "The Boss"
    Nov. 3, 1934 (24-28)
    Vol. 10 No. 38
    Helena Huntington Smith

Gordon, David
    Dancer
    "Making Work"
    Nov. 29, 1982 (51-107)
    Vol. 58 No. 41
    Arlene Croce

Gordon, John
    American folk art dealer
    "A Great Flowering of
    Free Spirits"
    February 3, 1973 (39-58)
    Vol. 48 No. 50
    Whitney Balliett

Gordon, Max
    Theatrical producer
    "The Old Max"
    March 29, 1941 (22-30)
    Vol. 17 No. 7
    Margaret Case Harriman

Gordon, Max
    Nightclub proprietor
    "Night Clubs"
    October 9, 1971 (50-92)
    Vol. 47 No. 34
    Whitney Balliett

Gordon, Mazie Phillips
("Bowery Angel")
    Ticket seller, Venice
    Theatre on Bowery
    "Mazie"
    Dec. 21, 1940 (22-36)
    Vol. 16 No. 45
    Joseph Mitchell

Goudsmit, Samuel A.
    Chairman, Physics
    Department, Brookhaven
    National Laboratory
    "A Farewell to String and
    Sealing Wax"
    Nov. 7, 1953 (47-72)
    Nov. 14, 1953 (46-67)
    Vol. 29 Nos. 38-39
    Daniel Lang

Goudy, Frederick William
    Type designer
    "Glorifer of the Alphabet"
    January 14, 1933 (20-24)
    Vol. 8 No. 48
    Milton MacKaye

Gould, Glenn
    Pianist
    "Apollonian"
    May 14, 1960 (51-93)
    Vol. 36 No. 13
    Joseph Roddy

Gould, Joe (Joseph
Ferdinand)
    Author (unpublished)
    "Professor Sea Gull"
    Dec. 12, 1942 (28-43)
    Vol. 18 No. 43
    Joseph Mitchell

    "Joe Gould's Secret"
    Sept. 19, 1964 (61-125)
    Sept. 26, 1964 (53-125)
    Vol. 40 Nos. 31-32
    Joseph Mitchell

Gould, Samuel B.
    Chancellor, State
    University of New York
    "A Certain Attitude
    Toward Change"
    Nov. 18, 1967 (67-128)
    Vol. 43 No. 39
    Calvin Tomkins

Goulding, Raymond Walter
    Ray of "Bob and Ray"
    comedy team
    "Their Own Gravity"
    Sept. 24, 1973 (42-65)
    Vol. 49 No. 31
    Whitney Balliett

Graebner, Clark
    Tennis player
    "Levels of the Game"
    June 7, 1969 (45-111)
    June 14, 1969 (45-81)
    Vol. 45 Nos. 16-17
    John McPhee

Graham, Florence Nightingale
("Elizabeth Arden")
Founder, Elizabeth Arden
"Glamour, Inc."
April 6, 1935 (24-30)
Vol. 11 No. 8
Margaret Case Harriman

Graham, Martha
Dancer, choreographer
"The Absolute Frontier"
Dec. 27, 1947 (28-37)
Vol. 23 No. 45
Angelica Gibbs

Grainger, Percy
Composer; pianist
"Musician"
January 31, 1948 (29-37)
Feb. 7, 1948 (32-39)
Feb. 14, 1948 (32-43)
Vol. 23 Nos. 51-52
Robert Lewis Taylor

Grange, Harold E. (Red)
All-America halfback
"All-American"
Oct. 31, 1925 (11-12)
Vol. 31 No. 37
J. R. Tunis

Grant, Cary
Motion picture actor
"The Man From
Dream City"
July 14, 1975 (40-68)
Vol. 51 No. 21
Pauline Kael

Grappelli, Stéphane
Concert violinist
"You Must Start Well and
You Must End Well"
January 19, 1976 (36-42)
Vol. 51 No. 48
Whitney Balliett

Green, Aaron
Psychoanalyst
"Impossible Profession"
Nov. 24, 1980 (55-133)
Dec. 1, 1980 (54-152)
Vol. 56 Nos. 40-41
Janet Malcolm

Green, Cecil
Fishing guide,
Florida Keys
"La Belle Dame
Sans Merci"
Feb. 11, 1961 (39-70)
Feb. 18, 1961 (45-90)
Vol. 36 No. 52 and
Vol. 37 No. 1
Robert Lewis Taylor

Green, Edward Howland
Robinson
Owner, Round Hill
Experimental
Laboratories
"Hetty Green's Son"
January 5, 1929 (24-27)
Vol. 4 No. 46
John K. Winkler

Greene, Graham
Author
"The Dangerous Edge"
March 26, 1979 (43-50)
Vol. 55 No. 6
Penelope Gilliatt

Greenspan, Benjamin E.
New York City Magistrate
"The Human Side"
April 28, 1934 (24-27)
Vol. 10 No. 11
St. Clair McKelway

Greer, Joseph
Roman Catholic priest
"Parish Priest"
June 13, 1988 (39-71)
Vol. 64 No. 17
Paul Wilkes

Greer, Sonny
Drummer
"New York Drummers"
Nov. 5, 1979 (52-76)
Vol. 55 No. 38
Whitney Balliett

Gregorian, Vartan
President, New York
Public Library
"Searching for Gregorian"
April 14, 1986 (45-61)
April 21, 1986 (53-68)
Vol. 62 Nos. 8-9
Philip Hamburger

Grenet, Augustine J.
Bookmaker
"The Line"
July 24, 1937 (20-25)
Vol. 13 No. 23
A.J. Liebling

Grosman, Tatyana
Lithographer
"The Moods of a Stone"
June 7, 1976 (42-76)
Vol. 52 No. 16
Calvin Tomkins

Grossman, Harry
Process-server
"Place and Leave With"
August 24, 1935 (23-26)
August 31, 1935 (21-24)
Vol. 11 Nos. 28-29
St. Clair McKelway

Grosvenor, Gilbert H.
Editor, *National Geographic*
"Geography Unshackled"
Sept. 25, 1943 (26-34)
October 2, 1943 (27-37)
October 9, 1943 (27-36)
Vol. 19 Nos. 32-34
Geoffrey T. Hellman

Grosz, George
Artist
"Artist"
Nov. 27, 1943 (32-43)
Dec. 4, 1943 (35-44)
Dec. 11, 1943 (37-44)
Vol. 19 Nos. 41-43
Richard Owen Boyer

Guérard, Michel
   Chef
   "La Nature des Choses"
   July 28, 1975 (34-48)
   Vol. 51 No. 23
   Joseph Wechsberg

Guitry, Sacha
   Playwright
   "Essence of Chic Paris"
   Dec. 18, 1926 (29-32)
   Vol. 2 No. 44
   Ferdinand Tuohy

Gumpert, Martin
   Physician
   "Geriatrician"
   June 10, 1950 (30-42)
   June 17, 1950 (34-47)
   Vol. 26 Nos. 16-17
   Daniel Lang

Gumpertz, Samuel W.
   Director, Ringling
   Brothers & Barnum &
   Bailey Circus
   "Boss of the Circus - I"
   May 6, 1933 (23-26)
   "Boss of the Big Top - II"
   May 13, 1933 (21-23)
   Vol. 9 Nos. 12-13
   Alva Johnston

Gunther, John
   Author
   "Inside"
   August 23, 1947 (30-40)
   Vol. 23 No. 27
   Richard H. Rovere

Guthrie, William Norman
   Rector, St. Mark's-in-the-
   Bouwerie
   "Lights, Please!"
   January 31, 1931 (22-25)
   Vol. 6 No. 50
   Geoffrey T. Hellman

Gutman, Walter Knowlton
   Investment counselor;
   art critic
   "A Proust in Wall Street"
   June 20, 1959 (41-70)
   Vol. 35 No. 18
   John Brooks

Hackett, Bobby
   Trumpet player
   "More Ingredients"
   August 12, 1972 (36-49)
   Vol. 48 No. 25
   Whitney Balliett

Hackscher, August
   Industrialist;
   philanthropist
   "What is a Merchant?"
   August 2, 1930 (20-23)
   Vol. 6 No. 24
   Babette Deutsch

Haft, Louis
   Owner, Haft Glass
   Company
   "Pause for Reflection"
   May 23, 1953 (39-55)
   Vol. 29 No. 14
   Berton Roueché

Hagen, Walter C.
Golfer
"Portrait of a Dutchman"
June 11, 1927 (17-19)
Vol. 3 No. 17
Niven Busch, Jr.

Haggard, Merle
Country musician
"Ornery"
Feb. 12, 1990 (39-77)
Vol. 65 No. 52
Bryan DiSalvatore

Hagstrom, Andrew Gunnar
Cartographer
"A Short, Squat Island"
April 9, 1949 (39-52)
Vol. 25 No. 7
Robert Rice

Hague, Frank
Mayor, Jersey City, N.J.;
Democratic Committee
Chairman, New Jersey
"Evolution of a
Problem Child"
July 16, 1932 (17-21)
Vol. 8 No. 22
Donald Moffat

"Evolution of a Problem
Child "
Feb. 12, 1938 (20-25)
Feb. 19, 1938 (23-28)
Vol. 13 No. 52 and
Vol. 14 No. 1
John McCarten

Haldeman-Julius, Emanuel
Publisher
"After June 30, the
Deluge"
June 20, 1925 (7-8)
Vol. 1 No. 18
Alexander Woollcott

Hale, Robert Beverly
Art teacher
"All in the Artist's Head"
June 13, 1977 (41-68)
Vol. 53 No. 17
Philip Hamburger

Hall, James Jefferson Davis
Street preacher
"A Spism and a Spasm"
July 24, 1943 (23-37)
Vol. 19 No. 23
Joseph Mitchell

Hall, Jim
Guitarist
"The Answer is Yes"
March 31, 1975 (34-41)
Vol. 51 No. 6
Whitney Balliett

Hallett, George Hervey, Jr.
Executive Secretary,
Citizens Union
"Cit"
August 22, 1953 (31-49)
Vol. 29 No. 27
Dwight MacDonald

Hallock, Joseph Theodore
First Lieutenant, U.S.
Army Air Force
"Young Man Behind
Plexiglass"
August 12, 1944 (26-37)
Vol. 20 No. 26
Brendan Gill

Hamid, George A.
Owner of acrobat agency
for state and county fairs
"Agriculture's Acrobatic
Friend"
Sept. 26, 1936 (18-21)
Vol. 12 No. 32
A.J. Liebling

Hammer, Armand
Entrepreneur
"The Innocents Abroad"
Dec. 23, 1933 (18-21)
Vol. 9 No. 45
Geoffrey T. Hellman

Hammerstein, Oscar, II
Lyricist
"The Perfect Glow"
May 12, 1951 (35-48)
May 19, 1951 (45-63)
Vol. 27 Nos. 13-14
Philip Hamburger

Hammond, John Hays
Inventor
"A Harvest of Inventions"
July 2, 1932 (16-20)
Vol. 8 No. 20
Gilbert Seldes

Hammond, John Henry
Director, Columbia
Recording Corporation
"Young Man With a Viola"
July 29, 1939 (19-24)
Vol. 15 No. 24
E.J. Kahn, Jr.

Hannon, Bryan
Historian; streetcar driver
"The Rolling Historian"
March 2, 1946 (28-39)
Vol. 22 No. 3
Robert Lewis Taylor

Harbach, Otto Abels
Musical comedy writer
"Learned Lyricist"
Feb. 27, 1937 (22-27)
Vol. 13 No. 2
A.J. Liebling

Harburger, John
Milliner, John-Frederics,
Inc.
"The Boys"
Dec. 28, 1935 (21-24)
Vol. 11 No. 46
Margaret Case Harriman

Harding, Edward Forrest
Major General, U.S. Army
"Two-Star General"
Dec. 26, 1942 (21-32)
January 2, 1943 (24-31)
Vol. 18 Nos. 45-46
E.J. Kahn, Jr.

Hardwicke, Cedric
Actor
"The Player - II"
Oct. 28, 1961 (109-120)
Vol. 37 No. 37
Lillian Ross

Harrigan, (Ned) Edward
Green
Entertainer
"Partners"
March 19, 1955 (42-67)
March 26, 1955 (39-72)
April 2, 1955 (45-67)
April 9, 1955 (41-81)
Vol. 31 Nos. 5-8
E.J. Kahn, Jr.

Harriman, W. Averell
Governor, New York State
"Plenipotentiary"
May 3, 1952 (41-67)
May 10, 1952 (36-57)
Vol. 28 Nos. 11-12
E.J. Kahn, Jr.

Harris, Cyril Manton
University professor
"A Quiet Man"
June 17, 1972 (39-67)
Vol. 48 No. 17
Bruce Bliven Jr.

Harrison, Wallace Kirkman
Director of Planning,
United Nations
"Architect"
Nov. 20, 1954 (51-79)
Nov. 27, 1954 (51-85)

Dec. 4, 1954 (55-85)
Vol. 30 Nos. 40-42
Herbert Warren Wind

Hart, Lorenz
Lyricist
"Words and Music"
May 28, 1938 (19-23)
June 4, 1938 (23-27)
Vol. 14 Nos. 15-16
Margaret Case Harriman

Hart, Moss
Playwright; producer
"Hi-yo, Platinum!"
Sept. 11, 1943 (29-43)
Vol. 19 No. 30
Margaret Case Harriman

Hart, Richard Olney
Window-washer, Empire
State Building
"It's Nice Out There This
Morning"
April 24, 1948 (35-49)
Vol. 24 No. 9
Mark Murphy

Hart, Tony
Entertainer
"Partners"
March 19, 1955 (42-67)
March 26, 1955 (39-72)
April 2, 1955 (45-67)
April 9, 1955 (41-81)
Vol. 31 Nos. 5-8
E.J. Kahn, Jr.

Hartmann, Alfred
Chef
"Two Waiters and a Chef"
June 1, 1935 (20-24)
June 8, 1935 (22-26)
Vol. 11 Nos. 16-17
Margaret Case Harriman

Hartzog, George
Director, National Park
Service
"Ranger"
Sept. 11, 1971 (45-89)
Vol. 47 No. 30
John McPhee

Harvey, George Upton
Borough president, Queens
"On the Up"
May 31, 1930 (24-27)
Vol. 6 No. 15
Richard F. Warner

Hayes, Helen
Actress
"Veni, Vidi, Vicky"
May 20, 1939 (24-30)
May 27, 1939 (28-38)
Vol. 15 Nos. 14-15
Margaret Case Harriman

Hayes, Cardinal (Patrick
Joseph)
Cardinal, Archdiocese of
New York
"Cardinal Shepherd"
Feb. 17, 1934 (22-27)
Vol. 10 No. 1
Thomas Sugrue

Haynes, James E.
Liaison officer, New York
City Democratic Party
"The Great Spectator"
Sept. 10, 1932 (21-25)
Vol. 8 No. 30
Stanley Walker

Hays, Will H.
U.S. Postmaster General,
censorship advocate
"Doctor of Movies"
May 8, 1926 (21-22)
Vol. 2 No. 12
Arthur Krock

"Czar and Elder "
June 10, 1933 (18-21)
June 17, 1933 (16-19)
Vol. 9 Nos. 17-18
Alva Johnston

Hayward, Leland
Theatrical and
movie agent
"Hollywood Agent"
July 11, 1936 (20-24)
Vol. 12 No. 21
Margaret Case Harriman

Hearst, William Randolph
  Publisher
  "Notes on an American
  Phenomenon "
  April 23, 1927 (25-27)
  April 30, 1927 (25-28)
  May 7, 1927 (23-26)
  May 14, 1927 (24-27)
  May 21, 1927 (23-26)
  Vol. 3 Nos. 10-14
  John K. Winkler

Heatter, Gabriel
  Radio commentator
  "The Crier"
  January 20, 1945 (23-33)
  Vol. 20 No. 49
  Philip Hamburger

Hedley, Frank
  President, Interborough
  Rapid Transit Company
  "Wheels in His Head"
  Dec. 31, 1927 (17-19)
  Vol. 3 No. 46
  Henry F. Pringle

Heifetz, Jascha
  Violinist
  "Genius About Town"
  Feb. 25, 1928 (23-25)
  Vol. 4 No. 1
  Helena Huntington Smith

Helburn, Theresa
  Director, The Theatre
  Guild
  "Behind the Throne"
  Dec. 6, 1930 (31-34)
  Vol. 6 No. 42
  Marya Mannes

Hellman, Daphne
  Concert harpist
  "Harp Lady"
  Dec. 24, 1990 (40-44)
  Vol. 66 No. 45
  Whitney Balliett

Hellman, Lillian
  Playwright
  "Miss Lily of New
  Orleans"
  Nov. 8, 1941 (22-35)
  Vol. 17 No. 39
  Margaret Case Harriman

Helms, Richard
  Former director, CIA
  *Reflections
  "Secrets"
  April 10, 1978 (44-86)
  Vol. 54 No. 8
  Richard Harris

Hemingway, Ernest
  Author
  "The Artist's Reward"
  Nov. 30, 1929 (28-31)
  Vol. 5 No. 41
  Dorothy Parker

Hemingway, Ernest *cont.*
"How Do You Like It Now,
Gentlemen?"
May 13, 1950 (36-62)
Vol. 26 No. 12
Lillian Ross

Henderson, William James
Music critic
"Opera and the Dean"
October 30, 1926 (23-25)
Vol. 2 No. 37
Hollister Noble

Henrich, Thomas David
Baseball player
"Old Reliable"
June 4, 1949 (33-45)
Vol. 25 No. 15
Richard O. Boyer

Herrick, Myron T.
U.S. Ambassador
to   France
"Master of Ceremonies"
July 21, 1928 (19-22)
Vol. 4 No. 22
James Thurber

Herrmann, Emil
Violin dealer
"Trustee in Fiddledale"
October 17, 1953 (38-59)
October 24, 1953 (39-63)
Vol. 29 Nos. 35-36
Joseph Wechsberg

Hertz, Mr. And Mrs. John D.
Horse owners
"Crazy Over Horses"
June 7, 1930 (22-25)
Vol. 6 No. 16
Helena Huntington Smith

Hewitt, Don
Producer, CBS'
60 Minutes
"The Candy Factory"
July 19, 1982 (40-61)
July 26, 1982 (38-55)
Vol. 58 Nos. 22-23
E.J. Kahn, Jr.

Hewitt, Edward Ringwood
Mack truck heir;
fly fisherman
"Compleat Angler"
Feb. 24, 1934 (23-26)
Vol. 10 No. 2
Geoffrey T. Hellman

Heydenryk, Henry
Picture framer
"An Enhancing Adjunct"
April 27, 1963 (49-81)
Vol. 39 No. 10
John Brooks

Hicks, Ray
Story teller
"Overgrown Jack"
July 18, 1988 (33-41)
Vol. 64 No. 22
Gwen Kinkead

Hildreth, Samuel
Race horse trainer
"All the King's Horses"
August 24, 1929 (20-23)
Vol. 5 No. 27
Niven Busch, Jr.

Hines, ("Father") Earl
Jazz pianist, band leader
"Rhythm in My Mind"
January 2, 1965 (39-57)
Vol. 40 No. 46
Whitney Balliett

Hines, Jimmy (James J.)
Leader, N.Y.C. 16th
Assembly District
"District Leader "
July 25, 1936 (21-26)
August 1, 1936 (18-23)
August 8, 1936 (18-24)
Vol. 12 Nos. 23-25
Jack Alexander

Hirst, Frederic
Milliner, John-Frederics,
Inc.
"The Boys"
Dec. 28, 1935 (21-24)
Vol. 11 No. 46
Margaret Case Harriman

Hitchcock, Alfred
Film director
"What Happens
After That"
Sept. 10, 1938 (28-32)
Vol. 14 No. 30
Russell Maloney

Hitchcock, Tommy
Polo player
"The Galloping
Hitchcocks"
August 14, 1926 (17-18)
Vol. 2 No. 26
Herbert Reed

Hitler, Adolf
German dictator
"Führer "
Feb. 29, 1936 (20-24)
March 7, 1936 (27-31)
March 14, 1936 (22-26)
Vol. 12 Nos. 2-4
Janet Flanner

Hockney, David
Artist
"Special Effects"
July 30, 1979 (35-69)
Vol. 55 No. 24
Anthony Bailey

Hodge, Paul
Chief Petty Officer,
U.S. Navy
"C.P.O."
January 30, 1943 (22-28)
Vol. 18 No. 50
John Kirkpatrick

Hoffer, Eric
Longshoreman; author
"The Creative Situation"
January 7, 1967 (34-77)
Vol. 42 No. 46
Calvin Tomkins

Holden, William
  Motion picture actor
  "The Player - I"
  Oct. 21, 1961 (111-118)
  Vol. 37 No. 36
  Lillian Ross

Hollins, Albert
  Bomb factory worker
  "The Spinner of
  Bomb Bay"
  March 7, 1942 (20-26)
  Vol. 18 No. 3
  St. Clair McKelway

Holtzmann, Fanny
  Attorney
  "Miss Fixit "
  January 30, 1937 (21-25)
  February 6, 1937 (22-25)
  Vol. 12 Nos. 50-51
  Margaret Case Harriman

Hood, Fredrick E.
  Sailmaker
  "Sailmaker"
  August 26, 1967 (34-73)
  Vol. 43 No. 27
  Anthony Bailey

Hood, Raymond Mathewson
  Architect
  "Man Against the Sky"
  April 11, 1931 (24-27)
  Vol. 7 No. 8
  Allene Talmey

Hoopingarner, Newman
Leander
  Business professor,
  New York University
  "Cubit-Adder"
  April 16, 1932 (21-24)
  Vol. 8 No. 9
  Russell Robbins Lord

Hoover, Herbert
  U.S. President
  "The President"
  Dec. 27, 1930 (20-23)
  January 3, 1931 (22-25)
  January 10, 1931 (22-25)
  Vol. 6 Nos. 45-47
  Henry F. Pringle

Hopkins, Arthur
  Theater director
  "A Timid Little Man"
  March 21, 1925 (9-10)
  Vol. 1 No. 5
  R. Hale (no byline)

Hopkins, Harry L.
  Advisor to President
  Franklin D. Roosevelt
  "House Guest"
  August 7, 1943 (25-31)
  August 14, 1943 (27-35)
  Vol. 19 Nos. 25-26
  Geoffrey T. Hellman

Hoppe, William Fredrick
Billiard player
"A Powerful Cue"
Nov. 16, 1940 (24-33)
Vol. 16 No. 40
Robert Lewis Taylor

Hopps, Walter
Museum director; found
ing director, Menil
Collection, Metropolitan
Museum of Art
"A Touch for the Now"
July 29, 1991 (33-57)
Vol. 67 No. 23
Calvin Tomkins

Horne, Marilyn
Singer
"When I Open Up
Down There, You'd
Better Look Out"
Sept. 2, 1972 (31-43)
Vol. 48 No. 28
Winthrop Sargeant

Hougen, Rev. Edward Thomas
Pastor, Central Congre-
gational Church (Mass.)
"The Good News"
May 12, 1973 (45-64)
Vol. 49 No. 12
Berton Roueché

Houston, James
Artist, designer, author
"Man"
August 29, 1988 (33-47)
Vol. 64 No. 28
Mary D. Kierstead

Hoving, Thomas P.F.
New York City Parks
Commissioner; director,
Metropolitan Museum
of Art
"A Roomful of Hovings"
May 20, 1967 (49-137)
Vol. 43 No. 13
John McPhee

Howard, Roy Wilson
Publisher, Scripps-Howard
newspapers
"Publisher"
August 2, 1941 (21-28)
August 9, 1941 (20-31)
August 16, 1941 (20-27)
August 23, 1941 (23-33)
Vol. 17 Nos. 25-28
A.J. Liebling

Howe, William F.
Lawyer
"89 Centre Street"
Nov. 23, 1946 (36-54)
Nov. 30, 1946 (44-57)
Dec. 7, 1946 (46-64)
Dec. 14, 1946 (47-59)
Vol. 22 Nos. 41-44
Richard H. Rovere

Huggins, Miller
    Manager, New York Yankees
    "A Small Package"
    October 8, 1927 (25-27)
    Vol. 3 No. 34
    Henry F. Pringle

Hughes, Charles Evans
    U.S. Supreme Court
    Chief Justice
    "Chief Justice"
    June 29, 1935 (20-24)
    July 6, 1935 (18-22)
    July 13, 1935 (18-22)
    Vol. 11 Nos. 20-22
    Henry F. Pringle

Hulten, Pontus
    Director, Centre
    Pompidou (Beaubourg)
    Museum, Paris
    "A Good Monster"
    January 16, 1978 (37-67)
    Vol. 53 No. 48
    Calvin Tomkins

Humes, Helen
    Popular singer
    * Our Local
    Correspondents
    "Helen Humes"
    Feb. 24, 1975 (98-103)
    Vol. 51 No. 1
    Whitney Balliett

Hummel, Abraham H.
    Lawyer
    "89 Centre Street"
    Nov. 23, 1946 (36-54)
    Nov. 30, 1946 (44-57)
    Dec. 7, 1946 (46-64)
    Dec. 14, 1946 (47-59)
    Vol. 22 Nos. 41-44
    Richard H. Rovere

Humphrey, Elliott (Jack)
    Director, The Seeing Eye
    (guide dogs for the blind)
    "The House That
    Jack Built"
    Dec. 26, 1936 (20-25)
    Vol. 12 No. 45
    Alexander Woollcott

Humphreys, Joe (Joseph E.)
    Fight announcer
    "Stentor "
    October 14, 1933 (24-27)
    October 21, 1933 (27-30)
    Vol. 9 Nos. 34-35
    Meyer Berger

Humphries, Barry
    Entertainer, "Dame Edna
    Everage"
    "Playing Possum"
    July 1, 1991 (38-66)
    Vol. 67 No. 19
    John Lahr

Hunt, Linda
  Actor
  "A Part in the Play"
  July 30, 1990 (37-54)
  Vol. 66 No. 24
  Cynthia Zarin

Hunter, George H.
  Trustee, African
  Methodist Church
  "Mr. Hunter's Grave"
  Sept. 22, 1956 (50-89)
  Vol. 32 No. 31
  Joseph Mitchell

Huntley, Chet
  Television news
  correspondent
  "An Accident of Casting"
  August 3, 1968 (34-60)
  William Whitworth

Hupfer, William
  Piano tuner
  "Piano Man"
  May 9, 1953 (39-63)
  Vol. 29 No. 12
  Bruce Bliven

Hussein bin Htalal
  King of Jordan
  "Monarch"
  Sept. 19, 1983 (49-120)
  Vol. 59 No. 31
  John Newhouse

Illich, Ivan
  Roman Catholic priest;
  educator; author
  "The Rules of the Game"
  April 25, 1970 (40-92)
  Vol. 46 No. 10
  Francine du Plessix Gray

Ingersoll, Ralph McAllister
  Editor, *PM*
  "A Very Active Type Man"
  May 2, 1942 (21-30)
  May 9, 1942 (21-30)
  Vol. 18 Nos. 11-12
  Wolcott Gibbs

Irwin, Bill
  Clown
  "Clown"
  Nov. 11, 1985 (51-87)
  Vol. 61 No. 38
  Mel Gussow

Irwin, Robert
  Artist
  "Taking Art to Point Zero"
  March 8, 1982 (48-95)
  March 15, 1982 (52-105)
  Vol. 58 Nos. 3-4
  Lawrence Weschler

Isaacs, Gary
  Scientist
  "Bells and Whistles"
  October 8, 1990 (76-97)
  Vol. 66 No. 34
  Lawrence Weschler

Isaacs, Stanley M.
    Member, N.Y.C. Council
    "The Public Be Served"
    Dec. 12, 1959 (59-96)
    Dec. 19, 1959 (41-71)
    Vol. 35 Nos. 43-44
    J.M. Flagler

Istel, Jacques André
    Skydiver
    "No Feeling of Falling"
    January 24, 1959 (42-73)
    Vol. 34 No. 49
    Robert Lewis Taylor

Jackson, David Sidney
    Specialist, New York
    Stock Exchange
    "The True Mobility"
    October 1, 1955 (41-72)
    Vol. 31 No. 33
    John Brooks

Jackson, Edward N.
    Photographer, *New York*
    Daily News
    "News Photographer"
    Dec. 1, 1934 (28-31)
    Dec. 8, 1934 (28-31)
    Vol. 10 Nos. 42-43
    Alva Johnston

Jackson, Jesse
    Politician
    "Outsider"
    Feb. 3, 1992 (36-69)
    Feb. 10, 1992 (41-75)
    Vol. 67 Nos. 50-51
    Marshall Frady

Jacobs, Hirsch
    Race horse trainer
    "Pigeon Man's Progress"
    August 5, 1939 (20-24)
    Vol. 15 No. 25
    G.F.T. Ryall

Jaeckel, Richard
    Furrier
    "Mr. Jaeckel and a Few
    Hides"
    April 9, 1932 (22-25)
    Vol. 8 No. 8
    S.N. Behrman

James, Edwin Leland
    European correspondent,
    New York Times
    "The Man Who Ruined
    Paris"
    October 2, 1926 (25-26)
    Vol. 2 No. 33
    Alexander Woollcott

Janis, Sidney
    Art dealer
    "Why Fight It?"
    Nov. 12, 1960 (59-101)
    Vol. 36 No. 39
    John Brooks

Jannings, Emil
    Motion picture actor
    "The Cinema Cherub"
    January 28, 1928 (20-33)
    Vol. 3 No. 50
    Elsie McCormick

Biographical Articles 1925-1992   79

Janssen, Werner
Conductor
"American Maestro"
October 20, 1934 (22-26)
October 27, 1934 (23-26)
Vol. 10 Nos. 36-37
Alva Johnston

Javits, Jacob K.
U.S. Senator (R-N.Y.)
"The Gentleman From
New York"
January 21, 1950 (31-45)
January 28, 1950 (30-42)
Vol. 25 Nos. 48-49
E.J. Kahn, Jr.

Jeannert, Charles Edouard
see Le Corbusier

Jeffers, Henry William
Milk distributor
"Milkman"
Dec. 3, 1932 (22-26)
Vol. 8 No. 42
Russell Robbins Lord

Jensen, Knud
Director, Louisiana
Museum, Humlebaek,
Denmark
"Louisiana in Denmark"
August 30, 1982 (36-61)
Vol. 58 No. 28
Lawrence Weschler

Jeritza, Maria
Singer, Metropolitan
Opera Company
"Viennese Tomboy"
January 24, 1931 (21-24)
Vol. 6 No. 49
Pitts Sanborn

Jerome, William Travers
Manhattan District
Attorney
"St. George of
Manhattan"
January 30, 1932 (19-23)
Vol. 7 No. 50
Milton MacKaye

Johnson, Chic
Comedian; stager of
Hellz-a-Poppin
"No Suave Inflections"
January 28, 1939 (20-25)
Vol. 14 No. 50
A.J. Liebling

Johnson, Edward
General Director,
Metropolitan Opera
Company
"General Director"
Dec. 14, 1935 (30-33)
Vol. 11 No. 44
Robert Alfred Simon

Johnson, Frederick
Captain, S.S. *Josiah Crabtree*
"Long After Bligh"
Sept. 30, 1944 (27-37)
Vol. 20 No. 33
John McCarten

Johnson, Hugh K.
Anthropologist
"Who You Are and What You Think You're Doing"
Dec. 23, 1961 (32-56)
Vol. 37 No. 45
Robert Rice

Johnson, Hugh Samuel
Brigadier General, U.S. Army; Director, National Recovery Administration
"The General"
August 18, 1934 (19-23)
August 25, 1934 (23-28)
Sept. 1, 1934 (22-28)
Vol. 10 Nos. 27-29
Matthew Josephson

Johnson, James Jay
Boxing promoter; assis tant to president of Madison Square Garden
"Compleat Angler"
January 23, 1932 (21-24)
Vol. 7 No. 49
Joel Sayre

Johnson, James Weldon
Author, NAACP leader
"Dark Leader"
Sept. 30, 1933 (20-24)
Vol. 9 No. 33
Robert Wohlforth

Johnson, James William
Collector, Internal Revenue Service
"The Friendly Attitude"
March 15, 1947 (36-50)
Vol. 23 No. 4
E.J. Kahn, Jr.

Johnson, Philip
Architect
"Forms Under Light"
May 23, 1977 (43-80)
Vol. 53 No. 14
Calvin Tomkins

Johnson, Robert J. (pseud.)
Insurance salesman
"Insurance Man"
July 7, 1934 (20-26)
Vol. 10 No. 21
St. Clair McKelway

Jones, Bassett
Chairman, Display Board, New York World's Fair
"Day-Before-Yesterday Man"
April 29, 1939 (24-30)
Vol. 15 No. 11
Geoffrey T. Hellman

Jones, Bobby (Robert Tyre)
Golfer
"Golf's Chevalier Bayard"
July 17, 1926 (17-20)
Vol. 2 No. 22
Herbert Reed

Jones, Elvin
Jazz drummer
"A Walk to the Park"
May 18, 1968 (45-70)
Vol. 44 No. 13
Whitney Balliett

Jones, Robert Edmond
Stage designer
"The Emperor Jones"
May 9, 1931 (25-28)
Vol. 7 No. 12
Gilbert Seldes

Jones, Robert Trent
Golf course architect
"Linksland and
Meadowland"
August 4, 1951 (28-43)
Vol. 27 No. 25
Herbert Warren Wind

Josephs, Louis ("Joe Frisco")
Broadway comedian
"Young Man From
Dubuque"
Sept. 26, 1925 (9-10)
Vol. 1 No. 32
Jo Swerling

Josephson, Barney
Nightclub proprietor
"Night Clubs"
October 9, 1971 (50-92)
Vol. 47 No. 34
Whitney Balliett

Julian, Hubert
Aviator; skydiver
"The Black Eagle"
July 11, 1931 (22-25)
July 18, 1931 (20-23)
Vol. 7 Nos. 21-22
Morris Markey

Kahn, Otto H.
Banker; arts patron;
manabout-town;
"...the ultimate New
Yorker."
"In Tune With the Finite"
Feb. 20, 1926 (23-24)
Vol. 2 No. 1
"Search-Light"
(Waldo Frank)

Kapp, Jack
President, Decca Records
"Pulse on the Public"
August 24, 1940 (22-26)
Vol. 16 No. 28
Howard Whitman

Katz, Hymie
Hustler, opener of
nightclubs
"Tummler"
Feb. 26, 1938 (24-29)
Vol. 14 No. 2
A.J. Liebling

Kauffman, Bernie, Ike and
Jake
Owners, H. Kauffman
Saddlery Company
"Three Men and the
Horse"
Sept. 4, 1943 (24-34)
Vol. 19 No. 29
John McCarten and
Robert Lewis Taylor

Kaufman, George S.
Playwright
"The Deep, Tangled
Kaufman"
May 18, 1929 (26-29)
Vol. 5 No. 13
Alexander Woollcott

Kayshus, Mme. Effie (pseud.)
(Satire)
Shoe manufacturer;
socialite
"Vamp in Violet"
January 16, 1937 (20-25)
Vol. 12 No. 48
Sinclair Lewis

Kazan, (Joe) A.E.
Author; rug merchant
"The Red and the Blue"
April 21, 1945 (30-45)
Vol. 21 No. 10
S.N. Behrman

Keane, Molly
Novelist
"Great Old
Breakerawayer"
Oct. 13, 1986 (97-112)
Vol. 62 No. 34
Mary D. Kierstead

Keaton, Diane
Motion picture actress
"Her Own Best
Disputant"
Dec. 25, 1978 (38-43)
Vol. 54 No. 45
Penelope Gilliatt

Keeler, Elisha
Square-dance caller
"Forward Six, Balance
Six, Side Gents Do-Si-Do"
February 9, 1957 (39-69)
Vol. 32 No. 51
Robert Lewis Taylor

Kellems, Vivian
Electrical parts
manufacturer
"Grips and Taxes"
Feb. 3, 1951 (36-54)
Feb. 10, 1951 (39-57)
Vol. 26 Nos. 50-51
Andy Logan

Keller, Helen
Author; lecturer
"Blind...Deaf...Dumb"
January 25, 1930 (24-26)
Vol. 5 No. 49
Robert M. Coates

Kelly, Alvin "Shipwreck"
Flagpole sitter
"Up From Hell's Kitchen"
April 26, 1930 (22-25)
Vol. 6 No. 10
Charles Robbins

Kemp, Harry
Poet
"Poet's Progress"
August 8, 1925 (9-10)
Vol. 1 No. 25
Murdock Pemberton

Kenlon, John
Chief, New York City
Fire Department
"A Cocky Mick"
June 12, 1926 (15-16)
Vol. 2 No. 17
Henry F. Pringle

Kennedy, Edward M.
U.S. Senator (D-Mass.)
* A Reporter at Large
"Senator From
Massachusetts"
August 25, 1975 (52-77)
Vol. 51 No. 27
James Stevenson

Kennedy, Edward M., *cont.*
* Our Far-Flung
Correspondents
"Watching the Shore"
Oct. 8, 1979 (102-116)
Vol. 55 No. 34
James Stevenson

Kenny, Nick
Poet-columnist, *New York
Daily Mirror*
"The Swan in the Mirror"
March 7, 1953 (35-54)
Vol. 29 No. 3
John McCarten

Kenny, William Frank
Construction magnate;
Tammany connections
"I'd Give My Shirt for Al"
June 23, 1928 (19-22)
Vol. 4 No. 18
Malcolm Ross

Kern, Jerome
Composer; lyricist
"Words and Music"
February 8, 1930 (21-23)
Vol. 5 No. 51
Franklin P. Adams

Ketcham, Howard
Color, design and
illumination engineer
"An Emolument
for Heliotrope"
March 8, 1952 (39-53)
Vol. 28 No. 3
Geoffrey T. Hellman

Kheel, Theodore
    Lawyer; labor mediator
    "Mediator"
    August 1, 1970 (36-58)
    Vol. 46 No. 24
    Fred C. Shapiro

Kiely, John J.
    Postmaster, New York
    City
    "Good and Faithful"
    Dec. 17, 1927 (25-27)
    Vol. 3 No. 44
    Foster Ware

Kilpatrick, John Reed
    President, Madison
    Square Garden
    "For God, Country, Yale,
    and Garden"
    January 28, 1956 (35-57)
    Vol. 31 No. 50
    E.J. Kahn, Jr.

Kimball, Dr. James H.
    Meteorologist
    "Forecaster to the Fliers"
    July 28, 1928 (20-23)
    Vol. 4 No. 23
    Foster Ware

King, Charles Brady
    Automobile designer,
    builder, racer
    "To Spare the Obedient
    Beast"
    May 18, 1946 (30-40)
    Vol. 22 No. 14
    Brendan Gill

King, Teddi
    Singer
    "American Singers"
    Feb. 27, 1978 (41-63)
    Vol. 54 No. 2
    Whitney Balliett

Kirstein, Lincoln
    Director, New York
    City Ballet
    "Conversations With
    Kirstein"
    Dec. 15, 1986 (44-80)
    Dec. 22, 1986 (37-63)
    Vol. 62 Nos. 43-44
    W. McNeil Lowry

Klein, Samuel
    Clothing manufacturer
    "On the Square"
    June 25, 1932 (17-21)
    Vol. 8 No. 19
    Milton MacKaye

Klem, Bill
    National League umpire
    "Man in a Blue Suit"
    October 5, 1929 (31-33)
    Vol. 5 No. 33
    Niven Busch, Jr.

Knepper, Jimmy
    Trombonist
    "A Trombone Mouth"
    May 20, 1991 (52-58)
    Vol. 67 No. 19
    Whitney Balliett

Knopf, Alfred A.
Publisher
"The Trinity–and a Dog"
August 21, 1926 (15-17)
Vol. 2 No. 27
Lurton Blassingame

"Publisher"
Nov. 20, 1948 (44-57)
Nov. 27, 1948 (36-52)
Dec. 4, 1948 (40-53)
Vol. 24 Nos. 39-41
Geoffrey T. Hellman

Knopf, Blanche
Publisher
"The Trinity–and a Dog"
August 21, 1926 (15-17)
Vol. 2 No. 27
Lurton Blassingame

Knopf, Samuel
Publisher
"The Trinity–and a Dog"
August 21, 1926 (15-17)
Vol. 2 No. 27
Lurton Blassingame

Knudsen, William Signius
President, General Motors
Corporation; Member,
Advisory Commission to
National Defense Council
"Production Man"
March 8, 1941 (22-32)
March 15, 1941 (26-34)
March 22, 1941 (23-34)
Vol. 17 Nos. 4-6
Matthew Josephson

Koch, Edward I.
Mayor of New York City
"The Mayor"
Sept. 10, 1979 (54-119)
Sept. 17, 1979 (50-123)
Vol. 55 Nos. 30-31
Ken Auletta

Koenig, Sam (Samuel S.)
Chairman, Republican
County Committee of N.Y.
"Nize Sam, Et Opp All the
G.O. P."
March 26, 1926 (15-16)
Vol. 2 No. 3
Oliver H.P. Garrett

Komar, Vitaly
Artist
"Partners"
Dec. 29, 1986 (33-54)
Vol. 62 No. 45
Ian Frazier

Kommer, Rudolf
Journalist, impresario
"The Mysteries of
Rudolfo"
March 18, 1933 (20-23)
Vol. 9 No. 5
Alexander Woollcott

Korman, Murray
Photographer
"The One Big Name"
October 3, 1942 (19-29)
Vol. 18 No. 33
Robert Lewis Taylor

Korotich, Vitaly
    Editor, Soviet weekly
    Ogonyok
    "Chronicling the Chaos"
    Dec. 31, 1990 (38-72)
    Vol. 66 No. 46
    John Newhouse

Kreisler, Fritz
    Violinist
    "A Gentleman From
    Vienna"
    Nov. 24, 1928 (29-32)
    Vol. 4 No. 40
    Helena Huntington Smith

Kroyt, Boris
    Member, Budapest String
    Quartet
    "The Budapest"
    Nov. 14, 1959 (59-112)
    Vol. 35 No. 39
    Joseph Wechsberg

Krudy, Gyula
    Poet
    "Sound of a Cello"
    Dec. 1, 1986 (43-60)
    Vol. 62 No. 41
    John Lukacs

Kubrick, Stanley
    Film director
    "How About a Little
    Game?"
    Nov. 12, 1966 (70-110)
    Vol. 42 No. 38
    Jeremy Bernstein

Kurosawa, Akira
    Film director
    "Kurosawa Frames"
    Dec. 21, 1981 (51-78)
    Vol. 57 No. 44
    Lillian Ross

Kusse, Ron
    Fishing rod maker
    "The Only Way"
    June 22, 1987 (34-44)
    Vol. 63 No. 18
    C.P. Crow

La Guardia, Fiorello H.
    Congressman; mayoral
    candidate
    "Italian Table D'Hote"
    August 31, 1929 (26-29)
    Vol. 5 No. 28
    Henry F. Pringle

Lachaise, Gaston
    Sculptor
    "Hewer of Stone"
    April 4, 1931 (28-31)
    Vol. 7 No. 7
    Gilbert Seldes

Lacoste, René
    Tennis player
    "Winning Against Time"
    Sept. 5, 1925 (10-11)
    Vol. 1 No. 29
    John R. Tunis

Lamb, Thomas
Designer of handles
"Come, Let Me Clutch
Thee"
May 29, 1954 (33-51)
Vol. 30 No. 15
E.J. Kahn, Jr.

Lambert, Gerard Barnes
President, Lambert
Company; yachtsman
"Ahoy, Listerine!"
July 16, 1938 (22-28)
Vol. 14 No. 22
Jack Alexander

Landolf, Bluch
Clown
"Here Come the Clowns"
April 15, 1939 (25-29)
Vol. 15 No. 9
A.J. Liebling

Langer, Susanne K.
Author
"Philosopher in a New Key"
Dec. 3, 1960 (67-100)
Vol. 36 No. 42
Winthrop Sargeant

Langner, Lawrence
Lawyer; Theatre
Guild co-director
"Business and Show
Business"
October 1, 1949 (34-48)
October 8, 1949 (34-51)
Vol. 25 Nos. 32-33
Robert Rice

Langlois, Henri
Film archivist,
Cinématheque Française
"The Decoy Fanatic"
March 24, 1975 (44-56)
Vol. 51 No. 5
Penelope Gilliatt

Larkins, Ellis
Jazz pianist
"Einfühlung"
Dec. 18, 1978 (41-48)
Vol. 54 No. 44
Whitney Balliett

La Rocque, Gene Robert
Director, Center for
Defense Information
"Sentinel"
October 6, 1986 (88-103)
Vol. 62 No. 33
Herbert Mitgang

La Rosa, Julius
Singer
"The Man Who Lost His
Humility"
Sept. 28, 1987 (57-62)
Vol. 63 No. 32
Whitney Balliett

Lasky, Jesse L.
Motion picture executive
"A Bugler's Progress"
July 10, 1937 (18-24)
Vol. 13 No. 21
Alva Johnston

Lasser, Jacob Kay
    Author; income
    tax expert
    "Tax Angler"
    March 14, 1953 (36-58)
    Vol. 29 No. 4
    E.J. Kahn, Jr.

Lastfogel, Abraham Isaac
    Theatrical agent, U.S.O.
    "The Quiet Guy in
    Lindy's"
    April 20, 1946 (34-46)
    April 27, 1946 (27-41)
    Vol. 22 Nos. 10-11
    E.J. Kahn, Jr.

Latham, Natalie Wales
    Founder, Bundles for
    Britain
    "Active Sparker"
    April 19, 1941 (21-26)
    Vol. 17 No. 10
    Geoffrey T. Hellman

Laubach, Frank Charles
    Congregational minister;
    educator
    "The Thousand Silver
    Threads"
    February 16, 1952 (38)
    Vol. 27 No. 53
    Robert Rice

Laughlin, James
    Founder, New Directions
    Books
    "Jaz"
    March 23, 1992 (41-64)
    Vol. 68 No. 5
    Cynthia Zarin

Laurence, William L.
    Science reporter, *The
    New York Times*
    "The Infinitesimal and
    the Infinite"
    August 18, 1945 (26-35)
    Vol. 21 No. 27
    Robert Simpson

Lawes, Lewis E.
    Warden, N.Y. State Prison
    "Counsel for the Defense"
    July 10, 1926 (15-17)
    Vol. 2 No. 21
    Helena Huntington Smith

Lawrence, Charles Lanier
    Airplane engine inventor
    "Deus ex Machina"
    August 13, 1927 (16-19)
    Vol. 3 No. 26
    Foster Ware

Le Corbusier (Charles
Edouard Jeannert)
    Architect
    "From Within to Without"
    April 26, 1947 (31-45)
    May 3, 1947 (36-53)
    Vol. 23 Nos. 10-11
    Geoffrey T. Hellman

Le Gallienne, Eva
Actress; director/prod-
ucer, Civic Repertory
Theatre
"Lady of Fourteenth
Street"
April 6, 1929 (29-32)
Vol. 5 No. 7
Djuna Barnes

Lea, Barbara
Singer
"American Singers"
Feb. 27, 1978 (41-63)
Vol. 54 No. 2
Whitney Balliett

Leader, Edwin O.
Crew coach, Yale
University
"Grim-visaged Victory"
June 26, 1926 (17-18)
Vol. 2 No. 19
Herbert Reed

Leblang, Joe (Joseph)
Broadway ticket salesman
January 2, 1926 (11-12)
Vol. 1 No. 46
Brock Pemberton

Ledoux, Urbain "Mr. Zero"
Soup kitchen director
"Snow Man"
February 5, 1927 (27-29)
Vol. 2 No. 51
Niven Busch, Jr.

Lee, Tsung-Dao
Theoretical physicist:
Nobel Prize winner
"A Question of Parity"
May 12, 1962 (49-104)
Vol. 38 No. 12
Jeremy Bernstein

Lefebvre, Channing
Choirmaster and organist,
Trinity Church
"685 Voices"
May 1, 1937 (26-29)
Vol. 13 No. 11
Robert Alfred Simon

Lefkowitz, Dave
Autograph collector
"Are You In Show
Business?"
Dec. 18, 1971 (38-44)
Vol. 47 No. 44
William Whitworth

Lehman, Herbert Henry
Governor of New York
"The Governor"
May 2, 1936 (21-26)
May 9, 1936 (25-30)
Vol. 12 Nos. 11-12
Hickman Powell

Lehmann, Lotte
Soprano, Metropolitan
Opera Company
"Song and Sentiment"
Feb. 23, 1935 (20-24)
Vol. 11 No. 2
Marcia Davenport

Leibowitz, Samuel S.
  Lawyer
  "Let Freedom Ring"
  June 4, 1932 (21-24)
  June 11, 1932 (18-23)
  Vol. 8 No. 16-17
  Alva Johnston

Leigh, Douglas
  Lighted sign designer
  "Lights, Lights, Lights"
  June 7, 1941 (23-31)
  Vol. 17 No. 17
  E.J. Kahn, Jr.

Leigh, William Colston
  Owner, Leigh Bureau
  of Lectures and
  Entertainment
  "Fifty Per Cent"
  January 25, 1941 (23-30)
  Vol. 16 No. 50
  B.A. Heggie and
  J.J. O'Malley

Leitzel, Lillian (Alize)
  Aerialist, Ring Brothers &
  Barnum & Bailey Circus
  "Star"
  April 21, 1956 (45-72)
  April 28, 1956 (47-69)
  Vol. 32 Nos. 9-10
  Robert Lewis Taylor

Lenglen, Suzanne
  Tennis player
  "The Temperamental
  Suzanne"
  Feb. 27, 1926 (15-17)
  Vol. 2 No. 2
  Ferdinand Tuohy

Lescaze, William
  Modernist architect
  "Modern"
  Dec. 12, 1936 (28-34)
  Vol. 12 No. 43
  Robert M. Coates

Leterman, Elmer G.
  Insurance salesman
  "The Master"
  May 4, 1940 (24-29)
  Vol. 16 No. 12
  Geoffrey T. Hellman

Levine, Joe (Joseph E.)
  Motion picture producer
  "The Very Rich Hours of
  Joe Levine"
  Sept. 16, 1967 (55-136)
  Vol. 43 No. 30
  Calvin Tomkins

Levine, Rubin
  Street musician
  "Winging It"
  March 28, 1983 (41-63)
  Vol. 59 No. 6
  Mark Singer

Lewis, Joseph
   Publisher
   "The Atheist Pope"
   October 8, 1932 (22-25)
   Vol. 8 No. 34
   Alva Johnston

Lewis, Rosa
   "'Orrible Woman"
   Proprietor, The Cavendish
   (London)
   Sept. 16, 1933 (23-26)
   Vol. 9 No. 31
   Joseph Bryan III

Lewis, Sinclair
   Author
   "In America's Image"
   July 18, 1925 (10-11)
   Vol. 1 No. 22
   "Search-light"
   (Waldo Frank)

   "The World and Sauk
   Center"
   January 27, 1934 (24-27)
   February 3, 1934 (24-27)
   Vol. 9 Nos. 50-51
   W.E. Woodward

Lewis, Wilmarth Sheldon
   Horace Walpole scholar
   "The Steward of
   Strawberry Hill"
   August 6, 1949 (26-37)
   August 13, 1949 (31-41)
   Vol. 25 Nos. 24-25
   Geoffrey T. Hellman

Lhevinne, Rosina
   Pianist, teacher
   "The Leaves of a Tree"
   January 12, 1963 (37-72)
   Vol. 38 No. 47
   Winthrop Sargeant

Libman, Emanuel
   Physician; diagnostician
   "Hyper or Hypo?"
   April 8, 1939 (23-29)
   Vol. 15 No. 8
   S.N. Behrman

Lichine, Alexis
   Vintner; wine merchant
   "A Dreamer of Wine"
   May 17, 1958 (48-86)
   May 24, 1958 (37-72)
   Vol. 34 Nos. 13-14
   Joseph Wechsberg

Lie, Trygve
   Secretary-General, U.N.
   "The Idea is Everything"
   October 11, 1947 (39-49)
   October 18, 1947 (39-52)
   Vol. 23 Nos. 34-35
   Philip Hamburger

Lilienthal, David Eli
   Financier; corporation
   director; author; chair-
   man, U.S. Atomic Energy
   Commission
   "A Second Sort of Life"
   April 29, 1961 (45-90)
   Vol. 37 No. 11
   John Brooks

Lillie, Beatrice
Actress; comedian
"Britain's Best"
Sept. 19, 1931 (22-25)
Vol. 7 No. 31
Henry F. Pringle

Lindbergh, Charles
Aviator
"Young Man of Affairs"
Sept. 20, 1930 (26-29)
Sept. 27, 1930 (30-33)
Vol. 6 No. 31-32
Morris Markey

Lindgren, Astrid
Author
"Astonishment of Being"
Feb. 28, 1983 (46-63)
Vol. 59 No. 2
Jonathan Cott

Lindsay, John V.
Mayor of New York City
"The Mayor"
Oct. 7, 1967 (56-128)
Oct. 14, 1967 (61-148)
Vol. 43 Nos. 33-34
Nat Hentoff

"The Mayor"
May 3, 1969 (44-104)
May 10, 1969 (42-118)
Vol. 45 Nos. 11-12
Nat Hentoff

Lippold, Richard
Sculptor
"A Thing Among Things"
March 30, 1963 (47-107)
Vol. 39 Nos. 6
Calvin Tomkins

Lipton, Sir Thomas Johnstone
Tea magnate
"Boy Wanted"
Sept. 13, 1930 (30-33)
Vol. 6 No. 30
Anthony Gibbs

Little, Lou
Football coach,
Columbia University
"Drive! Drive! Drive!"
October 9, 1948 (37-59)
Vol. 24 No. 33
Richard Owen Boyer

Littleton, Martin Wiley
Orator
"Reformed Spellbinder"
August 20, 1932 (18-22)
Vol. 8 No. 27
Alva Johnston

Liveright, Horace B.
Publisher
"One Hundred Per Cent
American"
October 10, 1925 (9-10)
Vol. 1 No. 34
"Search-light"
(Waldo Frank)

Lloyd, Harold
Motion picture actor;
comedian
"The Perennial
Freshman"
January 30, 1926 (15-16)
Vol. 1 No. 50
R.E. Sherwood

Logan, Joshua
Playwright, director,
producer
"The Tough Guy and the
Soft Guy"
April 4, 1953 (38-65)
April 11, 1953 (37-67)
Vol. 29 Nos. 7-8
E.J. Kahn, Jr.

Lombardo, Guy
Bandleader, Guy
Lombardo and His
Royal Canadians
"Powder Your Face With
Sunshine"
January 5, 1957 (35-49)
January 12, 1957 (35-57)
Vol. 32 Nos. 46-47
E.J. Kahn, Jr.

London, George
Singer, Metropolitan
Opera Company
"The Vocal Mission"
October 26, 1957 (49-92)
Nov. 2, 1957 (47-81)
Vol. 33 Nos. 36-37
Joseph Wechsberg

Londos, Jim
Wrestler
"The Pullman Theseus"
March 5, 1932 (26-29)
Vol. 8 No. 3
Joel Sayre

Lonergan, Anna
Head of stevedores union
"Lady in Crepe"
October 5, 1935 (28-32)
October 12, 1935 (25-29)
Vol. 11 Nos. 34-35
Meyer Berger

Longworth, Alice Roosevelt
Washington socialite,
daughter of TR
"Princess Alice"
February 28, 1925 (9-10)
Vol. 1 No. 2
"Quid"
(Marquis James)

Longworth, Nicholas
Speaker of the U.S. House
of Representatives
"The Playboy of Politics"
April 10, 1926 (15-16)
Vol. 2 No. 8
John K. Winkler

Looper, Leroy and Kathy
Proprietors, board-and-
care home
"Board-and-Care"
October 12, 1987 (51-90)
Vol. 63 No. 34
Bill Barich

Loos, Anita
Author; playwright
The Child Wonder"
Nov. 6, 1926 (25-28)
Vol. 2 No. 38
Edward E. Paramore

Lord, Mary Stinson Pillsbury
U.S. member, U.N.
Human Rights Commission
"One Thing Led to
Another"
May 16, 1953 (37-56)
Vol. 29 No. 13
Robert Rice

Loree, Leonor F.
President, Delaware and
Hudson Railroad
"Neanderthal"
June 3, 1933 (18-21)
Vol. 9 No. 16
Dwight MacDonald

Lorenz, Konrad Z.
Zoologist; author
"A Condition of
Enormous Improbability"
March 8, 1969 (39-93)
Vol. 45 No. 3
Joseph Alsop

Loring, John
Design director,
Tiffany & Co.
"Giving Good Value"
August 10, 1992 (34-58)
Vol. 68 No. 25
Holly Brubach

Lovett, Robert A.
U.S. Asst. Secretary of War
"The Thirteenth Labor
of Hercules"
Nov. 6, 1943 (30-39)
Nov. 13, 1943 (29-34)
Vol. 19 Nos. 38-39
Margaret Case Harriman
and John Bainbridge

Lucas, Diane Wilson
Cooking school proprietor
"With Palette Knife
and Skillet"
May 28, 1949 (34-53)
Vol. 25 No. 14
Angelica Gibbs

Luce, Clare Boothe see
Boothe, Clare

Luce, Henry Robinson
Publisher
"Time...Fortune...Life
...Luce"
Nov. 28, 1936 (20-25)
Vol. 12 No. 41
Wolcott Gibbs

Ludlam, Charles
Theater writer, producer,
director
"Ridiculous"
Nov. 15, 1976 (55-98)
Vol. 52 No. 39
Calvin Tomkins

Ludwig, Leopold
Pianist; conductor
"Down There"
October 2, 1954 (36-60)
Vol. 30 No. 33
Joseph Wechsberg

Lukas, D. Wayne
Race horse trainer
"Intensity Factor"
Dec. 26, 1988 (36-68)
Vol. 64 No. 45
Carol Flake

Luks, George
Artist, instructor at Art
Students' League
"The Illustrious George"
May 9, 1925 (13-14)
Vol. 1 No. 12
J. Hansuld (no byline)

Lunt, Alfred
English actor
"General Utility"
April 28, 1928 (25-27)
Vol. 4 No. 10
Timothy Vane

Lydig, Rita de Alba de Acosta
Socialite; author
"Lady of an Antique
World"
Nov. 19, 1927 (28-30)
Vol. 3 No. 40
"M.K.L."
(Margaret K. Leech)

Lyons, Harry
Barge owner
"The Rivermen"
April 4, 1959 (42-111)
Vol. 35 No. 7
Joseph Mitchell

Lyons, Leonard
Newspaper gossip
columnist
"These Things are Fated"
April 7, 1945 (28-37)
Vol. 21 No. 8
Russell Maloney

MacArthur, Charles Gordon
"The Young Monk of
Siberia"
March 9, 1929 (23-26)
Vol. 5 No. 3
Alexander Woollcott

McBride, John S.
Theater ticket agent
"Two on the Aisle"
August 6, 1927 (18-21)
Vol. 3 No. 25
Kenneth Mcgowan

McBride, Mary Margaret
Radio personality
"The Forty-Five-Minute
Tempo"
Dec. 19, 1942 (27-34)
Vol. 18 No. 44
Barbara Heggie

McClellan, George
    Mayor of New York City;
    historian
    "Out of the Past"
    May 28, 1932 (21-25)
    Vol. 8 No. 15
    Milton MacKaye

McCooey, John H.
    Democratic leader, Kings
    County, Brooklyn
    "The Emerald Boss"
    March 12, 1927 (25-28)
    Vol. 3 No. 4
    Niven Busch, Jr.

MacCormick, Austin H.
    N.Y. Commissioner of
    Correction
    "The Four-Eyed Kid"
    May 26, 1934 (24-27)
    Vol. 10 No. 15
    Arthur C. Bartlett

MacDougall, Alice Foote
    Restaurateur
    "Romance, Incorporated"
    February 4, 1928 (21-23)
    Vol. 3 No. 51
    Margaret K. Leech

Macfadden, Bernarr
    Health crusader
    "Another True Story"
    Sept. 19, 1925 (9-10)
    Vol. 1 No. 31
    Oliver H. P. Garrett

Macfadden, Bernarr *cont.*
    "Physical Culture"
    October 14, 1950 (39-51)
    October 21, 1950 (39-52)
    October 28, 1950 (37-51)
    Vol. 26 Nos. 34-36
    Robert Lewis Taylor

McGoldrick, Joseph Daniel
    N.Y.C. Comptroller
    "Professor in Politics"
    August 11, 1934 (19-22)
    Vol. 10 No. 26
    Milton MacKaye

McGoorty, John Patrick
    Tramp
    "Bowery Bum"
    October 31, 1931 (23-26)
    Vol. 7 No. 37
    Russell Crouse

McGovern, Artie (Arthur)
    Owner, McGovern's
    Gymnasium; prizefighter
    "Artie"
    May 22, 1937 (25-29)
    Vol. 13 No. 14
    Robert M. Coates

McGraw, John
    Manager, New York Giants
    "Mister Muggsy"
    March 28, 1925 (9-10)
    Vol. 1 No. 6
    William Slavens McNutt
    (no byline)

McGuinness, Peter J.
Democratic leader,
Greenpoint, Brooklyn
"The Big Hello"
January 12, 1946 (29-38)
January 19, 1946 (26-38)
Vol. 21 Nos. 48-49
Richard H. Rovere

Mack, Walter S., Jr.
Chairman, Pepsi-Cola Co.
"More Bounce to the
Ounce"
July 1, 1950 (32-49)
July 8, 1950 (28-43)
Vol. 26 Nos. 19-20
E.J. Kahn, Jr.

McKee, Joseph Vincent
President, N.Y.C. Board
of Aldermen
"Bringing Up the City
Fathers"
Sept. 10, 1927 (19-22)
Vol. 3 No. 30
Henry F. Pringle

McKenna, Dave
Jazz pianist
"Super Chops"
January 29, 1979 (37-44)
Vol. 54 No. 50
Whitney Balliett

McLaughlin, George V.
N.Y.C. police commissioner
"Tammany in Modern
Clothes"
January 16, 1926 (11-12)
Vol. 1 No. 48
Oliver H.P. Garrett

McLean, Alice Throckmorton
Founder, American Women's
Voluntary Services
"Ladies in Uniform"
July 4, 1942 (21-29)
Vol. 18 No. 20
Janet Flanner

MacLeish, Archibald
Poet
"The Omelet of
A. MacLeish"
January 14, 1939 (23-24)
Vol. 14 No. 48
Edmund Wilson

McNair, Lesley James
Lieutenant-general,
U.S. Army
"Education of an Army"
October 14, 1944 (28-39)
October 21, 1944 (34-47)
Vol. 20 No. 35-36
E.J. Kahn, Jr.

McNamee, Graham
Radio announcer
"Courtesy of Coca-Cola"
August 9, 1930 (20-22)
Vol. 6 No. 25
Geoffrey T. Hellman

McPartland, Marian
Jazz pianist
"The Key of D is Daffodil
Yellow"
January 20, 1973 (43-57)
Vol. 48 No. 48
Whitney Balliett

MacPhail, Larry
President, Brooklyn
Dodgers
"Borough Defender"
July 12, 1941 (20-28)
July 19, 1941 (20-30)
Vol. 17 Nos. 22-23
Robert Lewis Taylor

Macy, William Kingsland
Leader, Republican Party,
New York State
"The King"
Sept. 12, 1931 (25-28)
Vol. 7 No. 30
Alva Johnston

Madden, Joe
Saloonkeeper
"The Markee"
Nov. 4, 1939 (20-27)
Vol. 15 No. 38
Joseph Mitchell

Makiya, Kanan
Architect
"Architects Amid the
Ruins"
January 6, 1992 (40-65)
Vol. 67 No. 46
Lawrence Wechsler

Makiya, Mohamed
Architect
"Architects Amid the
Ruins"
January 6, 1992 (40-65)
Vol. 67 No. 46
Lawrence Wechsler

Mallon, Mary
Cook; typhoid carrier
"Typhoid Carrier No. 36"
January 26, 1935 (21-25)
Vol. 10 No. 50
Stanley Walker

Malraux, André
Author, French cabinet
minister
"The Human Condition"
Nov. 6, 1954 (45-81)
Nov. 13, 1954 (46-100)
Vol. 30 Nos. 38-39
Janet Flanner

"Man O' War"
Race horse
"Big Red"
Dec. 18, 1937 (24-31)
Vol. 13 No. 44
Arthur Bartlett

Maney, Richard Sylvester
Broadway press agent
"The Customer is Always
Wrong"
October 11, 1941 (27-42)
Vol. 17 No. 35
Wolcott Gibbs

Mann, Thomas
Author
"Goethe in Hollywood"
Dec. 13, 1941 (31-42)
Dec. 20, 1941 (22-31)
Vol. 17 Nos. 44-45
Janet Flanner

Manning, Gordon
Staff consultant, NBC News
"Initiator"
May 30, 1988 (49-66)
Vol. 64 No. 15
Mark Singer

Manning, William Thomas
Bishop, Protestant
Episcopal Diocese of
New York
"The First Churchman"
Feb. 28, 1931 (24-36)
Vol. 7 No. 2
Alva Johnston

Manship, Paul
Sculptor
"The Compleat Sculptor"
Sept. 1, 1928 (21-23)
Vol. 4 No. 28
Cameron Rogers

Mara, Tim
Founder, Turf and
Gridiron Club
"Turf and Gridiron"
Sept. 18, 1937 (25-29)
Vol. 13 No. 31
A.J. Liebling

Marbury, Elisabeth
National Democratic
Committeewoman, New
York City
"Seventy Years Young"
Dec. 24, 1927 (19-21)
Vol. 3 No. 45
Margaret K. Leech

Mardersteig, Giovanni
Publisher; printer; scholar
"A Good Eye"
July 11, 1970 (32-47)
Vol. 46 No. 21
Winthrop Sargeant

Marie of Roumania
Queen Consort of
Ferdinand I of Roumania
"Roumania's Royal
Saleslady"
October 23, 1926 (26-27)
Vol. 2 No. 36
John K. Winkler

Marin, John
Painter
"Leprechaun on the
Palisades"
March 14, 1942 (26-35)
Vol. 18 No. 4
A.J. Liebling

Mark, Herman F.
Scientist
"Polymers Everywhere"
Sept. 13, 1958 (48-71)
Sept. 20, 1958 (46-79)
Vol. 34 Nos. 30-31
Morton M. Hunt

Markova, Alicia (Lillian Alice
Marks)
Ballet dancer
"Inhabitant of the Air"
April 15, 1944 (33-44)
Vol. 20 No. 9
Barbara Heggie

Marquand, John P.
Author
"There's No Place"
March 29, 1952 (37-57)
April 5, 1952 (43-67)
April 12, 1952 (39-64)
Vol. 28 Nos. 6-8
Philip Hamburger

Marshall, George Catlett
U.S. Secretary of State
"Chief of Staff"
October 26, 1940 (26-35)
Vol. 16 No. 37
A.J. Liebling

Martin, Ernest H.
Theatrical producer
"The Hit's the Thing"
January 7, 1956 (29-53)
January 14, 1956 (33-59)
Vol. 31 Nos. 47-48
E.J. Kahn, Jr.

Martin, Glenn L.
Airplane manufacturer
"Hero for Business
Reasons"
Nov. 28, 1942 (24-32)
Dec. 5, 1942 (26-34)
Vol. 18 Nos. 41-42
Alva Johnston

Marx, Harpo (Arthur)
Comedian; musician
"Portrait of a Man With
Red Hair"
Dec. 1, 1928 (33-36)
Vol. 4 No. 41
Alexander Woollcott

Mary of England
Queen Consort of
George V of England
"Her Majesty, the Queen"
May 4, 1935 (20-24)
May 11, 1935 (28-32)
Vol. 11 Nos. 12-13
Janet Flanner

Mason, Jackie
Comedian
"The Casualness Of It"
Sept. 19, 1988 (51-58)
Vol. 64 No. 31
Whitney Balliett

Matheus, J.B.
Consulting expert, U.S.
House Committee on Dies
"The Testimony of a
Sinner"
April 22, 1944 (26-36)
Vol. 20 No. 10
Matthew Josephson and
Russell Maloney

Matisse, Henri
Painter
"King of the Wild Beasts"
Dec. 22, 1951 (30-46)
Dec. 29, 1951 (26-49)
Vol. 27 Nos. 45-46
Janet Flanner

Matthau, Walter
Motion picture actor
"The Player - III"
Nov. 4, 1961 (98-110)
Vol. 37 No. 38
Lillian Ross

Mattioli, Raffaele
Publisher; historian
"An Abstract Art"
April 30, 1966 (52-76)
Vol. 42 No. 10
Joseph Wechsberg

Maugham, W. Somerset
Author; playwright
"Very Old Party"
Dec. 30, 1944 (24-34)
January 6, 1945 (28-38)
Vol. 20 Nos. 46-47
Hamilton Basso

Maury, Reuben
Chief editorial writer,
New York Daily News
"Editorial Writer"
May 24, 1947 (36-51)
May 31, 1947 (31-41)
June 7, 1947 (38-52)
Vol. 23 Nos. 14-16
John Bainbridge

Maxim, Hudson
Inventor
"A White Hot Tamale"
October 16, 1926 (25-27)
Vol. 2 No. 35
Janet Flanner

Maxwell, Elsa
Socialite
"Come As Somebody
Else"
Nov. 25, 1933 (24-27)
Vol. 9 No. 40
Janet Flanner

May, Elaine
Comedian; actress;
playwright
"A Tilted Insight"
April 15, 1961 (47-75)
Vol. 37 No. 9
Robert Rice

Mayer, Arthur Loeb
Film professor, U.S.C.
"Boffos and Bustos"
Dec. 9, 1974 (46-66)
Vol. 50 No. 42
E.J. Kahn, Jr.

Mayer, Louis B.
President, Metro-
Goldwyn-Mayer Corp.
"Yes, Mr. Mayer"
March 28, 1936 (26-31)
April 4, 1936 (26-30)
Vol. 12 Nos. 6-7
Henry F. Pringle

Mayer, Robert
Concert impresario
"The Right People: The
Young"
April 21, 1980 (44-72)
Vol. 56 No. 9
Mollie Panter-Downes

Mayo, Mary
Singer
"American Singers"
Feb. 27, 1978 (41-63)
Vol. 54 No. 2
Whitney Balliett

Mead, Margaret
Anthropologist; author
"It's All Anthropology"
Dec. 30, 1961 (31-44)
Vol. 37 No. 46
Winthrop Sargeant

Medalie, George Z.
U.S. Attorney, Southern
District of N.Y.
"Last of the Prosecutors"
August 19, 1933 (18-22)
Vol. 9 No. 27
Alva Johnston

Meehan, Chick (John Francis)
Football coach, New York
University
"The Mantle of Rockne"
Nov. 14, 1931 (23-27)
Vol. 7 No. 39
Joel Sayre

Mehta, Amolak Ram
Ved Mehta's father
"Daddyji"
April 22, 1972 (47-107)
April 29, 1972 (45-100)
Vol. 48 Nos. 9-10
Ved Mehta

Mehta, Shanti Devi
Ved Mehta's mother
"Mamaji"
July 9, 1979 (40-74)
July 16, 1979 (40-72)
July 23, 1979 (34-71)
Vol. 55 Nos. 21-23
Ved Mehta

Mehta, Zubin
Conductor
"Powerful Sword"
Dec. 16, 1967 (53-92)
Vol. 43 No. 43
Winthrop Sargeant

Mekas, Jonas
Filmmaker
"All Pockets Open"
January 6, 1973 (31-49)
Vol. 48 No. 46
Calvin Tomkins

Melamid, Alexander
Artist
"Partners"
Dec. 29, 1986 (33-54)
Vol. 62 No. 45
Ian Frazier

Mellon, Andrew W.
Banking and steel tycoon;
Secretary of the Treasury
"Croesus in Politics"
August 4, 1928 (18-21)
Vol. 4 No. 24
Horner Joseph Dodge

Meltzer, Bernard
WOR radio talk show host
"What's Your Problem?"
"Paying Sam Back"
August 14, 1978 (39-47)
Vol. 54 No. 26
James Stevenson

Mengelberg, Willem
Conductor, New York
Philharmonic
"Apostle of Perfection"
December 5, 1925 (9-10)
Vol. 1 No. 41
"Tympani"
(Robert A. Simon)

Menjou, Adolphe
Motion picture actor
"Beautiful But Not Dumb"
January 15, 1927 (18-21)
Vol. 2 No. 48
Helena Huntington Smith

Menotti, Gian Carlo
Opera composer
"Orlando in Mount Kisco"
May 4, 1963 (49-89)
Vol. 39 No. 11
Winthrop Sargeant

Menuhin, Yehudi
Violinist
"Prodigy's Progress"
October 8, 1955 (50-90)
October 15, 1955 (49-72)
Vol. 31 Nos. 34-35
Winthrop Sargeant

Mercer, Mabel
Singer
"Queenly Aura"
Nov. 18, 1972 (55-64)
Vol. 48 No. 39
Whitney Balliett

Meredith, Burgess
Motion picture actor
"Up From Amherst"
April 3, 1937 (26-37)
Vol. 13 No. 7
Wolcott Gibbs

Merton, Robert K.
Professor of Sociology,
Columbia University
"How Does it Come
to Be So?"
January 28, 1961 (39-63)
Vol. 36 No. 50
Morton M. Hunt

Meyer, Alfred
  Physician
  "The Doctor, the Lady,
  and Columbia University"
  October 23, 1943 (27-32)
  October 30, 1943 (28-37)
  Vol. 19 Nos. 36-37
  Robert Lewis Taylor

Meyer, Annie Nathan
  Founder, Barnard College
  "The Doctor, the Lady,
  and Columbia University"
  October 23, 1943 (27-32)
  October 30, 1943 (28-37)
  Vol. 19 Nos. 36-37
  Robert Lewis Taylor

Meyer, Arthur Simon
  Chairman, New York
  State Board of Mediation
  "What Can I Do For You,
  Gentlemen?"
  February 8, 1947 (34-49)
  Vol. 22 No. 52
  E.J. Kahn, Jr.

Mielziner, Jo
  Theater set designer
  "Aider and Abettor"
  October 23, 1948 (37-51)
  October 30, 1948 (28-39)
  Vol. 24 Nos. 35-36
  Alva Johnston

Milburn, Devereaux
  Lawyer; polo player
  "Thor Plays Polo"
  June 5, 1926 (23-24)
  Vol. 2 No. 16
  Herbert Reed

Millay, Edna St. Vincent
  Poet
  "Vincent"
  Feb. 12, 1927 (25-27)
  Vol. 2 No. 52
  Griffin Barry

Miller, Alice Duer
  Writer; member of
  The New Yorker's original
  advisory board
  "A Lady Who Writes"
  Feb. 19, 1927 (25-27)
  Vol. 3 No. 1
  Harvey O'Higgins

Miller, Gilbert
  Playwright
  "Mr. Miller and Mr. Hyde"
  May 29, 1943 (25-30)
  June 5, 1943 (26-36)
  Vol. 19 Nos. 15-16
  Margaret Case Harriman

Miller, Mitch (Mitchell William)
  Orchestra leader; oboist
  "The Fractured Oboist"
  June 6, 1953 (43-63)
  Vol. 29 No. 16
  Robert Rice

Miller, Neal E.
Psychologist
"Visceral Learning"
August 19, 1972 (34-57)
August 26, 1972 (30-57)
Vol. 48 Nos. 26-27
Gerald Jonas

Miller, Roger
Songwriter; singer
"Why Don't We Just Hum
for Awhile?"
March 1, 1969 (38-66)
Vol. 45 No. 2
William Whitworth

Mills, William
Fishing tackle store
owner
"Hook, Line, and Sinker"
July 9, 1938 (16-20)
Vol. 14 No. 21
E.J. Kahn, Jr.

Mills, Ogden Livingston
U.S. Treasury official
"Up From Harvard"
Dec. 12, 1931 (25-28)
Vol. 7 No. 43
Robert S. Allen

Milnes, Sherrill
Baritone, Metropolitan
Opera Company
"Singing With the
Big Dads"
March 29, 1976 (36-61)
Vol. 52 No. 6
Winthrop Sargeant

Minsky, Marvin
Science professor
"A.I."
Dec. 14, 1981 (50-126)
Vol. 57 No. 43
Jeremy Bernstein

Mitropoulis, Dimitri
Conductor, New York
Philharmonic
"Maestro on a
Mountaintop"
April 15, 1950 (38-60)
Vol. 26 No. 8
Richard O. Boyer

Miyake, Issey
Clothing designer
"Great Moment"
Dec. 19, 1983 (48-87)
Vol. 59 No. 44
Kennedy Fraser

Mizner, Addison
Architect
"The Palm Beach
Architect"
Nov. 22, 1952 (46-93)
Nov. 29, 1952 (46-94)
Dec. 6, 1952 (48-64)
Dec. 13, 1952 (42-85)
Vol. 28 Nos. 40-43
Alva Johnston

Mizner, Wilson
Confidence man;
Broadway personality
"Legend of a Sport"
October 10, 1942 (21-28)
October 17, 1942 (26-34)
October 24, 1942 (25-32)
October 31, 1942 (25-28)
Vol. 18 Nos. 34-37
Alva Johnston

"Legend of a Sport"
note: non-sequential
Feb. 25, 1950 (39-67)
July 22, 1950 (30-45)
July 29, 1950 (26-41)
Dec. 23, 1950 (28-39)
Dec. 30, 1950 (26-41)
Vol. 26 Nos. 1, 22-23
and 44-45
Alva Johnston

Mock Sai Wing
President of the Hip Sing
tong (controlling agency
of "Chinatown" areas)
"Tong Leader"
Dec. 30, 1933 (18-22)
Vol. 9 No. 46
St. Clair McKelway

Molden, Otto
Founder, European Forum
"Somnambulistic
Certainty"
Sept. 16, 1961 (51-84)
Vol. 37 No. 31
Joseph Wechsberg

Molé, Paul
Barber
"Just a Little Off the Top"
October 21, 1967 (63-78)
Vol. 43 No. 35
William Whitworth

Molnar, Ferenc
Playwright
"Playwright"
May 25, 1946 (28-41)
June 1, 1946 (32-46)
June 8, 1946 (32-47)
Vol. 22 Nos. 15-17
S.N. Behrman

Monk, Julius
Nightclub owner
"Régisseur"
April 6, 1992 (38-44)
Vol. 68 No. 7
Whitney Balliett

Monro, John Usher
Education administrator
"A Whale of a Difference"
April 10, 1971 (43-64)
Vol. 47 No. 8
E.J. Kahn, Jr.

Moore, Alexander Pollock
Publisher; owner of *New
York Daily Mirror;* former
ambassador to Spain
"From Madrid to the
Mirror"
May 26, 1928 (23-26)
Vol. 4 No. 14
John K. Winkler

Moore, Archibald Lee
(Archie)
  Pugilist
  "The Mongoose"
  Nov. 11, 1961 (61-112)
  Vol. 37 No. 39
  Jack Murphy

Moore, Freddie
  Drummer
  "New York Drummers"
  Nov. 5, 1979 (52-76)
  Vol. 55 No. 38
  Whitney Balliett

Moore, Marianne Craig
  Poet
  "Humility, Concentration,
  and Gusto"
  Feb. 16, 1957 (38-77)
  Vol. 32 No. 52
  Winthrop Sargeant

Moore, Michael
  Jazz bassist
  "A Good, Careful Melody"
  January 14, 1980 (39-50)
  Vol. 55 No. 48
  Whitney Balliett

Moore, Paul Jr.
  Episcopal Bishop of
  New York
  "Standing Out There on
  the Issues"
  April 28, 1986 (41-95)
  Vol. 62 No. 10
  Jervis Anderson

Moran, Eugene F.
  President, Moran Towing
  & Transport Company
  "The Elegant Tugboater"
  Nov. 3, 1945 (32-38)
  Nov. 10, 1945 (33-43)
  Vol. 21 Nos. 38-39
  Robert Lewis Taylor

Moreau, Jeanne
  Motion picture actress
  "A Sense of Dream"
  March 13, 1978 (44-55)
  Vol. 54 No. 4
  Penelope Gilliatt

Morey, Sigmund M.
  Tool manufacturer
  "For Excellence"
  July 31, 1943 (25-32)
  Vol. 19 No. 24
  Brendan Gill

Morgan, Anne
  Philanthropist
  "Lady Into Dynamo"
  October 22, 1927 (21-23)
  Vol. 3 No. 36
  "M.K.L."
  (Margaret K. Leech)

Morgan, Charles, Jr.
  Attorney for A.C.L.U.
  "Something For a Lawyer
  to Do"
  Oct. 25, 1969 (63-134)
  Vol. 45 No. 36
  Fred Powledge

Morgan, John Pierpoint
Financier
"Mighty Dealer in Dollars"
February 2, 1929 (23-26)
February 9, 1929 (27-36)
Vol. 4 Nos. 50-51
John K. Winkler

Morgenthau, Henry, Jr.
U.S. Secretary of the
Treasury
"Any Bonds Today?"
January 22, 1944 (24-32)
January 29, 1944 (26-36)
Vol. 19 Nos. 49-50
Geoffrey T. Hellman

Morino, Louis
Restaurateur
"The Cave"
June 28, 1952 (32-55)
Vol. 28 No. 19
Joseph Mitchell

Morris, Errol
Film director
"Predilections"
February 6, 1989 (38-72)
Vol. 64 No. 51
Mark Singer

Morris, Newbold
President, New York City
Council
"Good Citizen"
October 28, 1944 (28-36)
Nov. 4, 1944 (28-38)
Vol. 20 Nos. 37-38
Richard H. Rovere

Morse, Father Walter P.
Missionary in China
"The Happy, Happy
Beggar"
May 11, 1946 (34-47)
Vol. 22 No. 13
John Hersey

Morton, Jelly Roll
Jazz musician
"Ferdinand La Menthe"
June 23, 1980 (38-49)
Vol. 56 No. 18
Whitney Balliett

Moses, Robert
Builder; city planner; N.Y.
Parks Council chairman
"Public Servant"
March 10, 1934 (24-27)
Vol. 10 No. 4
Milton MacKaye

* Annals of Politics
"The Power Broker"
July 22, 1974 (32-64)
August 5, 1974 (37-65)
August 12, 1974 (40-75)
August 19, 1974 (42-77)
Vol. 50 Nos. 22-23, 25-26
Robert A. Caro

Moskowitz, Belle Israels
Publicity director, N.Y.
Democratic Committee
"A Certain Person"
October 9, 1926 (26-28)
Vol. 2 No. 34
Oliver H.P. Garrett

Mostel, Zero
Actor
"The Player - II"
October 28, 1961 (72-82)
Vol. 37 No. 37
Lillian Ross

Mott, Stewart Rawlings
Philanthropist
"Blue Chip Off the
Old Block"
Nov. 27, 1971 (56-87)
Vol. 47 No. 41
E.J. Kahn, Jr.

Muldoon, William
Owner, Hygienic Institute;
N.Y. Boxing Commission
"Spartacus in
Westchester"
July 16, 1927 (18-21)
Vol. 3 No. 22
Stanley Walker

Mulligan, Gerry
Jazz saxophonist; composer
"In the Mainstream"
March 21, 1959 (51-84)
March 28, 1959 (39-84)
Vol. 35 Nos. 5-6
Nat Hentoff

Mulrooney, Edward Pierce
New York City Police
Commissioner
"Cop's Cop"
October 24, 1931 (22-26)
Vol. 7 No. 36
Milton MacKaye

Munn, Orson D.
Publisher, *Scientific
American*
"Black Duck - 40"
January 27, 1940 (20-25)
Vol. 15 No. 50
Geoffrey T. Hellman

Murphy, George and Sara
President, Mark Cross,
and wife
"Living Well is the Best
Revenge"
July 21, 1962 (31-69)
Vol. 38 No. 22
Calvin Tomkins

Murphy, Michael
Co-founder, Esalen
Institute
"New Paradigms"
January 5, 1976 (30-51)
Vol. 51 No. 46
Calvin Tomkins

Murray, Arthur
Dance instructor
"The Wallflower's Friend"
January 6, 1934 (27-30)
Vol. 9 No. 47
Milton MacKaye

Murrow, Edward R.
Radio and television news
correspondent
"The World on His Back"
Dec. 26, 1953 (28-45)
Vol. 29 No. 45
Charles Wertenbaker

Nader, Ralph
Consumer watchdog
"A Countervailing Force"
Oct. 8, 1973 (50-111)
Oct. 15, 1973 (46-101)
Vol. 49 Nos. 33-34
Thomas Whiteside

Nam June Paik
Video artist
"Video Visionary"
May 5, 1975 (44-79)
Vol. 51 No. 11
Calvin Tomkins

Narayan, R.K.
Author
"The Train Had Just
Arrived at Malgudi Station"
Sept. 15, 1962 (51-90)
Vol. 38 No. 30
Ved Mehta

Nash, Clarence "Ducky"
Voice of Donald Duck
"The Quack and Disney"
Dec. 29, 1975 (33-42)
Vol. 51 No. 45
Tony Hiss and
David McClelland

Nawkins, Angelina
Captain, Salvation Army
"A Good Hold on the Lord"
Sept. 21, 1946 (34-49)
Vol. 22 No. 32
Richard Owen Boyer

Nelson, Donald M.
Industrialist; chairman,
War Production Board
"A Businessman, Sir"
March 28, 1942 (25-34)
Vol. 18 No. 6
St. Clair McKelway

Nervi, Pier Luigi
Architect; engineer
"Maestro de
Construzione"
June 11, 1960 (40-64)
Vol. 36 No. 17
Winthrop Sargeant

Nessler, Charles
Hairdresser, inventor of
the artificial eyelash
"Hair Scientist"
April 29, 1933 (20-24)
Vol. 9 No. 11
Geoffrey T. Hellman

Newsom, David
U.S. State Dept. official
"The Eye of the Storm"
June 2, 1980 (43-89)
June 9, 1980 (48-111)
June 16, 1980 (44-95)
Vol. 56 Nos. 15-17
Robert Shaplen

Newstead, Helaine
English professor
"A Giant in Her Field"
March 30, 1957 (39-80)
Vol. 33 No. 6
Morton M. Hunt

Nyerere, Julius Kambarage
    President, United
    Republic of Tanzania
    "The President"
    Oct. 16, 1971 (42-100)
    Oct. 23, 1971 (47-106)
    Oct. 30, 1971 (53-99)
    Vol. 47 Nos. 35-37
    William Edgett Smith

Nyswander, Marie
    Pssychoanalyst
    "The Treatment of
    Patients"
    June 26, 1965 (32-77)
    July 3, 1965 (32-57)
    Vol. 41 Nos. 19-20
    Nat Hentoff

O'Brien, John P.
    Mayor of New York City
    "The Scholar in Politics"
    July 1, 1933 (18-21)
    July 8, 1933 (17-20)
    Vol. 9 Nos. 20-21
    Alva Johnston

O'Brien, "Philadelphia" Jack
    Pugilist, boxing instructor
    "Boxing Taught Without
    Punishment"
    January 8, 1938 (22-28)
    Vol. 13 No. 47
    A.J. Liebling

Ochs, Adolph Simon
    Publisher, *New York
    Times*
    "The Lone Prospector:
    Thirty Years After"
    Nov. 21, 1925 (11-12)
    Vol. 1 No. 39
    Elmer Davis

O'Connor, John J.
    Archbishop of New York
    "I'm Finally Going to
    be a Pastor"
    March 23, 1987 (59-76)
    March 30, 1987 (37-92)
    Vol. 63 Nos. 5-6
    Nat Hentoff

Odets, Clifford
    Playwright; anti-capitalist
    revolutionary
    "Revolution's Number
    One Boy"
    January 22, 1938 (21-27)
    Vol. 13 No. 49
    John McCarten

Odlum, Floyd B.
    President, Atlas
    Corporation
    "Trust-Gobbler"
    August 26, 1933 (20-24)
    Vol. 9 No. 28
    Geoffrey T. Hellman

O'Keeffe, Georgia
    Artist
    "Abstraction-Flowers"
    July 6, 1929 (21-24)
    Vol. 5 No. 20
    Robert M. Coates

    "The Rose in the Eye
    Looked Pretty Fine"
    March 4, 1974 (40-66)
    Vol. 50 No. 2
    Calvin Tomkins

Okie, William Bayard, Jr.
    Window display designer
    "The Magnificent Touch"
    May 30, 1942 (20-31)
    Vol. 18 No. 15
    Eugene Kinkead and
    Russell Maloney

Oldenburg, Claes
    Sculptor
    "Look What I've
    Got Here"
    Dec. 12, 1977 (55-88)
    Vol. 53 No. 43
    Calvin Tomkins

Oliphant, Patrick
    Editorial cartoonist
    "Endless Possibilities"
    Dec. 31, 1979 (38-46)
    Vol. 55 No. 46
    James Stevenson

Olsen, Ole
    Comedian; stager of
    Hellz-a-Poppin
    "No Suave Inflections"
    January 28, 1939 (20-25)
    Vol. 14 No. 50
    A.J. Liebling

Olvany, George Washington
    Judge, New York Court of
    General Sessions
    "No More Lawyers"
    January 9, 1932 (22-25)
    Vol. 7 No. 47
    Alva Johnston

O'Neill, Eugene
    Playwright
    "Roughneck and
    Romancer"
    February 6, 1926 (17-18)
    Vol. 1 No. 51
    Maxwell Bodenheim

    "The Tragic Sense"
    Feb. 28, 1948 (34-45)
    March 6, 1948 (34-49)
    March 13, 1948 (37-47)
    Vol. 24 Nos. 1-3
    Hamilton Basso

O'Neill, Rose
    Designer of the
    Kewpie doll
    "Kewpie Doll"
    Nov. 24, 1934 (22-26)
    Vol. 10 No. 41
    Alexander King

Opie, Iona and Peter
    Authors
    "Finding Out is Better"
    April 4, 1983 (47-91)
    Vol. 59 No. 7
    Jonathan Cott

Oppong, Kwabena
    Monarch, U.S. African
    Ashanti tribe
    "Gentle Reign"
    Dec. 12, 1988 (50-76)
    Vol. 64 No. 43
    Susan Orlean

Ordinas, Juan March
    Spanish robber-baron
    "Privateer"
    May 21, 1979 (42-102)
    May 28, 1979 (42-91)
    Vol. 55 Nos. 14-15
    John Brooks

Ornstein, Leo
    Pianist
    "Rare as Music"
    Dec. 19, 1925 (9-10)
    Vol. 1 No. 43
    "Search-Light"
    (Waldo Frank)

O'Rourke, William
    Diplomatic courier, U.S.
    State Department
    "The Hand on the Pouch"
    February 1, 1947 (30-41)
    Vol. 22 No. 51
    A.J. Liebling

Otis, Harry
    Life insurance salesman
    "An Answer to
    Everything"
    Feb. 3, 1945 (28-37)
    Vol. 20 No. 51
    Hubbard Hoover

Ottinger, Lawrence
    President, United States
    Plywood Corporation
    "The Plywood Baron"
    Dec. 22, 1945 (28-35)
    Dec. 29, 1945 (24-33)
    Vol. 21 Nos. 45-46
    Alva Johnston

Padarewski, Ignace
    Pianist; Premier of Poland
    "Double Life"
    Nov. 29, 1930 (29-32)
    Vol. 6 No. 41
    Helena Huntington Smith

Page, Geraldine
    Actress
    "The Player - III"
    Nov. 4, 1961 (62-72)
    Vol. 37 No. 38
    Lillian Ross

Pagliaro, Louis
    Ping-pong champion
    "The Terrible Midget"
    January 31, 1942 (20-26)
    Vol. 17 No. 51
    Robert Lewis Taylor

Panassié, Hugues
Jazz critic
"Panassié, Delaunay
et cie"
Feb. 14, 1977 (43-52)
Vol. 52 No. 52
Whitney Balliett

Park, Charles
Geologist
"Encounters With the
Archdruid - I"
March 20, 1971 (42-91)
Vol. 47 No. 5
John McPhee

Park, Daphne
Principal, Somerville
College, Oxford
"Vital Powers"
January 30, 1989 (57-71)
Vol. 64 No. 50
Caroline Alexander

Parkinson, Norman
Fashion photographer
"A Light in the Eye"
Dec. 10, 1984 (57-115)
Vol. 60 No. 43
Kennedy Fraser

Parsons, Betty
Art dealer
"A Keeper of the
Treasure"
June 9, 1975 (44-66)
Vol. 51 No. 16
Calvin Tomkins

Pate, Maurice
Executive director,
UNICEF
"At the Heart of UNICEF"
Dec. 2, 1961 (69-112)
Vol. 37 No. 42
Joseph Wechsberg

Paterno, Charles Vincent
Building contractor
"Maker of Castles"
July 2, 1927 (19-20)
Vol. 3 No. 20
Foster Ware

Patterson, Joseph Medill
Publisher, *New York
Daily News*
"Vox Populi"
August 6, 1938 (16-21)
August 13, 1938 (19-24)
August 20, 1938 (19-23)
Vol. 14 Nos. 25-27
Jack Alexander

Paul, Maury H.B.
Society newspaper
columnist
"Dolly and Polly,
Billy and Cholly"
October 16, 1937 (23-27)
October 23, 1937 (22-27)
Vol. 13 Nos. 35-36
Margaret Case Harriman

Peabody, Ernest Henry
President, Peabody
Engineering Corporation;
anti-noise campaigner
"The Sound and the Fury"
Nov. 22, 1941 (28-36)
Vol. 17 No. 41
Robert Lewis Taylor

Pennington, Mary Engle
Refrigeration expert
"Ice Woman"
Sept. 6, 1941 (23-30)
Vol. 17 No. 30
Barbara Heggie

Penzias, Arno A.
Physicist
"Three Degrees
Above Zero"
August 20, 1984 (42-70)
Vol. 60 No. 27
Jeremy Bernstein

Percy, Walker
Author
"The Search"
October 2, 1978 (43-110)
October 9, 1978 (52-125)
Vol. 54 Nos. 33-34
Robert Coles

Perkins, Anthony
Actor
"The Player - III"
Nov. 4, 1961 (83-89)
Vol. 37 No. 38
Lillian Ross

Perkins, Frances
U.S. Secretary of Labor
"Madame Secretary"
Sept. 2, 1933 (16-19)
Sept. 9, 1933 (20-23)
Vol. 9 Nos. 29-30
Russell Lord

Perkins, Maxwell Evarts
Vice president and editor,
Charles Scribner's Sons
"Unshaken Friend"
April 1, 944 (32-42)
April 8, 1944 (30-43)
Vol. 20 Nos. 7-8
Malcolm Cowley

Pershing, John J.
General, U.S. Army
"Notes on a Soldier"
Nov. 7, 1925 (11-12)
Vol. 1 No. 37B
*note: No. 38 omitted
in Vol. 1*
"Captain Quid"
(Marquis James)

Persky, Daniel
Hebrew scholar; member,
Herzliah Institute
"The Slave of Hebrew"
Nov. 28, 1959 (57-105)
Vol. 35 No. 41
Dwight MacDonald

Pétain, Henri Philippe
Marshall of France; head
of Vichy government
"La France et le Vieux"
Feb. 12, 1944 (27-40)
Feb. 19, 1944 (27-43)
Feb. 26, 1944 (28-41)
March 4, 1944 (27-41)
Vol. 19 No. 52 and
Vol. 20 Nos. 1-2
Janet Flanner

Peters, Clinton
Artist, art teacher
"The Daddy of
Sunday Painters"
July 11, 1925 (11-12)
Vol. 1 No. 21
Murdock Pemberton

Petit, Philippe
High-wire performer
"Alone and In Control"
June 15, 1987 (35-45)
Vol. 63 No. 17
Gwen Kinkead

Petrunkevitch, Alexander I.
Spider expert
"Arachnologist"
April 22, 1950 (38-59)
April 29, 1950 (37-55)
Vol. 26 Nos. 9-10
Eugene Kinkead

Petzold, Theodore
Boy scout
"Trustworthy, Loyal,
Helpful, Friendly"
July 25, 1942 (19-24)
Vol. 18 No. 23
St. Clair McKelway

Phelps, William Lyon
Literary critic; Professor
of English, Yale University
"A Kind Man"
October 24, 1925 (11-12)
Vol. 1 No. 36
"Search-Light"
(Waldo Frank)

Philippe, Claudius Charles
Vice president, catering,
Waldorf-Astoria Hotel
"Very, Very Cordial"
Feb. 19, 1955 (35-75)
Vol. 31 No. 1
Geoffrey T. Hellman

Phillips, Harvey
Tubist; music professor,
Indiana University
"Goodbye Oompah"
Dec. 15, 1975 (46-62)
Vol. 51 No. 43
Whitney Balliett

Picasso, Pablo
Painter
"One-Man Group"
Dec. 9, 1939 (32-37)
Vol. 15 No. 43
Janet Flanner

Picasso, Pablo *cont.*
"The Surprise of
the Century"
March 9, 1957 (37-63)
March 16, 1957 (39-74)
Vol. 33 Nos. 3-4
Janet Flanner

Pickford, Mary
Motion picture actress
"Sweetheart"
April 7, 1934 (29-33)
Vol. 10 No. 8
Margaret Case Harriman

Pierce, John R.
Executive Director of
Communications
Research, Bell Telephone
"Woomera Has It!"
Sept. 21, 1963 (49-110)
Vol. 39 No. 31
Calvin Tomkins

Pitkin, Walter B.
Author, self-help books;
journalism professor,
Columbia University
"Designer For Living"
May 12, 1934 (25-28)
May 19, 1934 (24-28)
Vol. 10 Nos. 13-14
Milton MacKaye

Platzker, Joseph
Director, N.Y.C. Vacancy
Listing Bureau
"C'est la Guerre and
Laissez Faire"
March 31, 1945 (28-39)
Vol. 21 No. 7
Philip Hamburger

Plimpton, Francis T.P.
Lawyer
"Period-Piece Fellow"
Dec. 4, 1971 (61-126)
Vol. 47 No. 42
Geoffrey T. Hellman

Plummer, Brian
Sportsman
"Ratcatcher"
Feb. 15, 1988 (41-57)
Vol. 63 No. 52
R.C. Smith

Point, Marie Louise Mado
Manager, Restaurant
de la Pyramide
"Hors Concours"
October 5, 1963 (57-130)
Vol. 39 No. 33
Joseph Wechsberg

Poiret, Paul
Clothing designer
"The Egotist"
October 29, 1927 (23-25)
Vol. 3 No. 37
"Hippolyta"
(Janet Flanner)

Poliziano, Angelo
  Poet
  "The Angel in May"
  Feb. 24, 1951 (34-65)
  Vol. 27 No. 2
  Alan Moorehead

Pollock, Channing
  Playwright
  "A Devout Mountebank"
  April 3, 1926 (17-18)
  Vol. 2 No. 7
  Percy Hammond

Pond, James Burton
  Owner, speakers bureau
  "The Culture Business"
  August 27, 1932 (18-22)
  Sept. 3, 1932 (22-25)
  Vol. 8 Nos. 28-29
  Milton MacKaye

Pons, Lily
  Soprano, Metropolitan
  Opera Company
  "The French Lily"
  January 16, 1932 (20-23)
  Vol. 7 No. 48
  Janet Flanner

Pope, Arthur Upham
  "Under the Rug"
  July 14, 1945 (28-34)
  July 21, 1945 (22-29)
  Vol. 21 Nos. 22-23
  Robert Lewis Taylor

Porter, Cole
  Composer, lyricist
  "Words and Music"
  Nov. 23, 1940 (24-34)
  Vol. 16 No. 41
  Margaret Case Harriman

  "Wouldn't It Be Fun?"
  Sept. 18, 1971 (48-64)
  Vol. 47 No. 31
  Brendan Gill

Post, Emily
  Author; authority on
  etiquette
  "Lady Chesterfield"
  August 16, 1930 (22-25)
  Vol. 6 No. 26
  Helena Huntington Smith

Post, Marjorie Meriwether *see*
  Marjorie Post Davies

Powell, Mel
  Pianist, composer
  "What Ever Happened to
  Mel Powell?"
  May 25, 1987 (37-43)
  Vol. 63 No. 14
  Whitney Balliett

Powers, Bertram A.
  President, New York
  Typographical Union
  No. 6
  "Printer"
  March 7, 1970 (43-81)
  Vol. 46 No. 3
  Geoffrey T. Hellman

Prajadhipok, King of Siam *see*
Rama VII, King of Siam

Pratt, Ruth Sears Baker
    Member, New York City
    Board of Aldermen
    "One of the Boys"
    April 24, 1926 (21-22)
    Vol. 2 No. 10
    Oliver H.P. Garrett

Preminger, Otto
    Film producer and
    director
    "Anatomy of a
    Commercial Interruption"
    Feb. 19, 1966 (42-129)
    Vol. 41 No. 53
    Lillian Ross

Prendergast, Charles
    Artist
    "A Glimpse of Heaven"
    July 27, 1946 (24-30)
    August 3, 1946 (28-39)
    Vol. 22 Nos. 24-25
    Hamilton Basso

Prendiville, Joseph P.
    Staff Sergeant, U.S. Army
    "The Regular"
    August 5, 1944 (23-31)
    Vol. 20 No. 25
    George Woodward

Previn, André
    Music Director, Pittsburgh
    Symphony Orchestra
    "A Way of Making
    Things Happen"
    January 10, 1983 (36-79)
    January 17, 1983 (44-85)
    Vol. 58 Nos. 47-48
    Helen Drees Ruttencutter

Printemps, Yvonne
    Actress
    "Essence of Chic Paris"
    Dec. 18, 1926 (29-32)
    Vol. 2 No. 44
    Ferdinand Tuohy

Purobayev, Pavel Petrovich
    Secret agent
    "Ukrainian Shadow"
    April 12, 1947 (36-45)
    Vol. 23 No. 8
    John Fischer

Pyle, C. C.
    Sports promoter
    "Cash and Carry"
    Dec. 8, 1928 (31-34)
    Vol. 4 No. 42
    Alva Johnston

Qualtinger, Helmut
    Actor; playwright
    "Enemy of
    Gemütlichkeit"
    April 20, 1963 (53-95)
    Vol. 39 No. 9
    Joseph Wechsberg

Quisenberry, Dan
Pitcher, Kansas City
Royals
"Quis"
Sept. 30, 1985 (41-72)
Vol. 61 No. 32
Roger Angell

Rabi, I.I. (Isidor Isaac)
Physicist
"Physicist"
Oct. 13, 1975 (47-110)
Oct. 20, 1975 (47-101)
Vol. 51 Nos. 34-35
Jeremy Bernstein

Rabkin, William
Manufacturer of coin-
operated amusement
machines
"Penny-Arcade
Philanthropist"
October 16, 1948 (36-48)
Vol. 24 No. 34
Robert Rice

Rachmaninoff, Sergei
Vassilievitch
Composer
"An Aristocrat"
January 9, 1926 (15-16)
Vol. 1 No. 47
Esther Carples

Ragozin, Leonard
Turf handicapper
"By the Numbers"
Dec. 21, 1987 (56-83)
Vol. 63 No. 44
Jeff Coplon

Rama VII (Prajadhipok)
King of Siam
"Little Monarch"
April 18, 1931 (24-26)
Vol. 7 No. 9
Andrew A. Freeman

Ramey, John Daniel
American soldier
"The Brilliant Jughead"
July 28, 1945 (25-37)
Vol. 21 No. 24
John Hersey

Ramsay, Peggy
Play agent
"Play Agent"
May 23, 1988 (35-60)
Vol. 64 No. 14
Mel Gussow

Randolph, A. Philip
Black leader
"Early Voice; From
Florida to Harlem"
Dec. 2, 1972 (60-120)
Dec. 9, 1972 (48-106)
Dec. 16, 1972 (40-85)
Vol. 48 Nos. 41-43
Jervis Anderson

Rapee, Erno
Orchestra conductor,
Radio City Music Hall
"Idea Flourisher"
February 5, 1944 (28-40)
Vol. 19 No. 51
Barbara Heggie and
Robert Lewis Taylor

Rauschenberg, Robert
Artist
"Moving Out"
Feb. 29, 1964 (39-105)
Vol. 40 No. 2
Calvin Tomkins

Ray, Dean Randolph
Rector, Little Church
Around the Corner
"A Downtown Gabriel"
July 27, 1929 (20-23)
Vol. 5 No. 23
Niven Busch, Jr.

Redgrave, Michael
Actor
"The Player - I"
October 21, 1961 (73-90)
Vol. 37 No. 36
Lillian Ross

Reilly, Edward J.
Lawyer
"For the Defense"
January 12, 1935 (18-22)
Vol. 10 No. 48
Robert M. Coates

Reiselin, Walter
Milkman, Sheffield Farms
"Route Salesman"
June 22, 1935 (18-22)
Vol. 11 No. 19
Robert M. Coates

Reisner, Christian Fichthorne
Pastor, Broadway Temple
"Just the Old-Time
Religion"
Dec. 16, 1939 (32-38)
Vol. 15 No. 44
Richard Owen Boyer

Renoir, Jean
Film director
"Le Meneur de Jeu"
August 23, 1969 (34-61)
Vol. 45 No. 27
Penelope Gilliatt

Riboud, Jean
Chairman, Schumberger,
Ltd.
"Certain Poetry"
June 6, 1983 (46-109)
June 13, 1983 (50-91)
Vol. 59 Nos. 16-17
Ken Auletta

Rich, Buddy
Jazz drummer
"Beautiful"
January 21, 1967 (35-66)
Vol. 42 No. 48
Whitney Balliett

Richardson, Sir Ralph
  Actor
  "At Three Minutes Past
  Eight You Must Dream"
  Feb. 21, 1977 (45-72)
  Vol. 53 No. 1
  Kenneth Tynan

Richter, Mike
  Hockey goalie
  "Facing the Shooter"
  Nov. 23, 1992 (110-125)
  Vol. 68 No. 40
  Alec Wilkinson

Rickard, Tex (George L.)
  Director, Madison Square
  Garden
  "Rickard Rounds Up the
  Rubes"
  Dec. 12, 1925 (17-18)
  Vol. 1 No. 42
  W.O. McGeehan

Rickey, Branch
  President, Brooklyn
  Dodgers
  "Thoughts on Baseball"
  May 27, 1950 (32-46)
  June 3, 1950 (30-47)
  Vol. 26 Nos. 14-15
  Robert Rice

Rieto, Vittorio
  Composer
  "A Kind of Dancer"
  January 9, 1989 (32-50)
  Vol. 64 No. 47
  Suzannah Lessard

Rifkind, Simon
  Lawyer
  "Advocate"
  May 23, 1983 (46-81)
  Vol. 59 No. 14
  John Brooks

Ringling, Charles and John
  Owners, Ringling Brothers
  & Barnum & Bailey
  Circus
  "A Two-Ringling Circus"
  May 1, 1926 (19-20)
  Vol. 2 No. 11
  Helena Huntington Smith

Ripley, Robert L.
  "Believe It or Not!"
  cartoonist; radio
  personality
  "Odd Man"
  August 31, 1940 (20-24)
  Sept. 7, 1940 (27-30)
  Vol. 16 Nos. 29-30
  Geoffrey T, Hellman

Ripley, Sidney Dillon II
  Associate Curator of
  Zoology, Peabody
  Museum; authority on
  birds of Asia
  "Curator Getting Around"
  August 26, 1950 (31-49)
  Vol. 26 No. 27
  Geoffrey T. Hellman

Rivera, Dennis
    President, Local 1199
    Drug, Hospital and Health
    Care Employees Union
    "Getting Things Done"
    Dec. 10, 1990 (54-85)
    Vol. 66 No. 43
    A.H. Raskin

Rivera, Diego
    Mural painter
    "Enfant Terrible"
    May 20, 1933 (21-24)
    Vol. 9 No. 14
    Geoffrey T. Hellman

Robards, Jason
    Actor
    "The Player - III"
    Nov. 4, 1961 (72-83)
    Vol. 37 No. 38
    Lillian Ross

Robbins, William J.
    Director, New York
    Botanical Gardens
    "Square Deal Among
    the Fungi"
    July 19, 1947 (30-41)
    Vol. 23 No. 22
    Geoffrey T. Hellman

Robeson, Paul
    Singer; actor
    "King of Harlem"
    Sept. 29, 1928 (26-29)
    Vol. 4 No. 32
    Mildred Gilman

Robinson, Bill
    Dancer
    "Bojangles"
    October 6, 1934 (26-28)
    October 13, 1934 (26-30)
    Vol. 10 Nos. 34-35
    St. Clair McKelway

Robinson, Dr. Frederick B.
    President, College of the
    City of New York
    "Educator"
    Nov. 18, 1933 (26-29)
    Vol. 9 No. 39
    Geoffrey T. Hellman

Robinson-Duff, Frances
    Drama coach
    "Do or Diaphragm"
    May 25, 1935 (22-27)
    Vol. 11 No. 15
    S.N. Behrman

Rockefeller, David
    President, Chase
    Manhattan Bank
    "Resources and
    Responsibilities"
    January 9, 1965 (37-83)
    January 16, 1965 (40-73)
    Vol. 40 Nos. 47-48
    E.J. Kahn, Jr.

Rockefeller, John D.
Industrialist; oil tycoon
"Notes on a Well-Known
Citizen"
January 22, 1927 (16-20)
January 29, 1927 (24-29)
Vol. 2 Nos. 49-50
John K. Winkler

Rockefeller, John D., Jr.
Industrialist;
philanthropist
"A Scientific Santa Claus"
June 2, 1928 (27-31)
June 9, 1928 (20-24)
Vol. 4 Nos. 15-16
John K. Winkler

Rockefeller, John D. III
Foundation executive
"Out of the Cocoon on
the Fifty-sixth Floor"
Nov. 4, 1972 (56-103)
Vol. 48 No. 37
Geoffrey T. Hellman

Rockefeller, Nelson A.
Governor, New York
State; expert on Latin
America
"Best Neighbor"
April 11, 1942 (23-30)
April 18, 1942 (22-32)
Vol. 18 Nos. 8-9
Geoffrey T. Hellman

Rockwell, Norman
Artist; illustrator
"U.S. Artist"
March 17, 1945 (34-45)
March 24, 1945 (36-47)
Vol. 21 Nos. 5-6
Rufus Jarman

Rodgers, Richard
Composer
"Words and Music"
May 28, 1938 (19-23)
June 4, 1938 (23-27)
Vol. 14 Nos. 15-16
Margaret Case Harriman

"You Can't Force It"
Nov. 18, 1961 (58-95)
Vol. 37 No. 40
Winthrop Sargeant

Rogers, Anne Hone
Show dog handler and
breeder
"The Touch"
April 9, 1960 (49-87)
Vol. 36 No. 8
Robert Rice

Rogers, Joe
Midway concessionaire,
New York World's Fair
"Masters of the Midway"
August 12, 1939 (22-25)
August 19, 1939 (23-27)
Vol. 15 Nos. 26-27
A.J. Liebling

Rogers, Richard
    Architect
    "Architecture of
    Possibilities"
    Nov. 14, 1988 (47-96)
    Vol. 64 No. 39
    Lincoln Caplan

Rohatyn, Felix
    Chairman, Municipal
    Assistance Corporation
    "Allocating Sacrifice"
    January 24, 1983 (45-78)
    Vol. 58 No. 49
    Jeremy Bernstein

Romanoff, Prince Dmitri
Michl Oblenski *see* Gerguson,
Harry F.

Roosevelt, Eleanor (Mrs.
Franklin D.)
    Wife of recently-elected
    Governor of New York
    "Noblesse Oblige"
    April 5, 1930 (23-25)
    Vol. 6 No. 7
    Helena Huntington Smith

    "The Years Alone"
    June 12, 1948 (30-43)
    June 19, 1948 (30-42)
    Vol. 24 Nos. 16-17
    E.J. Kahn, Jr.

Roosevelt, Franklin Delano
    Governor of New York
    [U.S. President, 1933-45]
    "The Governor"
    August 15, 1931 (19-22)
    August 22, 1931 (24-29)
    Vol. 7 Nos. 26-27
    Milton MacKaye

    "The President"
    June 16, 1934 (20-25)
    June 23, 1934 (20-24)
    June 30, 1934 (20-24)
    Vol. 10 Nos. 18-20
    Henry F. Pringle

Root, Elihu
    U.S. Senator (D-N.Y.);
    U.S. Secretary of State;
    U.S. Ambassador to
    Russia
    "De Senectute"
    Feb. 1, 1936 (21-26)
    Feb. 8, 1936 (21-25)
    Feb. 15, 1936 (22-27)
    Vol. 11 Nos. 51-53
    Henry F. Pringle

Roper, William W.
    Football coach, Princeton
    University; politician
    "The Roper Complex"
    Nov. 13, 1926 (25-27)
    Vol. 2 No. 39
    Sigmund Gottfried Spaeth

Rose, Billy
Stage show producer
"Mass Entertainment"
April 27, 1935 (22-29)
Vol. 11 No. 10
Alva Johnston

Rosen, Al
Hollywood agent
"The Great Expurgator"
March 29, 1947 (40-49)
Vol. 23 No. 6
Alva Johnston

Rosenbach, Dr. A. S. W.
Rare book dealer
"Napoleon of Books"
April 14, 1928 (25-28)
Vol. 4 No. 8
Avery Strakosch

Rosenberg, Anna
Labor mediator
"Middlewoman"
April 23, 1938 (24-29)
Vol. 14 No. 10
Richard Owen Boyer

Rosendahl, Charles E.
Aviator
"No Hero"
March 26, 1932 (22-25)
Vol. 8 No. 6
Henry F. Pringle

Rosenfeld, Henry Jonas
Dress manufacturer
"The Millionaire"
January 7, 1950 (30-41)
January 14, 1950 (32-44)
Vol. 25 Nos. 46-47
Lillian Ross

Rosenstein, Nettie
Fashion designer
"Very Terrific, Very
Divine"
October 19, 1940 (28-36)
Vol. 16 No. 36
Margaret Case Harriman

Rosenthal, Jean
Theater lighting expert
"Please, Darling, Bring
Three to Seven"
February 4, 1956 (33-39)
Vol. 31 No. 51
Winthrop Sargeant

Rosoff, Samuel
Contractor, Eighth
Avenue Subway
"A Master Ditch Digger"
June 4, 1927 (19-21)
Vol. 3 No. 16
Russell Owen

Ross, Glynn
Director, Seattle Opera
"Ring" festival
"The Ring's the Thing"
June 26, 1978 (35-50)
Vol. 54 No. 19
Winthrop Sargeant

Ross, Rita
    Cat-catcher
    "Lady of the Cats"
    May 14, 1938 (21-26)
    Vol. 14 No. 13
    Wolcott Gibbs and
    Eugene Kinkead

Rothafel, Samuel "Roxy"
    Manager, Roxy Theater
    "Deus ex Cinema"
    May 28, 1927 (20-22)
    Vol. 3 No. 15
    Kenneth Macgowan

Rothberg, Sam ("Stitch
McCarthy")
    Bondsman
    "Bail-Bond Baron"
    March 25, 1933 (18-21)
    Vol. 9 No. 6
    Meyer Berger

Rothschild, Miriam
    Naturalist
    "Fritillaries and Hairy
    Violets"
    October 19, 1987 (45-74)
    Vol. 63 No. 35
    Kennedy Fraser

Rovenstein, Emery Andrew
    Bellevue anesthesiologist
    "Anesthesiologist"
    October 25, 1947 (36-45)
    Nov. 1, 1947 (33-43)
    Nov. 8, 1947 (38-51)
    Vol. 23 Nos. 36-38
    Mark Murphy

Rowles, Jimmy
    Concert pianist
    * Our Local
    Correspondents
    "Dancing on the Carpet"
    April 1, 1974 (43-50)
    Vol. 50 No. 6
    Whitney Balliett

Royal, John F.
    Vice president, NBC
    "Vaudeville to Television"
    Sept. 28, 1946 (32-43)
    October 5, 1946 (36-47)
    October 12, 1946 (36-46)
    Vol. 22 Nos. 33-35
    Alva Johnston

Royce, William H.
    Balzac scholar, biographer
    "Thirty-Five Years of
    Balzac"
    April 1, 1933 (18-21)
    Vol. 9 No. 7
    Alva Johnston

Rubenstein, Helena
    Cosmetics magnate
    "Beauty in Jars and Vials"
    June 30, 1928 (20-23)
    Vol. 4 No. 19
    Jo Swerling

Rubin, Louis
    Marriage broker
    "Bearded Cupid"
    June 11, 1938 (16-21)
    Vol. 14 No. 17
    Meyer Berger

Rubin, William S.
Director of Collections,
MOMA
"Sharpening the Eye"
Nov. 4, 1985 (52-76)
Vol. 61 No. 37
Calvin Tomkins

Rubinstein, Artur
Pianist
"Metamorphosis"
Nov. 1, 1958 (47-99)
Vol. 34 No. 37
Joseph Wechsberg

Ruckdeschel, Carol
Biologist
"Travels in Georgia"
April 28, 1973 (44-103)
Vol. 49 No. 10
John McPhee

Rudel, Julius
Conductor, New York City
Opera
"A Feeling of Intense
Concentration"
October 20, 1962 (57-82)
Vol. 38 No. 35
Winthrop Sargeant

Rudkin, Margaret
President, Pepperidge
Farms, Inc.
"Striking a Blow for
Grandma"
May 22, 1948 (38-51)
Vol. 24 No. 13
John Bainbridge

Rudman, Kal
Popular music columnist
"Money Music"
Dec. 23, 1972 (32-49)
Vol. 48 No. 44
George W.S. Trow, Jr.

Ruml, Beardsley
Economist; author;
government advisor
"The National Idea Man"
Feb. 10, 1945 (28-35)
Feb. 17, 1945 (26-34)
Feb. 24, 1945 (30-41)
Vol. 20 No. 52 and
Vol. 21 Nos. 1-2
Alva Johnston

Runciman, Steven
Historian
"Historian"
Nov. 3, 1986 (53-80)
Vol. 62 No. 37
David Plante

Ruppert, Jacob
Brewer; owner, New York
Yankees; U.S.
Congressman
"Beer and Baseball"
Sept. 24, 1932 (20-24)
Vol. 8 No. 32
Alva Johnston

Russell, Pee Wee (Charles
Ellsworth)
Jazz clarinetist
"Even His Feet Look Sad"
August 11, 1962 (30-45)
Vol. 38 No. 25
Arthur Robinson

Russo, Susan Cook
High school teacher; anti-
Pledge of Allegiance
crusader
* A Reporter at Large
"Love of Country"
July 30, 1973 (35-48)
Vol. 49 No. 23
Daniel Lang

Ruth, Babe (George Herman)
Baseball player
"The Babe"
July 31, 1926 (15-17)
Vol. 2 No. 24
Arthur Robinson

Ryan, Bunny (Elizabeth)
Tennis player
"A Master of Her Art"
August 22, 1925 (9-10)
Vol. 1 No. 27
John R. Tunis

Ryan, George J.
President, New York City
Board of Education
"Pedagogue"
Feb. 22, 1930 (29-32)
Vol. 6 No. 1
Helena Huntington Smith

Sabin, Pauline Morton
Politician; president,
Women's Organization for
National Prohibition
Reform
"The New Crusade"
October 22, 1932 (20-24)
Vol. 8 No. 36
Milton MacKaye

Safford, Frank
Harness horse trainer
"Hymns on the Harness
Track"
October 15, 1949 (37-53)
Vol. 25 No. 34
Ricard Owen Boyer

Sagan, Carl
Astronomer
"A Resonance With
Something Alive"
June 21, 1976 (39-83)
June 28, 1976 (30-61)
Vol. 52 Nos. 18-19
Henry S.F. Cooper, Jr.

Sahl, Mort
Comedian
"The Fury"
July 30, 1960 (31-53)
Vol. 36 No. 24
Robert Rice

Saito, Hirosi
Japanese Ambassador to
the United States
"Diplomat in the
Doghouse"
April 30, 1938 (22-27)
Vol. 14 No. 11
Jack Alexander

Salveson, Magda
Artist
"City Voices"
Feb. 25, 1985 (35-51)
Vol. 61 No. 1
Whitney Balliett

Sandburg, Carl
Poet
"Peasant by Paradox"
Nov. 14, 1925 (13-14)
Vol. 1 No. 38
"Search-Light"
(Waldo Frank)

Sande, Earle
Jockey
"Silk and Leather"
July 30, 1927 (15-18)
Vol. 3 No. 24
Niven Busch, Jr.

Sanders, Colonel Harland
Founder, Kentucky Fried
Chicken restaurant chain
"Kentucky-Fried"
Feb. 14, 1970 (40-52)
Vol. 45 No. 52
William Whitworth

Sanger, Margaret
Author; birth control
crusader
"The Child Who Was
Mother to a Woman"
April 11, 1925 (11-12)
Vol. 1 No. 8
R. Hale (no byline)

"They Were Eleven"
July 5, 1930 (22-25)
Vol. 6 No. 20
Helena Huntington Smith

Santana, Carmen
Recipient of government
assistance
"A Welfare Mother"
Sept. 29, 1975 (42-99)
Vol. 51 No. 32
Susan Sheehan

Santelli, George (Giorgio)
Fencing master
"To Touch and Not Be
Touched"
January 10, 1953 (30-42)
January 17, 1953 (32-48)
Vol. 28 Nos. 47-48
Robert Lewis Taylor

Saracini, Count Guido Chigi
Music patron
"Torna! Torna!"
Sept. 3, 1960 (37-77)
Vol. 36 No. 29
Winthrop Sargeant

Sarra, Valentino
Photographer; advertising
executive
"Master of the Before and
the After"
Sept. 1, 1951 (29-42)
Vol. 27 No. 29
Andy Logan

Saunders, Blanche
Dog obedience trainer
"Down the Leash"
Nov. 24, 1951 (42-64)
Vol. 27 No. 41
Angelica Gibbs

Sawyer, Peter Roland
British police constable
"Constable"
August 14, 1971 (40-53)
Vol. 47 No. 26
John Bainbridge

Scammon, Richard M.
Statistician
"One-Man Think Tank"
Sept. 20, 1969 (50-89)
Vol. 45 No. 31
William Whitworth

Schaffer, Kenny
Businessman
"Opening Windows"
Dec. 2, 1991 (48-115)
Vol. 67 No. 41
David Owen

Scheepers, John T.
Flower bulb broker
"Flower Lover No. 1"
June 25, 1938 (20-26)
Vol. 14 No. 19
Richard Owen Boyer

Scheer, George Fabian
Trade book publishers'
representative
"Book Traveller"
Nov. 12, 1973 (51-113)
Vol. 49 No. 38
Bruce Bliven, Jr.

Scheff, Fritzi
Broadway actress;
light-opera singer
"The Mascot of the
Troop"
Nov. 16, 1929 (30-32)
Vol. 5 No. 39
Alison Smith

Schell, Maria
Actress
"The Player - II"
Oct. 28, 1961 (100-109)
Vol. 37 No. 37
Lillian Ross

Schenck, Nicholas M.
President, Loew's Inc. and
Metro-Goldwyn-Mayer
"Business is Business"
April 30, 1932 (22-25)
Vol. 8 No. 11
Henry F. Pringle

Scher, Louis
  Book scout
  "Book Scout"
  Nov. 8, 1952 (39-84)
  Vol. 28 No. 38
  Stanley Edgar Hyman

Schiaparelli, Elsa
  Fashion designer
  "Comet"
  June 18, 1932 (19-23)
  Vol. 8 No. 18
  Janet Flanner

Schiff, Dorothy
  Owner and publisher,
  New York Post
  "Publisher"
  August 10, 1968 (37-65)
  Vol. 44 No. 25
  Geoffrey T. Hellman

Schindler, Raymond C.
  Head of private detective
  agency
  "Private Detective"
  July 3, 1943 (26-36)
  July 10, 1943 (26-37)
  July 17, 1943 (27-33)
  Vol. 19 Nos. 20-22
  Alva Johnston

Schlemmer, William
  President, Hammacher
  Schlemmer & Co.
  "Metamorphic Merchant"
  July 8, 1939 (25-31)
  Vol. 15 No. 21
  Dwight MacDonald

Schling, Max
  Florist, started vogue for
  Bordeaux carnations
  "For Any Occasion"
  July 18, 1936 (18-23)
  Vol. 12 No. 22
  Margaret Case Harriman

Schmidt, Elwood L.
  Physician
  "Solo"
  January 1, 1972 (30-40)
  Vol. 47 No. 46
  Berton Roueché

Schnabel, Artur
  Pianist
  "Music's Faithful Servant"
  April 2, 1938 (23-27)
  Vol. 14 No. 7
  César Saerchinger

Schneider, Hannes
  Inventor of skiing
  techniques
  "A Way of Life"
  Feb. 28, 1942 (21-27)
  Vol. 18 No. 2
  C. Lester Walker

Schueler, Jon
  Artist
  "City Voices"
  Feb. 25, 1985 (35-51)
  Vol. 61 No. 1
  Whitney Balliett

Schultes, Richard Evans
    Botanist
    "Jungle Botanist"
    June 1, 1992 (35-58)
    Vol. 68 No. 15
    E.J. Kahn, Jr.

Schultz, Sam
    Sidewalk grate
    "fisherman"
    "Sidewalk Fisherman"
    July 23, 1938 (16-20)
    Vol. 14 No. 23
    Meyer Berger

Schumann-Heink, Ernestine
    Contralto
    "Hausfrau Prima Donna"
    March 20, 1926 (17-18)
    Vol. 2 No. 5
    Helena Smith

Schuster, M. Lincoln
    Publisher
    "How to Win Profits and
    Influence Literature"
    Sept. 30, 1939 (22-28)
    October 7, 1939 (24-30)
    October 14, 1939 (25-29)
    Vol. 15 Nos. 33-35
    Geoffrey T. Hellman

Schwab, Charles M.
    President, U.S. Steel Corp.
    "Steel"
    April 25, 1931 (23-26)
    May 2, 1931 (26-35)
    Vol. 7 Nos. 10-11
    John K. Winkler

Schwartz, A. Charles
    Financier
    "The Lucky Stiff"
    July 24, 1926 (15-17)
    Vol. 2 No. 23
    Arthur Krock

Schwartz, Louis G.
    Waiter; war bond salesman
    "The Bard in the
    Delicatessen"
    March 18, 1944 (32-45)
    Vol. 20 No. 5
    Philip Hamburger

Scotti, Antonio
    Singer, Metropolitan
    Opera Company
    "Villain of Villains"
    Feb. 13, 1926 (15-16)
    Vol. 1 No. 52
    George White Garland

Scull, Robert Cooper
    Art dealer; owner of taxi
    cab company
    "Man Who is Happening
    Now"
    Nov. 26, 1966 (64-120)
    Vol. 42 No. 40
    Jane Kramer

Scully, Vince
    Art history professor
    "What Seas, What
    Shores"
    Feb. 18, 1980 (43-69)
    Vol. 55 No. 53
    James Stevenson

Seabury, Samuel
  Politician; judge
  "Inquisitor"
  June 27, 1931 (20-23)
  Vol. 7 No. 19
  Richard Owen Boyer

Segalla, Stanley J.
  Stunt pilot
  "Aerobat"
  August 27, 1984 (38-59)
  Vol. 60 No. 28
  Burton Bernstein

Seiden, Irving
  President, Mercury
  Service Systems
  "Urgent! Rush!"
  July 5, 1958 (29-51)
  Vol. 34 No. 20
  Daniel Lang

Sell, Henry Blackman
  Maker of canned meat
  products
  "Specialities"
  March 27, 1948 (32-44)
  April 3, 1948 (34-47)
  April 10, 1948 (33-47)
  Vol. 24 Nos. 5-7
  Richard H. Rovere

Sendak, Maurice
  Author; illustrator of
  children's books
  "Among the Wild Things"
  January 22, 1966 (39-73)
  Vol. 41 No. 49
  Nat Hentoff

Service, John
  U.S. Diplomat
  "Foresight, Nightmare,
  and Hindsight"
  April 8, 1972 (43-95)
  Vol. 48 No. 7
  E.J. Kahn, Jr.

Service, Robert W.
  Poet
  "Whooping It Up"
  March 30, 1946 (34-41)
  April 6, 1946 (32-43)
  Vol. 22 Nos. 7-8
  Geoffrey T. Hellman

Setterfield, Valda
  Dancer
  "Making Work"
  Nov.29, 1982 (51-107)
  Vol. 58 No. 41
  Arlene Croce

Seuss, Dr. *see* Geisel,
  Theodore Seuss

Shaffer, Paul
  Musical director, "Late
  Night with David
  Letterman"
  "Stay Up Late"
  January 16, 1989 (36-60)
  Vol. 64 No. 48
  James Kaplan

Shannon, Hugh
  Cabaret singer
  "According to
  Where I Go"
  January 17, 1977 (36-42)
  Vol. 52 No. 48
  Whitney Balliett

Shapiro, Elliott
  Elementary school
  principal
  "The Principal"
  May 7, 1966 (52-119)
  Vol. 42 No. 11
  Nat Hentoff

Shattuck, Frank G.
  Owner, Schrafft's
  restaurants
  "Without Benefit of
  Tin Foil"
  May 19, 1928 (29-31)
  Vol. 4 No. 13
  Oliver H.P. Garrett

Shaw, Artie
  Jazz clarinetist; band
  leader
  "Middle-Aged Man
  Without a Horn"
  May 19, 1962 (47-98)
  Vol. 38 No. 13
  Robert Lewis Taylor

Sherover, Max
  President, Linguaphone
  Institute of America
  "At Home With the
  Durands"
  June 28, 1947 (30-43)
  Vol. 23 No. 19
  John Bainbridge

Sherwood, Robert Emmet
  Playwright
  "Old Monotonous"
  June 1, 1940 (33-41)
  June 8, 1940 (23-36)
  Vol. 16 Nos. 16-17
  S.N. Behrman

Shine, Benjamin
  Courtroom spectator
  "Court Buff"
  Dec. 15, 1980 (46-79)
  Vol. 56 No. 43
  Mark Singer

Shippey, Hartwell Stuart
  Barge captain
  "Socrates Afloat"
  August 25, 1945 (25-32)
  Vol. 21 No. 28
  Brendan Gill

Shor, Toots (Bernard)
  Restaurateur
  "Toot's World"
  Nov. 11, 1950 (50-76)
  Nov. 18, 1950 (54-74)
  Nov. 25, 1950 (42-61)
  Vol. 26 Nos. 38-40
  John Bainbridge

Shubert, Jacob J.
Theater owner
"The Boys From
Syracuse"
Nov. 18, 1939 (26-30)
Nov. 25, 1939 (23-37)
Dec. 2, 1939 (33-37)
Vol. 15 Nos. 40-42
A.J. Liebling

Shubert, Lee
Theater owner
"The Boys From
Syracuse"
Nov. 18, 1939 (26-30)
Nov. 25, 1939 (23-37)
Dec. 2, 1939 (33-37)
Vol. 15 Nos. 40-42
A.J. Liebling

Siegel, Morris
Insurance expert
"Mr. X and Mankind's
Greatest Blessing"
June 28, 1941 (19-28)
Vol. 17 No. 20
George Ross Leighton and
Strother Holland Walker

Sigornet, Simone
Actress
"The Player - III"
Nov. 4, 1961 (89-98)
Vol. 37 No. 38
Lillian Ross

Sikorsky, Igor Ivanovich
Airplane engineer
"The Winged - S"
August 10, 1940 (21-29)
August 17, 1940 (20-28)
Vol. 16 Nos. 26-27
Geoffrey T. Hellman

Sills, Beverly
Soprano, Metropolitan
Opera Company
"Superstar"
March 6, 1971 (42-64)
Vol. 47 No. 3
Winthrop Sargeant

Simenon, Georges
Author
"Out of the Dark"
January 24, 1953 (35-53)
Vol. 28 No. 49
Brendan Gill

Simon, Richard L.
Publisher
"How to Win Profits and
Influence Literature"
Sept. 30, 1939 (22-28)
October 7, 1939 (24-30)
October 14, 1939 (25-29)
Vol. 15 Nos. 33-35
Geoffrey T. Hellman

Simpson, Alan
U.S. Senator
"Taking It Personally"
March 16, 1992 (56-78)
Vol. 68 No. 4
John Newhouse

Simpson, Kenneth Farrand
   Chairman, N.Y. County
   Republican Party
   "Boss Without Cigar"
   October 28, 1939 (21-27)
   Vol. 15 No. 37
   Noel Fairchild Busch

Sinatra, Frank
   Popular singer
   "Phenomenon"
   October 26, 1946 (36-48)
   Nov. 2, 1946 (37-54)
   Nov. 9, 1946 (36-53)
   Vol. 22 Nos. 37-39
   E.J. Kahn, Jr.

Singh, Sirdar Jagjit
   President, India League
   of America; interpreter
   "One-Man Lobby"
   March 24, 1951 (35-55)
   Vol. 27 No. 6
   Robert Shaplen

Sirovich, William I.
   U.S. Congressman;
   physician
   "Boy Orator Grows
   Older"
   Nov. 5, 1938 (24-30)
   Vol. 14 No. 38
   Richard Owen Boyer

Sischy, Ingrid
   Editor, *Artforum*
   "Girl of the Zeitgeist"
   October 20, 1986 (49-89)
   October 27, 1986 (47-66)
   Vol. 62 Nos. 35-36
   Janet Malcolm

Sloan, John
   Historical artist
   "After Enough Years Have
   Passed"
   May 7, 1949 (36-51)
   Vol. 25 No. 11
   Robert M. Coates

Sloane, Carol
   Jazz singer
   "Carol Sloane and
   Julie Wilson"
   April 6, 1987 (72-80)
   Vol. 63 No. 7
   Whitney Balliett

Slonimsky, Nicolas
   Pianist; conductor
   "Boy Wonder"
   Nov. 17, 1986 (54-93)
   Nov. 24, 1986 (52-74)
   Vol. 62 Nos. 39-40
   Lawrence Weschler

Slotkin, Samuel
   President, Hygrade Foods
   "Dignified Meat"
   June 15, 1946 (28-39)
   June 22, 1946 (30-41)
   Vol. 22 Nos. 18-19
   Robert Lewis Taylor

Smith, Alfred E.
Governor of New York
"The Brown Derby and
the Bee"
May 29, 1926 (16-18)
Vol. 2 No. 15
Arthur Krock

Smith, Bernard E.
Stockbroker
"Jolly Bear"
May 14, 1932 (22-25)
May 21, 1932 (21-25)
Vol. 8 Nos. 13-14
Matthew Josephson

Smith, Bruce
Director, Institute of
Public Administration
"Not Like Taking the
Waters"
Feb. 27, 1954 (39-73)
Vol. 30 No. 2
Robert Shaplen

Smith, Elinor
Aviator
"New Woman"
May 10, 1930 (28-31)
Vol. 6 No. 12
Helena Huntington Smith

Smith, Kate
Contralto, radio star
"Home Girl"
March 3, 1934 (25-29)
Vol. 10 No. 3
Joseph Mitchell

Smith, Maynard
Staff sergeant,
U.S. Army Air Force
"The Deal"
Sept. 18, 1943 (30-40)
Vol. 19 No. 31
Sam Boal

Smith, Robert Lansing and
William W., II
Executives, Smith
Brothers (cough drops)
"The Boys"
Sept. 6, 1947 (32-45)
Vol. 23 No. 29
John Bainbridge

Snyder, Daniel
Captain, U.S.A.A.F.
"Young Captain Chips"
May 8, 1943 (23-30)
Vol. 19 No. 12
John Kirkpatrick

Sokoloff, Vladimir
Actor
"The Player - I"
Oct. 21, 1961 (118-124)
Vol. 37 No. 36
Lillian Ross

Solti, Georg
Chief conductor,
Chicago Symphony
"Absolute Trust"
May 27, 1974 (38-62)
Vol. 50 No. 14
Winthrop Sargeant

Somervell, Brehon Burke
W.P.A. administrator for
N.Y.C.; Col., U.S. Army
"Army Man at Work"
Feb. 10, 1940 (22-27)
Feb. 17, 1940 (27-30)
Vol. 15 No. 52 and
Vol. 16 No. 1
L.D. Dunbar

Sonnenberg, Benjamin
Public relations consultant
"A House on Gramercy
Park"
April 8, 1950 (40-61)
Vol. 26 No. 7
Geoffrey T. Hellman

Soss, Wilma Porter
Founder, Federation of
Women Shareholders in
American Business, Inc.
"Hoboken Must Go!"
March 17, 1951 (34-51)
Vol. 27 No. 5
Andy Logan

Soulé, Henri
Maître d'hotel
"The Ambassador in the
Sanctuary"
March 28, 1953 (37-64)
Vol. 29 No. 6
Joseph Wechsberg

Soyer, David
Cellist, Guarneri Quartet
"String Quartet"
Oct. 23, 1978 (45-131)
Vol. 54 No. 36
Helen Drees Ruttencutter

Spencer, Shirley
Graphologist, *New York
Daily News*
"T-bars and I-dots"
Dec. 24, 1949 (26-36)
Vol. 25 No. 44
Angelica Gibbs

Sperry, Elmer A.
Inventor
"Gadget-Maker"
April 19, 1930 (24-26)
Vol. 6 No. 9
Henry F. Pringle

Speyer, James
Banker; arts patron
"Banker, Old Style"
Feb. 27, 1932 (20-23)
Vol. 8 No. 2
Geoffrey T. Hellman

Stacy, Jess
Jazz/big band pianist
"Back From Valhalla"
August 18, 1975 (32-37)
Vol. 51 No. 26
Whitney Balliett

Stanley, Kim
Actress
"The Player - I"
October 21, 1961 (59-73)
Vol. 37 No. 36
Lillian Ross

Stanton, Frank
President, Columbia
Broadcasting System
"Let's Find Out"
January 18, 1947 (32-42)
January 25, 1947 (28-38)
Vol. 22 Nos. 49-50
Robert Lewis Taylor

Stapleton, Maureen
Actress
"The Player - II"
Oct. 28, 1961 (120-132)
Vol. 37 No. 37
Lillian Ross

Steel, David
Member of Parliament
"Breaking the Mold"
May 21, 1984 (48-96)
Vol. 60 No. 14
John Newhouse

Stefansson, Vilhjalmur
Arctic explorer
"Klondike Stef"
October 18, 1941 (26-38)
October 25, 1941 (25-36)
Vol. 17 Nos. 36-37
Robert Lewis Taylor

Steichen, Edward
Photographer; Navy officer
"Commander With
a Camera"
June 3, 1944 (30-36)
June 10, 1944 (29-41)
Vol. 20 Nos. 16-17
Matthew Josephson

Steiger, Rod
Actor
"The Player - II"
Oct. 28, 1961 (90-100)
Vol. 37 No. 37
Lillian Ross

Stein, Ben
Wallpaper hanger
"The Greatest Paper-
Hanger in the World"
Nov. 6, 1937 (22-26)
Vol. 13 No. 38
Henry Anton Steig

Steinhardt, Arnold
First violin,
Guarneri Quartet
"String Quartet"
Oct. 23, 1978 (45-131)
Vol. 54 No. 36
Helen Drees Ruttencutter

Stella, Frank
Artist
"The Space Around Real
Things"
Sept. 10, 1984 (53-97)
Vol. 60 No. 30
Calvin Tomkins

Stephens, Olin and Roderick
    Yacht designers
    "Up From Corker"
    Sept. 7, 1957 (39-71)
    Sept. 14, 1957 (49-88)
    Vol. 33 Nos. 29-30
    Morton M. Hunt

Steuer, Max D.
    Lawyer
    "A Symbol of Justice"
    May 16, 1925 (13-14)
    Vol. 1 No. 13
    "AGNI"
    (Alva Johnston)

    "My Lawyer"
    May 16, 1931 (24-27)
    May 23, 1931 (21-24)
    Vol. 7 Nos. 13-14
    Alva Johnston

Stevens, Harry S.
    Publisher; concessionaire
    "Red Hot"
    August 11, 1928 (23-25)
    Vol. 4 No. 25
    Niven Busch, Jr.

Stevens, Roger Lacey
    Theater producer;
    real estate tycoon
    "Closings and Openings"
    Feb. 13, 1954 (37-56)
    Feb. 20, 1954 (41-61)
    Vol. 29 No. 52 and
    Vol. 30 No. 1
    E.J. Kahn, Jr.

Stieglitz, Alfred
    Photographer
    "291"
    April 18, 1925 (9-10)
    Vol. 1 No. 9
    "Search-light"
    (Waldo Frank)

Stillman, Lou
    Owner, Stillman's Gym
    "Cauliflower King"
    April 8, 1933 (24-26)
    April 15, 1933 (18-20)
    Vol. 9 Nos. 8-9
    Alva Johnston

Stimson, Henry L.
    U.S. Secretary of State
    "Laird of Woodley"
    October 4, 1930 (30-33)
    Vol. 6 No. 33
    Henry F. Pringle

Stingo, John R. (pseud.)
    Columnist, *New York*
    Enquirer
    "Yea, Verily"
    Sept. 13, 1952 (46-72)
    Sept. 20, 1952 (45-71)
    Sept. 27, 1952 (34-61)
    Vol. 28 Nos. 30-32
    A.J. Liebling

Stipe, Gene
    Oklahoma state senator
    "Prince"
    April 2, 1979 (41-92)
    Vol. 55 No. 7
    Mark Singer

Stokowski, Leopold
  Conductor, Philadelphia
  Orchestra
  "Practical Orpheus"
  March 21, 1931 (22-26)
  Vol. 7 No. 5
  Samuel Chotzinoff

Stone, Edward D.
  Architect
  "From Sassafras
  Branches"
  January 3, 1959 (32-49)
  Vol. 34 No. 46
  Winthrop Sargeant

Stout, Rex
  Mystery writer
  "Alias Nero Wolfe"
  July 16, 1949 (26-41)
  July 23, 1949 (30-43)
  Vol. 25 Nos. 21-22
  Alva Johnston

Stoppard, Tom
  Playwright
  "Withdrawing With Style
  From the Chaos"
  Dec. 19, 1977 (41-111)
  Vol. 53 No. 44
  Kenneth Tynan

Strand, Paul
  Photographer, artist
  "Look to the Things
  Around You"
  Sept. 16, 1974 (44-94)
  Vol. 50 No. 30
  Calvin Tomkins

Stratas, Teresa
  Lyric soprano
  "Presence"
  January 26, 1981 (40-60)
  Vol. 56 No. 49
  Winthrop Sargeant

Straton, Dr. John Roach
  Pastor, Calvary Baptist
  Church
  "The Meshuggah of
  Manhattan"
  April 16, 1927 (25-27)
  Vol. 3 No. 9
  Stanley Walker

Strauss, Robert S.
  Ambassador-at-Large for
  Middle East negotiations
  "Equations"
  May 7, 1979 (50-129)
  Vol. 55 No. 12
  Elizabeth Drew

Stravinsky, Igor Fedorovich
  Composer; conductor
  "Russian Firebird"
  January 5, 1935 (23-28)
  Vol. 10 No. 47
  Janet Flanner

Strehler, Giorgio
  Theater director
  "The Storyteller"
  May 4, 1992 (40-67)
  Vol. 68 No. 11
  Harvey Sachs

Strom, Earl
  National Basketball
  Association referee
  "The Right Call"
  October 1, 1990 (48-72)
  Vol. 66 No. 33
  Jeff Coplon

Strong, Maurice Frederick
  Environmentalist
  "Environmentalist"
  June 3, 1972 (45-75)
  Vol. 48 No. 15
  E.J. Kahn, Jr.

Stryker, Lloyd Paul
  Lawyer
  "The Knight With the
  Rueful Countenance"
  January 21, 1939 (23-26)
  Vol. 14 No. 49
  Alexander Woollcott

Sulzberger, Arthur Ochs
  Publisher, *The New York
  Times*
  "Viewer From the
  Fourteenth Floor"
  January 18, 1969 (40-71)
  Vol. 44 No. 48
  Geoffrey T. Hellman

Sumner, John Saxton
  Censor; anti-vice crusader
  "Contented Crusader"
  Feb. 20, 1937 (22-27)
  Vol. 13 No. 1
  Alva Johnston

Sutherland, Joan
  Soprano, Metropolitan
  Opera Company
  "The Power and the
  Glory"
  April 1, 1972 (40-64)
  Vol. 48 No. 6
  Winthrop Sargeant

Suzman, Helen
  Member, South African
  House of Assembly
  "Hon. Member for
  Houghton"
  April 20, 1987 (50-74)
  Vol. 63 No. 9
  E.J. Kahn, Jr.

Suzuki, Daisetz Teitaro
  Zen Buddhism expert
  "Great Simplicity"
  August 31, 1957 (34-53)
  Vol. 33 No. 28
  Winthrop Sargeant

Swanson, Gloria
  Motion picture actress
  "Ugly Duckling"
  January 18, 1930 (24-27)
  Vol. 5 No. 48
  Helena Huntington Smith

Swift, J. Otis
  Nature editor, *New York
  World-Telegram*
  "The Sassafras Hawk"
  May 31, 1941 (21-29)
  Vol. 17 No. 16
  Geoffrey T. Hellman

Swinburne, Algernon Charles
  Poet
  "At the Pines"
  January 23, 1971 (40-65)
  January 30, 1971 (31-43)
  February 6, 1971 (40-71)
  Vol. 46 Nos. 49-51
  Mollie Panter-Downes

Swing, Raymond Gram
  Radio commentator
  "The Voice"
  Nov. 14, 1942 (24-31)
  Nov. 21, 1942 (24-35)
  Vol. 18 Nos. 39-40
  Richard O. Boyer

Syms, Sylvia
  Popular singer
  "Moonbeam Moscowitz"
  October 21, 1974 (47-56)
  Vol. 50 No. 35
  Whitney Balliett

Szell, George
  Conductor, Cleveland
  Orchestra
  "The Grace of the
  Moment"
  Nov. 6, 1965 (59-112)
  Vol. 41 No. 38
  Joseph Wechsberg

Szladits, Lola
  Curator, Berg Collection,
  New York Public Library
  "City Voices"
  Dec. 31, 1984 (32-37)
  Vol. 60 No. 46
  Whitney Balliett

Takamine, Hideko
  Actor
  "The Odor of Pickled
  Radishes"
  Nov. 5, 1990 (53-112)
  Vol. 66 No. 38
  Phyllis Birnbaum

Talley, Marion
  Singer, Metropolitan
  Opera Company
  "A Name is Made"
  Feb. 11, 1928 (18-20)
  Vol. 3 No. 52
  Elizabeth Armstrong

Tate, Jeffrey
  Conductor
  "Walking to the Pavilion"
  April 30, 1990 (51-81)
  Vol. 66 No. 11
  David Blum

Tati, Jacques
  Filmmaker
  "Playing"
  January 27, 1973 (35-49)
  Vol. 48 No. 49
  Penelope Gilliatt

Taylor, Deems
  Music critic, *New York World*
  "Versatility Personified"
  June 6, 1925 (9-10)
  Vol. 1 No. 16
  Newman Levy

Taylor, Marion Sayle
  Radio personality
  "The Voice"
  October 26, 1935 (26-29)
  Nov. 2, 1935 (24-28)
  Vol. 11 Nos. 37-38
  Margaret Case Harriman

Taylor, Theodore B.
  Nuclear physicist
  "The Curve of Binding Energy"
  Dec. 3, 1973 (54-145)
  Dec. 10, 1973 (50-108)
  Dec. 17, 1973 (60-97)
  Vol. 49 Nos. 41-43
  John McPhee

Teagarden, Jack
  Trombonist
  "Big T"
  April 2, 1984 (47-57)
  Vol. 60 No. 7
  Whitney Balliett

Teague, Walter Dorwin
  Industrial designer
  "Industrial Classicist"
  Dec. 15, 1934 (28-32)
  Vol. 10 No. 44
  Gilbert Seldes

Teal, John J., Jr.
  Explorer, author
  "The Friend of the Musk Ox"
  October 4, 1958 (49-79)
  October 11, 1958 (49-84)
  Vol. 34 Nos. 33-34
  Robert Lewis Taylor

Thatcher, Margaret
  British Prime Minister
  "Gamefish"
  Feb. 10, 1986 (68-99)
  Vol. 61 No. 51
  John Newhouse

Thomas, Lewis
  Essayist, president of Memorial Sloan-Kettering Cancer Center, New York
  "Biology Watcher"
  January 2, 1978 (27-46)
  Vol. 53 No. 46
  Jeremy Bernstein

Thomas, Norman
  Socialist candidate
  "Also Ran"
  Nov. 9, 1929 (28-31)
  Vol. 5 No. 38
  Henry F. Pringle

Thompson, Dorothy
  Newspaper columnist
  "The It Girl"
  April 20, 1940 (24-30)
  April 27, 1940 (23-29)
  Vol. 16 Nos. 10-11
  Margaret Case Harriman

Thompson, Ellery Franklin
  Captain in dragger fleet
  "Dragger Captain"
  January 4, 1947 (32-43)
  January 11, 1947 (30-42)
  Vol. 22 Nos. 47-48
  Joseph Mitchell

Tibbett, Lawrence
  Singer, Metropolitan
  Opera Company
  "Home Talent"
  January 21, 1933 (21-25)
  Vol. 8 No. 49
  Robert A. Simon

Tiebor, John W., Roland and
John W., Jr.
  Seal trainers
  "Captains Courageous"
  April 24, 1937 (24-29)
  Vol. 13 No. 10
  A.J. Liebling

Tilden, William Tatem
  Tennis player
  "The Iconoclast of the
  Courts"
  Sept. 18, 1926 (27-29)
  Vol. 2 No. 31
  John K. Winkler

Tilley, George Dudley
  Ornamental bird farmer
  "A Reputation in Swans"
  July 11, 1942 (21-27)
  Vol. 18 No. 21
  Mark Murphy

Tinguely, Jean
  Motion sculptor
  "Beyond the Machine"
  Feb. 10, 1962 (44-93)
  Vol. 37 No. 52
  Calvin Tomkins

Tobin, Ralph C.
  Colonel, Seventh
  Regiment, N.Y.C.; socialite
  "Colonel of the 7th"
  January 11, 1936 (20-24)
  Vol. 11 No. 48
  Victor Weybright

Todd, John R.
  Manager, Rockefeller
  Center
  "The Man Behind
  Prometheus"
  Nov. 14, 1936 (31-34)
  Nov. 21, 1936 (23-26)
  Vol. 12 Nos. 39-40
  Geoffrey T. Hellman

Tojo Hideki
  Premier of Japan
  "Razor on Horseback"
  April 17, 1943 (26-38)
  Vol. 19 No. 9
  John Bainbridge

Tolstoy, Alexandra Lvovna
  Founder of Russian
  welfare agency
  "From Yasnaya Polyana to
  Valley Cottage"
  March 15, 1952 (34-47)
  March 22, 1952 (36-59)
  Vol. 28 Nos. 4-5
  Robert Rice

Tomlinson, Homer A.
  Bishop, Church of God
  "On the Tide of the
  Times"
  Sept. 24, 1966 (67-108)
  Vol. 42 No. 31
  William Whitworth

Torme, Mel
  Singer, songwriter
  "A Vast Minority"
  March 16, 1981 (49-58)
  Vol. 57 No. 4
  Whitney Balliett

Toscanini, Arturo
  Conductor, Metropolitan
  Opera
  "Conducted by the
  Spirits"
  Feb. 23, 1929 (23-26)
  Vol. 5 No. 1
  Samuel Chotzinoff

Townsend, A.J. and William
  Advertising consultants
  "The Law and the
  Prophets"
  Sept. 16, 1939 (21-26)
  Vol. 15 No. 31
  Russell Maloney

Townsend, Edward T.
  Game warden
  "Hawkshaw in the
  Woods"
  Dec. 10, 1949 (42-53)
  Dec. 17, 1949 (35-49)
  Vol. 25 Nos. 42-43
  Eugene Kinkead

Tree, Michael Tree
  Viola, Guarneri Quartet
  "String Quartet"
  Oct. 23, 1978 (45-131)
  Vol. 54 No. 36
  Helen Drees Ruttencutter

Tremaine, Morris Sawyer
  Comptroller, State of
  New York
  "The Comptroller"
  August 29, 1936 (18-23)
  Vol. 12 No. 28
  Edward Angly

Tresca, Carlo
  Socialist; labor organizer
  "Troublemaker"
  Sept. 15, 1934 (31-36)
  Sept. 22, 1934 (26-29)
  Vol. 10 Nos. 30-31
  Max Eastman

Trudeau, Pierre
Canadian Prime Minister
"Prime Minister/Premier
Ministre"
July 5, 1969 (36-60)
Vol. 45 No. 20
Edith Iglauer

Truman, Harry S
U.S. President
"Mr. President"
April 7, 1951 (42-56)
April 14, 1951 (38-55)
April 21, 1951 (36-61)
April 28, 1951 (36-55)
May 5, 1951 (36-53)
Vol. 27 Nos. 8-12
John Hersey

Tsuji, Shizuo
Proprietor, École
Technique Hoteliere
(Osaka)
* Our Far-Flung
Correspondents
"A Worried Man"
Dec. 11, 1978 (86-93)
Vol. 54 No. 43
John Bainbridge

Tuckwell, Barry
Concert French hornist
"Something I Could Do"
March 14, 1977 (45-63)
Vol. 53 No. 4
Winthrop Sargeant

Tugwell, Rexford Guy
U.S. Under-Secretary of
Agriculture
"Rural New Yorker"
March 23, 1935 (20-24)
March 30, 1935 (22-26)
Vol. 11 Nos. 6-7
Russell Robbins

Tunney, Gene
Pugilist
"Gene the Genteel"
August 20, 1927 (16-19)
Vol. 3 No. 27
Kelly Coombs

Turner, Hilary F.
Ferryboat captain
"Harbor-Hopper"
Sept. 21, 1935 (25-29)
Vol. 11 No. 32
Robert M. Coates

Turner, Joe
Blues singer
* Our Local
Correspondents
"Majesty"
Nov. 29, 1976 (80-97)
Vol. 52 No. 41
Whitney Balliett

Turnesa, William
Golfer
"Amateur at Work"
Sept. 9, 1939 (21-26)
Vol. 15 No. 30
Noel F. Busch

Tuttle, Charles H.
    U.S. District Attorney
    "Saint in Politics"
    March 23, 1929 (23-26)
    Vol. 5 No. 5
    Alva Johnston

Twyeffort, Raymond G.
    Custom tailor
    "Color Nut"
    Sept. 23, 1939 (22-27)
    Vol. 15 No. 32
    Richard Owen Boyer

Twynam, Robert
    Groundskeeper at
    Wimbledon
    "The Laws of Wimbledon"
    June 22, 1968 (32-57)
    Vol. 44 No. 18
    John McPhee

Tysen, John Colquhoun
    Real estate executive
    "The Third Most
    Important Day"
    Nov. 17, 1956 (57-92)
    Vol. 32 No. 39
    E.J. Kahn, Jr.

Uno, Chiyo
    Author
    "Modern Girl"
    October 31, 1988 (39-59)
    Vol. 64 No. 37
    Phyllis Birnbaum

Untermyer, Samuel
    Attorney
    "Little Giant"
    May 17, 1930 (29-32)
    May 24, 1930 (24-27)
    Vol. 6 Nos. 13-14
    Alva Johnston

Urban, Joseph
    Stage designer; architect
    "Caprice Viennois"
    June 25, 1927 (21-23)
    Vol. 3 No. 19
    Kenneth Macgowan

Valdo, Patrick Francis
    Personnel director,
    Ringling Brothers &
    Barnum & Bailey Circus
    "Boss of the Kinkers"
    April 19, 1952 (39-57)
    April 26, 1952 (43-64)
    Vol. 28 Nos. 9-10
    Robert Lewis Taylor

Valentine, Lewis J.
    New York City Police
    Commissioner
    "Independent Cop"
    October 3, 1936 (21-27)
    October 10, 1936 (24-28)
    October 17, 1936 (28-34)
    Vol. 12 Nos. 33-35
    Jack Alexander

Van Anda, Carl Vatell
Managing editor,
New York Times
"V.A."
March 7, 1925 (7-8)
Vol. 1 No. 3
Alexander Woollcott
(no byline)

"The Anonymous Man"
Sept. 7, 1935 (26-32)
Vol. 11 No. 30
Alva Johnston

Van Dyke, Woodbridge Strong
Film director
"Lord Fauntleroy in
Hollywood"
Sept. 28, 1935 (20-24)
Vol. 11 No. 33
Alva Johnston

Van Loon, Hendrik Willem
Author, historian
"Poor Little Rich Boy"
June 19, 1926 (19-20)
Vol. 2 No. 18
"P.G.W."
(Waldo Frank)

"The Story of Everything"
March 20, 1943 (24-32)
March 27, 1943 (24-30)
April 3, 1943 (24-36)
Vol. 19 Nos. 5-7
Richard Owen Boyer

Vanderbilt, Alfred Gwynne, Jr.
Race track operator
"All in Fun"
Sept. 28, 1940 (26-33)
Vol. 16 No. 33
G.F.T. Ryall

Vanderbilt, Cornelius Jr.
Publisher, socialite
"A Fifth Avenue
Maverick"
Dec. 26, 1925 (11-12)
Vol. 1 No. 45
William Boardman Knox

Vanderbilt, Harold
Yachtsman; authority on
contract bridge
"Good at Games"
March 4, 1933 (21-25)
Vol. 9 No. 3
Milton MacKaye

Vereker, Elliot (Fictitious)
Author; dilettante
"Something to Say"
July 30, 1932 (17-19)
Vol. 8 No. 24
James Thurber

Verrett, Shirley
Singer, Metropolitan
Opera Company
"Doing Something"
April 14, 1975 (42-58)
Vol. 51 No. 8
Winthrop Sargeant

Villella, Edward
    Director, Miami City
    Ballet
    "Prodigal"
    Nov. 21, 1988 (59-94)
    Nov. 28, 1988 (42-66)
    Vol. 64 Nos. 40-41
    Arlene Croce

Vincent, George Robert
    Collector, voices of
    famous persons
    "Voices"
    May 17, 1941 (24-31)
    Vol. 17 No. 14
    Barbara Heggie

Vishniac, Roman
    Zoologist
    "The Tiny Landscape"
    July 2, 1955 (28-42)
    July 9, 1955 (31-56)
    Vol. 31 Nos. 20-21
    Eugene Kinkead

Von Karajan, Herbert
    Conductor
    "Space-Age Maestro"
    January 7, 1961 (36-62)
    Vol. 36 No. 47
    Winthrop Sargeant

Von Sternberg, Josef
    Film director
    "All For Art"
    March 28, 1931 (26-29)
    Vol. 7 No. 6
    Henry F. Pringle

Voorhis, John R.
    New York State
    Superintendent of
    Elections, aged 100
    "Centenarian"
    June 22, 1929 (23-26)
    Vol. 5 No. 18
    Alva Johnston

Wagner, Robert F., Sr.
    U.S. Senator
    "The Janitor's Boy"
    March 5, 1927 (24-26)
    Vol. 3 No. 3
    Henry F. Pringle

Wagner, Robert F. Jr.
    Mayor of New York City
    "The Mayor"
    January 26, 1957 (39-67)
    February 2, 1957 (39-69)
    Vol. 32 Nos. 49-50
    Philip Hamburger

Wahl, Jean
    Philosopher
    "Philosopher"
    May 12, 1945 (27-41)
    Vol. 21 No. 13
    Hamilton Basso

Wald, Lillian D.
    Socialist; founder, Henry
    Street Settlement
    "Rampant But
    Respectable"
    Dec. 14, 1929 (32-35)
    Vol. 5 No. 43
    Helena Huntington Smith

Walker, Charles
  Lobbyist
  * A Reporter at Large
  "Charlie"
  January 9, 1978 (32-58)
  Vol. 53 No. 47
  Elizabeth Drew

Walker, Jimmie (James John)
  Mayor of New York City
  (candidate in 1925)
  "Fourteenth Street and
  Broadway"
  August 29, 1925 (9-10)
  Vol. 1 No. 28
  Oliver H.P. Garrett

Walker, Mickey
  Prizefighter; artist
  "Glove and Palette"
  Nov. 12, 1955 (57-90)
  Vol. 31 No. 39
  Robert Lewis Taylor

Wallace, DeWitt
  Editor, *Reader's Digest*
  "Little Magazine"
  Nov. 17, 1945 (33-42)
  Nov. 24, 1945 (36-47)
  Dec. 1, 1945 (40-51)
  Dec. 8, 1945 (38-53)
  Dec. 15, 1945 (38-59)
  Vol. 21 Nos. 40-44
  John Bainbridge

Wallach, Eli
  Actor
  "The Player - I"
  Oct. 21, 1961 (90-100)
  Vol. 37 No. 36
  Lillian Ross

Walsh, Arthur
  Cigar store owner
  "A Man This Country
  Needed"
  Sept. 11, 1937 (24-29)
  Vol. 13 No. 30
  Sanderson Vanderbilt

Walsh, Christy
  Ghost writer
  "The Ghosting Business"
  Nov. 23, 1935 (20-25)
  Vol. 11 No. 41
  Alva Johnston

Walsh, Patrick
  New York City Fire Chief
  "The Chief"
  April 25, 1942 (21-29)
  Vol. 18 No. 10
  Robert Lewis Taylor

Wapner, Joseph A.
  Television personality
  ("People's Court")
  "People's Judge"
  March 31, 1986 (45-59)
  Vol. 62 No. 6
  E.J. Kahn, Jr.

Warburg, Siegmund G.
Merchant banker
"A Prince of the City"
April 9, 1966 (45-78)
Vol. 42 No. 7
Joseph Wechsberg

Warner, Albert, Harry, Jack
and Sam
Motion picture producers
"Kings of the Talkies"
Dec. 22, 1928 (21-24)
Vol. 4 No. 44
Alva Johnston

Warner, Karl C.
American soldier
"Quest for Mollie"
May 26, 1945 (28-36)
June 2, 1945 (24-35)
Vol. 21 Nos. 15-16
A.J. Liebling

Watson, Dr. John B.
Psychology professor,
Johns Hopkins University;
author
"The Adventure of the
Behaviorist"
October 6, 1928 (30-32)
Vol. 4 No. 33
Kenneth MacGowan

Watson, Phil
Hockey player
"Disorder on the Rink"
Feb. 15, 1947 (33-46)
Vol. 22 No. 53
Robert Lewis Taylor

Watts-Dunton, Walter
Theodore
Poet, novelist, critic
"At the Pines"
January 23, 1971 (40-65)
January 30, 1971 (31-43)
February 6, 1971 (40-71)
Vol. 46 Nos. 49-51
Mollie Panter-Downes

Weakland, Rembert George W.
Archbishop of Milwaukee
"The Education of an
Archbishop"
July 15, 1991 (38-59)
July 22, 1991 (46-65)
Vol. 67 Nos. 21-22
Paul Wilkes

Weaver, Sylvester L., Jr. (Pat)
President, National
Broadcasting Company
"The Communicator"
October 16, 1954 (37-64)
October 23, 1954 (43-76)
Vol. 30 Nos. 35-36
Thomas Whiteside

Webster, Harold Tucker
Comic-strip cartoonist
"The World of Caspar
Milquetoast"
Nov. 5, 1949 (40-61)
Vol. 25 No. 37
Hamilton Basso

Webster, Margaret
Actress; director
"We"
May 20, 1944 (32-43)
Vol. 20 No. 14
Barbara Heggie

Weil, Richard, Jr.
President, R.H. Macy
"White Sales and
Aristotle"
February 2, 1952 (30-47)
February 9, 1952 (39-55)
Vol. 27 Nos. 51-52
Dwight MacDonald

Weinberg, Sidney James
Investment banker;
corporation director
"Directors' Director"
Sept. 8, 1956 (49-74)
Sept. 15, 1956 (49-74)
Vol. 32 Nos. 29-30
E.J. Kahn, Jr.

Welles, Orson
Film director; actor;
radio personality
"This Ageless Soul"
October 8, 1938 (22-27)
Vol. 14 No. 34
Russell Maloney

Wellstood, Dick
Pianist
"Easier Than Working"
March 3, 1980 (46-56)
Vol. 55 No. 2
Whitney Balliett

Werrenrath, Reinald
Baritone
"A New Yorker Who
Sings"
October 3, 1925 (9-10)
Vol. 1 No. 33
Clare Peeler

West, Mae
Actress
"Diamond Mae"
Nov. 10, 1928 (26-29)
Vol. 4 No. 38
Thyra Samter Winslow

Westcott, Cynthia
Plant pathologist
"Physician in the
Flower Beds"
July 26, 1952 (26-43)
Vol. 28 No. 23
Eugene Kinkead

Westley, Helen
Actress; director of
The Theatre Guild
"Adventuress With a
Difference"
March 27, 1926 (15-16)
Vol. 2 No. 6
"Search-Light"
(Waldo Frank)

Whalen, Grover A.
N.Y.C. Police Commissioner
"The Gilded Copper"
January 12, 1929 (26-28)
Vol. 4 No. 47
Alva Johnston

Whalen, Grover A. *cont.*
"For City and for Coty"
July 14, 1951 (28-45)
July 21, 1951 (28-45)
Vol. 27 Nos. 22-23
Geoffrey T. Hellman

Wharton, Edith
Author
"Dearest Edith"
March 2, 1929 (26-28)
Vol. 5 No. 2
Janet Flanner

Wheeler, Elmer
Head, Tested Selling
Institute
"The Sizzle"
April 16, 1938 (21-25)
Vol. 14 No. 9
John McNulty

White, Walter Francis
Sociologist; author
"The Frontal Attack"
Sept. 4, 1948 (28-38)
Sept. 11, 1948 (38-54)
Vol. 24 Nos. 28-29
E.J. Kahn, Jr.

White, William Allen
Owner and editor,
Emporia Gazette
(Emporia, Kansas)
May 30, 1925 (9-10)
Vol. 1 No. 15
Edna Ferber

Whiteman, Paul
Orchestra leader
"The Paid Piper"
Nov. 27, 1926 (25-27)
Vol. 2 No. 41
Niven Busch, Jr.

Whitman, Lucilla Mara de
Vescovi (Countess Mara)
Owner of men's shop
"The Unusually Nice
Necktie"
Feb. 26, 1949 (34-47)
Vol. 25 No. 1
Geoffrey T. Hellman

Whitney, Cornelius Vanderbilt
(Sonny)
Corporation director; polo
player; racing stables
owner
"The Man Who is Not His
Cousin"
June 21, 1941 (21-29)
Vol. 17 No. 19
Geoffrey T. Hellman

Whitney, Harry Payne
Socialite; polo player
"Up From Fifth Avenue"
July 25, 1925 (8-9)
Vol. 1 No. 23
"Jack Frost"
(Carl Brandt)

Whitney, John Hay (Jock)
Foundation director;
philanthropist
"Man of Means"
August 11, 1951 (32-49)
August 18, 1951 (36-57)
Vol. 27 Nos. 26-27
E.J. Kahn, Jr.

Whitney, Richard
President, NYSE
"Gorton, Harvard, Wall
Street"
April 2, 1932 (19-22)
Vol. 8 No. 7
Matthew Josephson

Widener, Joseph E.
Horse breeder; owner,
Belmont Park
"Beau Belmont"
Sept. 3, 1927 (17-19)
Vol. 3 No. 29
George F.T. Ryall

Widmark, Richard
Actor
"The Player - III"
Nov. 4, 1961 (60-62)
Vol. 37 No. 38
Lillian Ross

Wiesner, Jerome B.
M.I.T. engineering professor
"A Scientist's Advice"
January 19, 1963 (39-59)
January 26, 1963 (38-71)
Vol. 38 Nos. 48-49
Daniel Lang

Wightman, Hazel Hotchkiss
Tennis player; coach;
author
"Run, Helen!"
August 30, 1952 (31-46)
Vol. 28 No. 28
Herbert Warren Wind

Wilber, Bob
Jazz musician, composer
"The Westchester Kids"
May 9, 1977 (45-54)
Vol. 53 No. 12
Whitney Balliett

Wilder, Alec
Songwriter
"The President of the
Derriere-Garde"
July 9, 1973 (36-46)
Vol. 49 No. 20
Whitney Balliett

Willebrandt, Mabel Walker
Asst. U.S. Attorney
General
"Mrs. Firebrand"
Feb. 16, 1929 (23-26)
Vol. 4 No. 52
John Stuart Martin

William, Maurice
Historian; author; dentist
"The Man Who Changed
the Course of Chinese
History"
August 22, 1942 (20-26)
Vol. 18 No. 27
John Kirkpatrick

Williams, Albert Moran
New York City patrolman
"Average Cop"
Feb. 10, 1934 (23-27)
Vol. 9 No. 52
St. Clair McKelway

Williams, Mary Lou
Jazz pianist; composer
"Out Here Again"
May 2, 1964 (52-85)
Vol. 40 No. 11
Whitney Balliett

Williamson, Nicol
Actor
"Are You the
Entertainment?"
January 15, 1972 (35-69)
Vol. 47 No. 48
Kenneth Tynan

Willis, Charles Fountain, Jr.
President, non-scheduled
airlines
"Squaring Away and
Turning To"
July 5, 1947 (28-36)
Vol. 23 No. 20
Lillian Ross

Willis, Gordon
Film crew photography
director
"Cinematographer"
October 16, 1978 (46-85)
Vol. 54 No. 35
James Stevenson

Willkie, Wendell Lewis
Business executive;
lawyer; presidential
candidate
"Rushville's Renowned
Son-in-Law"
October 12, 1940 (27-42)
Vol. 16 No. 35
Janet Flanner

Wills, Helen
Tennis player
"Another Glorified Girl"
August 27, 1927 (16-18)
Vol. 3 No. 28
Helena Huntington Smith

Wilson, Edmund
Author; critic
* Personal Recollections
"A Prelude"
April 29, 1967 (50-131)
May 6, 1967 (53-149)
May 13, 1967 (54-157)
Vol. 43 Nos. 10-12
Edmund Wilson

Wilson, Halsey William
Publisher, *Reader's Guide
to Periodical Literature*
"A Mousetrap in the Bronx"
October 29, 1938 (25-28)
Vol. 14 No. 37
Creighton Peet

Wilson, Julie
  Cabaret singer
  "Carol Sloane and
  Julie Wilson"
  April 6, 1987 (72-80)
  Vol. 63 No. 7
  Whitney Balliett

Wilson, Robert
  Director, School of Byrds
  theater company
  "Time to Think"
  January 13, 1975 (38-62)
  Vol. 50 No. 47
  Calvin Tomkins

Wilson, Robert W.
  Physicist
  "Three Degrees Above
  Zero"
  August 20, 1984 (42-70)
  Vol. 60 No. 27
  Jeremy Bernstein

Winchell, Walter
  Newspaper columnist
  "Gossip Writer"
  June 15, 1940 (26-40)
  June 22, 1940 (24-33)
  June 29, 1940 (23-26)
  July 6, 1940 (24-30)
  July 13, 1940 (21-26)
  July 20, 1940 (23-28)
  Vol. 16 Nos. 18-23
  St. Clair McKelway

Windsor, Edward, Duke of,
see Edward, Prince of Wales

Winlock, Herbert E.
  Director, Metropolitan
  Museum of Art
  "Egyptologist"
  July 29, 1933 (16-19)
  Vol. 9 No. 24
  Geoffrey T. Hellman

Winston, Harry
  Jewelry dealer
  "The Big Stone"
  May 8, 1954 (36-69)
  May 15, 1954 (45-73)
  Vol. 30 Nos. 12-13
  Lillian Ross

Winter, Benjamin
  Real estate speculator
  "Fifth Avenue's Nize
  Baby"
  July 3, 1926 (15-17)
  Vol. 2 No. 20
  Niven Busch, Jr.

Wise, Stephen S.
  Rabbi, Jewish Institute
  of Religion
  "Prophet, 1931"
  Nov. 7, 1931 (22-25)
  Vol. 7 No. 38
  Geoffrey T. Hellman

Wodehouse, P.G.
  Author
  "A Chap With a Good
  Story to Tell"
  May 15, 1971 (43-101)
  Vol. 47 No. 13
  Herbert Warren Wind

Wolff, Helen
  Publisher
  "Imprint"
  August 2, 1982 (41-73)
  Vol. 58 No. 24
  Herbert Mitgang

Woods, A.H. (Albert Herman)
  Theater producer
  "Saint Al"
  Feb. 26, 1927 (25-27)
  Vol. 3 No. 2
  Percy Hammond

Woollcott, Alexander
  Author; critic; radio
  personality
  "Big Nemo"
  March 18, 1939 (24-29)
  March 25, 1939 (22-27)
  April 1, 1939 (22-27)
  Vol. 15 Nos. 5-7
  Wolcott Gibbs

Woolley, Monty
  Actor
  "It's De-Lovely"
  January 20, 1940 (25-29)
  Vol. 15 No. 49
  Russell Maloney

Woolton, Fredrick James
  British Minister of
  Reconstruction
  "Great Provider"
  May 6, 1944 (32-48)
  Vol. 20 No. 12
  Mollie Panter-Downes

Work, Milton C.
  Auction bridge authority
  "Autocrat of the Card
  Table"
  January 14, 1928 (18-19)
  Vol. 3 No. 48
  Helena Huntington Smith

Worth, Charles Frederick
  Proprietor, Worth et Cie
  couture house
  "Those Were the Days"
  January 20, 1934 (17-20)
  Vol. 9 No. 49
  Janet Flanner

Wright, Bruce McMarion
  N.Y. Civil Court Judge
  * Our Local
  Correspondents
  "Judge Wright"
  Sept. 6, 1976 (76-86)
  Vol. 52 No. 29
  Fred C. Shapiro

Wright, Frank Lloyd
  Architect
  "The Prodigal Father"
  July 19, 1930 (22-25)
  Vol. 6 No. 22
  Alexander Woollcott

Wright, John Kirtland
  Director, American
  Geographical Society
  "Big Geographer"
  July 26, 1941 (20-30)
  Vol. 17 No. 24
  E.J. Kahn, Jr.

Wright, Orville
Airplane inventor;
manufacturer
"Heavier Than Air"
Dec. 13, 1930 (29-32)
Vol. 6 No. 43
Eric Hodgins

Wylie, Elinor
Poet
"Portrait in Black Paint,
With a Very Sparing Use
of Whitewash"
(in verse)
March 19, 1927 (24)
Vol. 3 No. 5
"E.W."
(E.B. White)

Yang, Chen Ning
Theoretical physicist
"A Question of Parity"
May 12, 1962 (49-104)
Vol. 38 No. 12
Jeremy Bernstein

Yereshevsky, Izzy (Isadore)
Cigar store owner
"Broadway Storekeeper"
October 15, 1938 (24-27)
Vol. 14 No. 35
A.J. Liebling

Young, Art
Editorial cartoonist
"Good Humorist"
March 2, 1935 (21-25)
Vol. 11 No. 3
Max Eastman

Youngman, Henny
Comedian
"Hurry, Hurry!"
Sept. 12, 1977 (46-92)
Vol. 53 No. 30
Tony Hiss

Zanuck, Darryl Francis
Motion picture producer;
co-founder of Twentieth
Century Pictures, Inc.
"The Wahoo Boy"
Nov. 10, 1939 (24-28)
Nov. 17, 1934 (24-29)
Vol. 10 Nos. 39-40
Alva Johnston

Zeckendorf, Williams
Realtor
"Big Operator"
Dec. 8, 1951 (46-61)
Dec. 15, 1951 (41-68)
Vol. 27 Nos. 43-44
E.J. Kahn, Jr.

Zeisel, Eva
Ceramist
"The Present Moment"
April 13, 1987 (36-59)
Vol. 63 No. 8
Suzannah Lessard

Zerbe, Jerome
Photographer
"Happy Times"
June 9, 1973 (39-68)
Vol. 49 No. 16
Brendan Gill

Ziegfeld, Florenz
  Theater producer
  "Glorifier"
  July 25, 1931 (19-22)
  August 1, 1931 (18-22)
  Vol. 7 Nos. 23-24
  Gilbert Seldes

Zimbalist, Efram
  Violinist
  "Con lenezza"
  Dec. 5, 1931 (24-27)
  Vol. 7 No. 42
  Marcia Gluck Davenport

Zolotow, Sam
  Messenger service owner;
  publisher, Advance
  Theatrical Guide
  "Office-Boy of Destiny"
  October 13, 1928 (28-30)
  Vol. 4 No. 34
  Alexander Woollcott

Zukor, Adolph
  President, Paramount-
  Famous Players-Lasky
  motion picture studio
  "Paramount's Patriarch"
  Sept. 7, 1929 (29-33)
  Vol. 5 No. 29
  Niven Busch, Jr.

COMPOSITES AND PARODIES

American Academy of Arts
and Letters/National Institute
of Arts and Letters
  "Some Splendid and
  Admirable People"
  Feb. 23, 1976 (43-81)
  Vol. 52 No. 1
  Geoffrey T. Hellman

The Chinos
  Japanese-American
  family; home gardeners
  "The Chinos' Artful
  Harvest"
  Nov. 30, 1992 (142-156)
  Vol. 68 No. 41
  Mark Singer

County Agent
  "Grower's Shadow"
  Unnamed Agricultural
  Extension Service Agent
  Sept. 3, 1973 (30-45)
  Vol. 49 No. 28
  Berton Roueché

The French of Algiers
  "Les Pieds Noirs"
  Nov. 25, 1972 (52-108)
  Vol. 48 No. 40
  Jane Kramer

Immigration Lawyers
  "Making Adjustments"
  May 28, 1984 (50-71)
  Vol. 60 No. 15
  Calvin Trillin

"Lotta Fairfax"
Satire on Beatrice
Kaufman, wife of George
S. Kaufman
"Dante and –"
July 7, 1928 (16-17)
Vol. 4 No. 20
Ring Lardner

Migrant Workers in Europe
"Invandrare"
March 22, 1976 (43-84)
Vol. 52 No. 5
Jane Kramer

Modern Jazz Quartet
"Room to Live"
Nov. 20, 1971 (62-108)
Vol. 47 No. 40
Whitney Balliett

"The Old Man"
Composite parody of
football coaches
Nov. 23, 1929 (30-32)
Vol. 4 No. 40
John R. Tunis

"Otto and Anne"
Pseudonymous farmhouse
inn restaurateurs near
New York City
"Brigade de Cuisine"
Feb. 19, 1979 (43-99)
Vol. 55 No. 1
John McPhee

"Pop"
Anonymous bookmaker
"Six, Two, and Even"
June 24, 1933 (18-21)
Vol. 9 No. 19
Niven Busch, Jr.

Showgirls as a Type
"Grayce"
October 15, 1932 (23-25)
Vol. 8 No. 35
John O'Hara

The Theater Guild: Mr. Beer,
Mr. Langner, Mr. Goodman,
Miss Helburn, Mr. Simonson,
Mr. Moeller, Miss Westley
"The Guild - A Composite
Photograph"
Dec. 25, 1926 (17-20)
Vol. 2 No. 45
Cuthbert Wright

Uganda Asians
Immigrants to England
"Uganda Asians"
April 8, 1974 (47-93)
Vol. 50 No. 7
Jane Kramer

Author Index

Franklin P. Adams: Jerome Kern
By Franklin Pierce Adams: *In Cupid's Court* (1902); *In Other Words* (1912) *By and Large* (1914); *Something Else Again* (1920); *Overset* (1922); *So Much Velvet* (1924); *The Conning Tower Book* (1926); *Half a Loaf* (1927); *Nods and Becks* (1944), others. See biography by Sally Ashley (1986).

Caroline Alexander: Daphne Park

Jack Alexander: Aherman Culver Amsden, Vincent Astor, Walter Sherman Gifford, Jimmy Hines, Gerald Barnes Lambert, Joseph Medill Patterson, Hirosi Saito, Lewis J. Valentine

Robert S. Allen: Sol Bloom, Ogden Livingston Mills
By Robert Sharon Allen: *Washington Merry-Go-Round* (1931); *More Washington Merry-Go-Round* (1932); *Nine Old Men at the Crosroads* (with Drew Pearson) (1937/74); *Lucky Forward: The History of Patton's Third U.S. Army* (1947); ed., *Our Fair City* (1947/74).

A. Alvarez: Mo Anthoine

Jervis Anderson: Ed Bullins, Ralph Ellison, Paul Moore, Jr., A. Philip Randolph
By Jervis Anderson: *The Meaning of Our Numbers* (1972); *A. Philip Randolph, A Biographical Portrait* (1973); *Guns in American Life* (1984); *This Was Harlem: A Cultural Portrait* (1982/93); *Bayard Rustin: Troubles I've Seen* (1997).

Roger Angell: Roy Eisenhardt, Dan Quisenberry
By Roger Angell: *The Stone Arbor* (1961); *A Day in the Life of Roger Angell* (1971); *The Summer Game* (1972); *Five Seasons* (1977); *Late Innings* (1982); *Season Ticket* (1988); *Once More Around the Park* (1991); ed., *Nothing But You: Love Stories from the New Yorker* (1997).

Edward Angly: Morris Sawyer Tremaine
By Edward Angly: *Oh, Yeah!* (1932); *Fifty Billion Dollars* (with Jesse Jones) (1950).

Hannah Arendt: W.H. Auden, Bertolt Brecht
By Hannah Arendt: *Rahel Vornhagen* (1957); *The Human Condition*

(1958); *On Revolution* (1963); *Eichmann in Jerusalem* (1964); *The Origins of Totalitarianism* (1968); *Men in Dark Times* (1968); *Between Past and Future* (1968); *Crises of the Republic* (1972), others. See biographies by Derwent May (1986) and Ingeborg Nordmann (1994).

Ken Auletta: Mario Cuomo, Edward I. Koch, Jean Riboud
By Ken Auletta: *The Streets Were Paved with Gold* (1977); *The Art of Corporate Success: The Story of Schlumberger* (1984); *Greed and Glory on Wall Street: The Fall of the House of Lehman* (1986); *Hard Feelings: Reporting on Pols, the Press, People and the City* (1980); *Three Blind Mice: How the T.V. Networks Lost Their Way* (1991); *Highwaymen: Warriors of the Information Superhighway* (1997); *Underclass* (1999).

Anthony Bailey: Elizabeth II of England, David Hockney, Frederick E. Hood, Erskine Hamilton Childers, Robert Erskine Childers

John Bainbridge: Daniel G. Arnstein, Harold Fredric Blackburn (1956, 1962), Kingman Brewster, Milton Caniff, Thomas Edmund Dewey (with Wolcott Gibbs), George Fielding Eliot, Bud Freeman, Alfred Carlton Gilbert, Louis Dusenbery Gilbert, Robert A. Lovett (with Margaret Case Harriman), Reuben Maury, Margaret Rudkin, Peter Roland Sawyer, Max Sherover, Toots Shor, Robert Lansing Smith, William W. Smith II, Tojo Hideki, Shizuo Tsuji, DeWitt Wallace
By John Bainbridge: *Little Wonder, or the* Reader's Digest *and How It Grew* (1946); *The Wonderful World of Toots Shor* (1951); *Biography of an Idea* (1952); *Garbo* (1955); *The Super-Americans* (1961); *Like a Homesick Angel* (1964); *Another Way of Living* (1968); *English Impressions* (1981).

Whitney Balliett: Henry "Red" Allen, Jean Bach, Tommy Benford, Tony Bennett, Ruby Braff, Doc Cheatham, Bradley Cunningham, Blossom Dearie, Charles Delaunay, Vic Dickenson, Robert Brackett Elliott, Anita Ellis, Art Farmer, Benny Goodman (1977), John Gordon, Max Gordon, Raymond Walter Goulding, Stéphane Grappelli, Sonny Greer, Bobby Hackett, Jim Hall, "Father" Earl Himes, Helen Humes, Elvin Jones, Barney Josephson, Teddi King, Ellis Larkins, Julius La

Rosa, Barbara Lea, Dave McKenna, Marian McPortland, Jackie Mason, Mary Mayo, Mabel Mercer, Freddie Moore, Michael Moore, Jelly Roll Morton, Red Norvo, Hugues Panassié, Harvey Phillips, Mel Powell, Buddy Rich, Jimmy Rowles, Magda Salveson, Jon Schueler, Hugh Shannon, Carol Sloane, Jess Stacy, Sylvia Sims, Lola Szladits, Jack Teagarden, Mel Torme, Joe Turner, Dick Wellstood, Bob Wilber, Alec Wilder, Mary Lou Williams, Julie Wilson; Modern Jazz Quartet
By Whitney Balliett: *The Sound of Surprise* (1959); *Dinosaurs in the Morning* (1962); *Such Sweet Thunder* (1966); *Super-Drummer: A Profile of Buddy Rich* (1968); *Ecstasy at the Onion* (1971); *Alec Wilder and His Friends* (1974); *New York Notes* (1976); *Improvising* (1977); *Night Creature* (1981); *Jelly Roll, Jabbo and Fats* (1983); *American Musicians: Fifty-Six Portraits in Jazz* (1986); *American Singers: Twenty-Seven Portraits in Song* (1988); *Barney, Bradley and Max: Sixteen Portraits in Jazz* (1989); *Goodbyes and Other Messages: A Journal of Jazz* (1981-91); *American Musicans II: Seventy-Two Portraits in Jazz* (1996).

Djuna Barnes: Eva Le Gallienne
By Djuna Barnes: *Night Among the Horses* (1929); *Nightwood* (1936); *The Antiphon* (play in verse) (1958); *Spillway* (stories) (1962); *Selected Works* (1962); illus., *A Book* (1923); *Ryder* (1928); *The Ladies Almanack* (1928/72). See biographies by Andrew Field (1983) and Phillip Herring (1995).

Griffin Barry: Edna St. Vincent Millay

Arthur C. Bartlett: Walter Cox, Marjorie Post Davies, John J. Dillon, Austin H. MacCormick, Man O' War
By Arthur Charles Bartlett: *Find Your Own Frontier* (1940); *Baseball and Mr. Spalding* (1951).

Hamilton Basso: W. Somerset Maugham, Eugene O'Neill (1948), Charles Prendergast, Jean Wahl, Harold Tucker Webster
By Hamilton Basso: *The World From Jackson Square* (with Etolia S. Basso) (1948); *The Green Room* (1948); *The View From Pompey's Head* (1954); *The Light Infantry Ball* (1959); *A Quota of Seaweed* (1961); *A Touch of the Dragon* (1964).

S.N. Behrman: Sir Max Beerbohm, Eddie Cantor, Max Dreyfus, Sir Joseph Duveen (1951), George Gershwin, Richard Jaeckel, Joe Kazan, Emanuel Libman, Perenc Molnar, Frances Robinson Duff, Robert E. Sherwood
By Samuel Nathaniel Behrman: Plays: *The Second Man* (1927); *Serena Blandish* (1928); *Meteor* (1929); *Brief Moment* (1932); *Biography* (1933); *Love Story* (1934); *Rain From Heaven* (1935); *End of Summer* (1936); *Amphitryon 38* (1937); *Wine of Choice* (1938); *No Time for Comedy* (1939); *The Talley Method* (1941); *The Pirate* (1942); *Jacobowsky and the Colonel* (with Franz Werfel) (1944); *Dunnigan's Daughter* (1945); *Fanny* (with Joshua Logan) (1954); *The Cold Wind and the Warm* (1958); *Lord Pengo* (1962); *But For Whom Charlie* (1964); Books: *The Worcester Account* (1954); *Duveen* (1952); *Portrait of Max* (1960); *The Suspended Drawing Room* (1965); *The Burning Glass* (1968); *People in a Diary–A Memoir* (1972); *Tribulations and Laughter–A Memoir* (1972).

Meyer Berger: Pete (George H.) Bostiwck, Marty Franklin, Joe Humphreys, Anna Lonergan, Stitch McCarthy (pseud.), Louis Rubin, Sam Schultz
By Meyer Berger: *The Eight Million* (1942); *Men of Maryknoll* (1943); *The Story of* The New York Times (1951); *City on Many Waters* (1955).

Burton Bernstein: Barry Goldwater, Stanley J. Segalla
By Burton Bernstein: *The Lost Art* (1963); *Thurber: A Biography* (1975); *Sinai: The Great and Terrible Wilderness* (1979); *Family Matters: Sam, Jennie, and the Kids* (1982).

Jeremy Bernstein: Hans Bethe, Yves Chouinard, Arthur C. Clarke, Albert Einstein (1973), Stanley Kubrick, Tsung-Dao Lee, Marvin Minsky, Arno A. Penzias, I.I. Rabi, Felix Rohatyn, Lewis Thomas, Robert W. Wilson, Chen Ning Yang

John Betjeman: John Betjeman
By John Betjeman: Poetry: *Mount Zion* (1931); *Continual Dew* (1937); *Old Lights for New Chancels* (1940); *New Bats in Old Belfries* (1945); *Selected Poems* (1950); *A Few Late Chrysanthemums* (1954); *Collected Poems* (1958). Prose: *Ghastly Good Taste* (1933); *First and Last Loves* (1953).

Lurton Blassingame: Walter P. Chrysler, Gertrude Ederle, Harry Fosdick, Alfred A. Knopf, Blanche Knopf, Samuel Knopf

Bruce Bliven, Jr.: Cyril Manton Harris, William Hupfer, George Fabian Scheer
By Bruce Bliven, Jr.: *The Wonderful Writing Machine* (1954); *Battle for Manhattan* (1956); *New York: The Story of the World's Most Exciting City* (with Naomi Bliven) (1969); *Under the Guns* (1972); *Book Traveller* (1975); *Volunteers, One and All* (1976); *The Finishing Touch* (1978); *New York: A Bicentennial History* (1981).

Sam Boal: Maynard Smith
By Sam Boal: ed. (with Matty Simmons), *The Best of the Diners' Club Magazine* (1962).

Maxwell Bodenheim: Eugene O'Neill (1926)
By Maxwell Bodenheim: *Minna and Myself* (1918); *Advice* (1920); *Replenishing Jessica* (1925); *Naked on Roller Skates* (1931), *Six A.M.* (1932), many others.

Louise Bogan: Willa Cather
By Louise Bogan: *Body of This Death* (1923); *Dark Summer* (1929); *The Sleeping Fury* (1937); *Poems and New Poems* (1941); *Achievement in American Poetry, 1900-1950* (1951); *Collected Poems, 1923-53* (1954); *Selected Criticism* (1955); *The Blue Estuaries: Poems 1923-68* (1968); *A Poet's Alphabet* (1970). Co-translator: *The Journal of Jules Renard* (1964); *The Glass Bees* (1961); *Elective Affinities* (Goethe) (1964); *The Sorrows of Young Werther and Novella* (Goethe) (1971). Ed. (with W.J. Smith), *The Golden Journey* (1965).

Richard Owen Boyer: Walter Russell Bowie, Joseph Curran, Meyer Davis, Charles De Zember, Arthur Urbane Dilley, Duke Ellington, Dizzy Gillespie, George Grosz, Lou Little, Angelina Nawkins, Christian Fichthorne Reisner, Anna Rosenberg, John T. Scheepers, Samuel Seabury, William I. Sirovich, Raymond G. Twyeffort, Hendrik Willem Van Loon
By Richard Owen Boyer: *The Legend of John Brown* (1972); *Labor's Untold Story* (with Herbert M. Morais) (1975).

Carl Brandt: Harry Payne Whitney

Bertolt Brecht: Hannah Arendt
Bertolt Brecht (1898-1956). See biographies by Martin Esslin (1969)
and Ronald Speirs (1987).

John Brooks: Hugh Bullock, Edward Russell Dewey, Walter
Knowlton Gutman, Henry Heydenryk, David Sidney Jackson,
Sidney Janis, David Eli Lilienthal, Juan March Ordinas, Simon
Rifkind
By John Brooks: *The Fate of the Edsel and Other Business Adventures*
(1963); *Once in Golconda: A True Drama of Wall Street, 1920-1938*
(1969); *The Games Players: Tales of Men and Money* (1979); *The
Takeover Game* (1987); *The Go-Go Years* (1973/98), others.

Heywood Broun: Heywood Broun, Charles Townsend Copeland
By Heywood Broun: *Seeing Things at Night* (1921); *Sun Field* (1923);
Shepherd (1924); *His Nose* (1926); *Christians Only, Study in
Prejudice* (with George Britt) (1931); *51st Dragon* (1968); *The
Collected Edition of Heywood Broun* (1969).

Joseph Bryan III: Rosa Lewis
By Joseph Bryan III: *Mission Beyond Darkness* (1945); *Admiral
Halsey's Story* (1947); *The World's Greatest Showman: The Life of P.T.
Barnum* (1956); *The Windsor Story* (1979); *Merry Gentlemen (And
One Lady)* (1985); *Hodgepodge Two: Another Commonplace Book*
(1989).

Paul A. Burns: Grace Coolidge

Niven Busch, Jr.: Winthrop Ames, David Belasco, Lucius
Boomer, Fanny Brice, Irving T. Bush, William F. Carey, Irwin
Salmon Chanin, Glenna Collett, Father John D. Coughlin (with
A. Barr Gray), Dr. John Frederick Erdmann, Henry Ford, Lou
Gehrig, Walter C. Hagen, Samuel Hildreth, Bill Klem, Urbain
Ledoux, John H. McCooey, Dean Randolph Ray, Earle Sande,
Harry Stevens, Paul Whiteman, Benjamin Winter, Adolph Zukor
By Niven Busch, Jr.: *Twenty One Americans* (*New Yorker* Profiles)
(1930); *The Carrington Incident* (1941), *Duel in the Sun* (1944), *The
San Franciscans* (1961), *The Takeover* (1977), *The Titan Game*
(1989), others.

Noel F. Busch: William Turnesa
By Noel F. Busch: *What Manner of Man* (FDR bio.) (1944); *Fallen Sun: A Report on Japan* (1948); *Theodore Roosevelt* (1963); *Winter Quarters: George Washington at Valley Forge* (1974).

David B. Campbell: Edward Riley Bradley

Lincoln Caplan: Richard Rogers

Truman Capote: Marlon Brando
Truman Capote: See biographies by Gerald Clarke (1988) and Marianne M. Moates (1989) and memoirs by John Malcolm Brinnin (1986), Jack Dunphy (1987) and Donald Windham (1989).

Esther Carples: Sergei Rachmaninoff

Samuel Chotzinoff: Abraham Flexner, Leopold Stokowski, Arturo Toscanini
By Samuel Chotzinoff: *Eroica* (1930); *A Lost Paradise: Early Reminiscences* (1955); *Toscanini: An Intimate Portrait* (1956); *A Little Nightmusic* (1964); *Day's at the Morn* (1965).

Robert M. Coates: J. Clarence Davies, Fred F. French, Helen Keller, William Lescaze, Artie McGovern, Georgia O'Keeffe (1929), Edward J. Reilly, Walter Reiselin, John Sloan, Hilary F. Turner
By Robert Myron Coates: *The Eater of Darkness* (1929); *The Outlaw Years* (1930); *Yesterday's Burdens* (1933); *All the Year Round* (1943); *The Bitter Season* (1946); *Wisteria Cottage* (1948); *The Farther Shore* (1955); *The Hour After Westerly* (1957); *The View From Here* (1960); *Beyond the Alps* (1961); *The Man Just Ahead of You* (1963).

Robert Coles: Dolores Garcia, Walker Percy
By Robert Coles: *Children of Crisis: A Study of Courage and Fear* (1967); *Uprooted Children: The Early Lives of Migrant Farmers* (1970); *Still Hungry in America* (1969); *Walker Percy: An American Search* (1978); *Flannery O'Connor's South* (1980).

Marc Connelly: Joe Cook
By Marc Connelley: *The Wisdom Tooth* (play) (1926); *The Green Pastures* (1930); *A Souvenir from Qam* (novel) (1965); *Voices Offstage* (memoir) (1968); *A Stitch in Time* (play) (1977).

Kelly Coombs: Gene Tunney, Bud Fisher

Henry S.F. Cooper. Jr.: Carl Sagan
By Henry S.F. Cooper, Jr.: *Apollo on the Moon* (1969); *Moon Rocks* (1970); *Thirteen: The Flight That Failed* (1973); *Before Liftoff: The Making of a Space Shuttle Crew* (1987).

Jonathan Cott: Iona Opie, Peter Opie, Astrid Lindgren
By Jonathan Cott: *Stockhausen: Conversations with the Composer* (1973); *City of Earthly Love* (1975); *Conversations with Glenn Gould* (1984); *Dylan* (1984); *Wandering Ghost: The Journey of Lafcadio Hearn* (1991); *Thirteen: A Journey Into the Number* (1996), others.

Arlene Croce: David Gordon, Valda Setterfield, Edward Villella
By Arlene Croce: *Afterimages* (1977); *Going to the Dance* (1982); *Sight Lines* (1987).

C.P. Crow: Steve Charney, Ron Kusse

Marcia Gluck Davenport: Lotte Lehmann, Efram Zimbalist
By Marcia Gluck Davenport: *Mozart* (1932/56); *Of Lena Geyer* (1939); *The Valley of Decision* (1944); *East Side, West Side* (1947); *My Brother's Keeper* (1954; *Too Strong for Fantasy* (1967).

Babette Deutsch: George Gray Barnard, Judge Benjamin Nathan Cardozo, August Hackscher
By Babette Deutsch: Poetry: *Banners* (1919); *Honey Out of the Rock* (1925); *Collected Poems 1919-1962* (1963). Novels: *A Brittle Heaven* (1926); *In Such a Night* (1927). Criticism: *Potable Gold* (1929); *This Modern Poetry* (1935); *The Reader's Shakespeare* (1946); *Poetry in Our Time* (1952/63); trans.: *The Twelve* (Blok); *Eugene Onegin* (Pushkin); *Poems From the Book of Hours* (Rilke) and *Two Centuries of Russian Verse* (1966).

Horner Joseph Dodge: Andrew W. Mellon

Elizabeth Drew: Zbigniew Brzezinski, John C. Culver, John Gardner, Robert S. Strauss, Charles Walker
By Elizabeth Drew: *Washington Journal* (1975); *American Journal* (1977); *Senator* (1979); *Portrait of an Election* (1981); *Politics and Money* (1983); *Campaign Journal* (1985); *Election Journal* (1989); *On the Edge: The Clinton Presidency* (1994); *Showdown: The Struggle Between the Gingrich Congree and the Clinton White House* (1996); *Whatever It Takes: The Real Struggle for Political Power in America* (1997).

Max Eastman: Carlo Tresca, Art Young
By Max Forrester Eastman: *Journalism versus Art* (1916), *The Sense of Humor* (1921), *Since Lenin Died* (1925), *The Enjoyment of Living* (1948) and *Seven Kinds of Goodness* (1967), many others; and translator of Trotsky and Lenin.

Edna Ferber: William Allen White
Edna Ferber: See biography by Julie Goldsmith Gilbert (1978).

J.M. Flagler: Allen Funt

Carol Flake: D. Wayne Lukas
By Carol Flake: *Redemptorama: Culture, Politics and the New Evangelicalism* (1984); *Tarnished Crown: The Race for a Racetrack Champion* (1987).

Janet Flanner: Margaret Anderson, Main Bocher, Georges Braque, Bernard Buffet, William Christian Bullitt, Gabrielle Chanel, François Coty, Cheryl Crawford, Bette Davis, Elsie de Wolfe, Isadora Duncan, Adolf Hitler, Alice Throckmorton McLean, Andre Malraux, Thomas Mann, Mary of England, Henri Matisse, Hudson Maxim, Elsa Maxwell, Henri Petain, Pablo Picasso (1939, 1957), Lily Pons, Elsa Schiaparelli, Igor Stravinsky, Edith Wharton, Charles Frederick Worth
By Janet Flanner: *The Cubical City* (novel) (1926); *American in Paris* (collection of *New Yorker* Profiles) (1940); *Men and Monuments* (art monographs) (1957); *Paris Journal I, 1944-65*; *Paris Journal II, 1965-71*; *Paris Was Yesterday* (with Irving Drutman) (1972); *London Was Yesterday* (1975); trans. *Claudine a L'Ecole* and *Cheri* (Colette).

Waldo Frank: Ernest Bloch, Abraham Arden Brill, Charlie Chaplin (1925); John Dewey; Theodore Dreiser; Otto H. Kahn; Sinclair Lewis (1925); Horace B. Liveright; Leo Ornstein; William Lyon Phelps; Carl Sandburg; Alfred Steiglitz; Hendrik Williem Van Loon (1926); Helen Westley
By Waldo David Frank: *Our America* (1919); *Time Exposures, by Search-Light* (1926); *City Block* (1932); *America and Alfred Stieglitz: A Collective Portrait* (1934); *In the American Jungle, 1925-1936* (1937); *America Hispana: South of Us* (1940); *The Jew in Our Day* (1944), *Birth of a World: Bolivar in Terms of His Peoples* (1951); *Bridgehead: The Drama of Israel* (1957); *Cuba: Prophetic Island* (1961).

Kennedy Fraser: Issey Miyake, Norman Parkinson, Miriam Rothschild
By Kennedy Fraser: *The Fashionable Mind: Reflections on Fashion, 1970-1982* (1985); *Ornament and Silence: Essays on Women's Lives* (1996).

Ian Frazier: Jim Deren, Ponce Cruse Evans, Vitaly Komar, Alexander Melamid
By Ian Frazier: *Dating Your Mom* (1986); *Great Plains* (1989); *They Went: The Art and Craft of Travel Writing* (ed. William Zinsser) (1991).

Gilbert W. Gabriel: Giulio Gatti-Casazza, Morris Gest
By Gilbert Wolf Gabriel: *The Seven-Branched Candlestick* (1916); *Jiminy* (1922); *Brownstone Front* (1924); *Famous Pianists and Composers* (1928); *I Got a Country* (1943) others.

Paul Gallico: Max Adalbert Baer
By Paul Gallico: *The Snow Goose* (1941); *Lou Gehrig: Pride of the Yankees* (1942); *Mrs. 'Arris Goes to Paris* (1958), many others.

George White Garland: Antonio Scotti

Oliver H.P. Garrett: Sam Koenig, George V. McLaughlin, Belle Israels Moskowitz, Ruth Sears Baker Pratt, Frank G. Shattuck, Jimmie Walker

Angelica Gibbs: Jessica Cosgrave, Agnes De Mille, Veronica McKenna Dengel, May Gadd, Martha Graham, Dione Wilson Lucas, Blanche Saunders, Shirley Spencer

Anthony Gibbs: Edward VIII of England, Sir Thomas Lipton
By Anthony Gibbs: *The Aunt of England: A Play in Three Acts* (1935).

Wolcott Gibbs: Kelcey Allen, Lucius Beebe, Thomas Edmund Dewey (with John Bainbridge), Ralph McAllister Ingersoll, Henry Robinson Luce, Rita Ross (with Eugene Kinkead), Richard Sylvester Maney, Burgess Merideth, Alexander Woollcott
By Wolcott Gibbs: *Bed of Neuroses* (1937); *Season in the Sun* (1946); *Season in the Sun* (play) (1950); *More in Sorrow* (1958).

Brendan Gill: Tallulah Bankhead, Philip Barry, Frederic Huntington Bartlett, Joseph Theodore Hallock, Charles Brady King, Sigmund M. Morey, Cole Porter (1971), Hartwell Stuart Shippey, Georges Simenon, Jerome Zerbe
By Brendan Gill: *The Trouble of One House* (1950); *Cole* (1971); *Tallulah* (1972); *The Malcontents* (1973); *Here at The New Yorker* (1975); *Lindbergh Alone* (1977); *Many Marks: A Life of Frank Lloyd Wright* (1987); *A New York Life: Of Friends and Others* (1990); *Late Bloomers* (1996).

Penelope Gilliatt: Woody Allen, Louis Buñuel, John Cleese, Jean-Luc Godard, Graham Greene, Diane Keaton, Henri Langlois, Jeanne Moreau, Jean Renoir, Jacques Tati
By Penelope Gilliatt: *A State of Change* (1968); *What's It Like Out* (1969); *Nobody's Business* (1972); *Sunday Bloody Sunday* (1972); *Three-Quarter Face: Reports and Reflections* (1980); *They Sleep Without Dreaming* (1985); *A Woman of Singular Occupation* (1988); *To Wit: Skin and Bones of Comedy* (1990).

Joseph Gollomb: B.L.M. Bates, Louis Dublin
By Joseph Gollomb: *Songs for Courage* (with Zoe Beckley) (1917); *That Year at Lincoln High* (1921); trans. *Brunet's German Constitution* (1923); *The Girl in the Fog* (1923), *Window on the World* (1947), others.

A. Barr Gray: Father John D. Coughlin (with Niven Busch, Jr.)

Geoffrey T. Hellman: Elisabeth Achelis, Stanley N. Arnold, Andrey Avinoff, Joseph Clark Baldwin III, George Gordon Battle, George Biddle, Bruce Blair, Victor Borge, Alexander Calder, Frank R. Capra, Bennett Cerf, Frank Mitchler Chapman, Peter Cooper, John C. Craig, Joe Crane, Frank Crowninshield, Howard S. "Stix" Cullman, Chester Dale, Joseph P. Day, Jean Delacour, Rene d'Harnoncourt, Joseph Donon, Leon Edel, Sherman Mills Fairchild, Hamilton Fish, Jr, Albert Eugene Gallatin, Augustus E. Giegengack, Robert S. Goelet, Gilbert H. Grosvenor, William Norman Guthrie, Armand Hammer, Edward Ringwood Hewitt, Harry L. Hopkins, Charles Edouard Jeannert ("Le Corbusier"), Bassett Jones, Howard Ketcham, Natalie Wales Latham, Elmer G. Leterman, Wilmarth Sheldon Lewis, Graham MacNamee, Henry Morgenthau, Jr., Orson Desaix Munn, Charles Nessler, Floyd B. Odlum, Claudius Charles Philippe, Francis T.P. Plimpton, Sidney Dillon Ripley, Diego Rivera, William J. Robbins, Dr. Frederick B. Robinson, John D. Rockefeller III, Nelson A. Rockefeller, Dorothy Schiff, Max Lincoln Schuster, Robert W. Service, Igor Sikorsky, Richard Leo Simon, Benjamin Sonnenberg, James Speyer, Orthur Ochs Sulzberger, J. Otis Swift, John R. Todd, Lucilla Mara de Vescovi Whitman ("Countess Mara"), Sonny Whitney, Herbert E. Winlock, Stephan Samuel Wise; American Academy of Arts and Letters, National Institute of Arts and Letters

By Geoffrey Theodore Hellman: *How to Disappear for an Hour* (1947); *Mrs. DePeyster's Parties* (1963); *The Smithsonian: Octopus on the Mall* (1967/78); *Bankers, Bones and Beetles: The First Century of the American Museum of Natural History* (1968); anthologies of *New Yorker* Profiles and other pieces.

Nat Hentoff: Henry Clark, Bob Dylan, John V. Lindsay (1967, 1969), Gerry Mulligan, Cardinal John J. O'Connor, Maurice Sendak, Elliott Shapiro

By Nathan Irving Hentoff: *The Jazz Life* (1961); *Jazz Country* (for children) (1965); *Peace Agitator: The Story of A.J. Muste* (1963); *A Political Life: The Education of John V. Lindsay* (1969); *State Secrets: Police Surveillance in America* (1973) *Boston Boy: A Memoir* (1986); *John Cardinal O'Connor at the Storm of a Changing American Church* (1988).

John Hersey: Bernard Mannes Baruch (1948), Father Walter P. Morse, John Daniel Ramey, Harry S Truman
John Hersey: *Men on Bataan* (1942); *A Bell for Adano* (1946); *Wall* (1950); *Marmot Drive* (1953); *War Lover* (1959); *Walnut Door* (1977); *Child Buyer* (1989); *Into the Valley: A Skirmish of Marines* (1989); *Antonietta* (1993); *Hiroshima* (1994). See biography by David Sanders (1990).

Henrik Hertzberg: Robert Freitas

Peter Heyworth: Pierre Boulez
By Peter Heworth: *Otto Klemperer: His Life and Times* (1983), *Conversations with Klemperer* (1985).

Tony Hiss: Clarence "Ducky" Nash (with David McClelland), Henny Youngman
By Anthony Hiss: *All Aboard with E.M. Frimbo, World's Greatest Railroad Buff* (with Rogers E.M. Whitaker) (1974); *Laughing Last* (1977); *The Experience of Place* (1990).

Eric Hodgins: Orville Wright
By Eric Hodgins: *Mr. Blandings Builds His Dream House* (1948), *Blandings' Way* (1950), *Episode* (1964).

Dan Hofstadter: Avigdor Arikha, Richard Diebenkorn
By Dan Hofstadter: trans., *Histoire de ma Vie* (George Sand) (1979); *Temperaments: Artists Facing Their Work* (1992); *The Love Affair as a Work of Art* (1996).

Raymond Holden: Robert Frost
By Raymond Peckham Holden: *Abraham Lincoln: The Politician and the Man* (1929).

Hubbard Hoover: Harry Otis
By Hubbard Hoover: *An Answer for Everything* (1948).

Morton M. Hunt: Mary A. Benjamin, Herman F. Mark, Robert K. Merton, Helaine Newstead, Olin Stephens, Roderick Stephens

Stanley Edgar Hyman: Louis Scher

Edith Iglauer: Arthur Erickson, Pierre Trudeau

Sulamith Ish-Kishor: Feodor Chaliapin
By Sulamith Ish-Kishor: *American Promise: A History of the Jews in the New World* (1947); *A Boy of Old Prague* (1963).

Marquis James: Capt. John H. Craige
By Marquis James: *History of the American Legion* (1923); *Six Feet Six, A Biography of Sam Houston* (with Bessie Rowland James) (1931); *Mr. Garner of Texas* (1939); *Andrew Jackson: Portrait of a President* (1964); *The Cherokee Strip: A Tale of an Oklahoma Boyhood* (1993), others.

Alva Johnston: Evangeline Smith Adams, Wallace Beery, Russell Juarez Birdwell, Alfred Cleveland Blumenthal, Charles V. Bob, Joe E. Brown, Frank Nathan Daniel Buchman, Gene Buck, Emory Roy Buckner, Nicholas Murray Butler, Charles Butterworth, Royal S. Copeland, Jack Curley, Sir Joseph Duveen, Thomas Alva Edison, Albert Einstein, James W. Elliott, James A. Farley, W.C. Fields, William Zebulon Foster, Daniel Frohman, Alpheus Geer, Harry F. Gerguson, Samuel W. Gumpertz, Will H. Hays (1933), Edward N. Jackson, Werner Janssen, Jesse Lasky, Samuel Simon Leibowitz, Joseph Lewis, Martin Wiley Littleton, William Kingsland Macy, William Thomas Manning, Glenn Luther Martin, George Z. Medalie, Jo Mielziner, John P. O'Brien, George Washington Olvany, Lawrence Ottinger, Billy Rose, Al Rosen, John J. Royal, William H. Royce, Beardsley Ruml, Jacob Ruppert, Raymond C. Schindler, Max Steuer (1925, 1931), Lou Stillman, Rex Stout, John Saxton Sumner, Charles H. Tuttle, Samuel Untermeyer, Carl Vatell Van Anda (1935), Woodbridge Strong Van Dyke, John R. Voorhis, Christy Walsh, Albert Warner, Harry Warner, Jack Warner, Morris Warner, Grover Whalen, Darryl Zanuck
By Alva Johnston: *The Great Goldwyn* (1937); *Wilson Mizner: The Legend of a Sport (1943)*.

Gerald Jonas: Neal E. Miller

Matthew Josephson: Harry C. Content, Felix Frankfurter, Leon Fraser, Brigadier General Hugh Samuel Johnson, William Signius Knudsen, J.B. Matheus, Bernard E. Smith, Edward Steichen, Richard Whitney
By Matthew Josephson: *Galamathias* (1923); *Zola and His Time* (1928); *Portrait of the Artist as an American* (1930); *Jean-Jacques Rousseau* (1932); *The Robber Barons* (1934); *The Politicos* (1938); *The President Makers* (1940); *Victor Hugo* (1942); *The Empire of the Air* (1944); *Stendhal: or, the Pursuit of Happiness* (1946); *Sidney Hillman: Statesman of American Labor* (1952); *Union House, Union Bar* (1956); *Edison: A Biography* (1959); *Life Among the Surrealists, a Memoir* (1962); *Infidel in the Temple: A Memoir of the 1930's* (1967); *Al Smith: Hero of the Cities* (with Hannah Josephson) (1969); *The Money Lords: The Great Finance Capitalists 1925-50* (1972).

Pauline Kael: Cary Grant
By Pauline Kael: *I Lost It at the Movies* (1965); *Kiss Kiss Bang Bang* (1968); *Going Steady* (1970); *Reeling* (1976); *5001 Nights at the Movies* (1982); *Hooked* (1989); *For Keeps* (1994), others.

E.J. Kahn, Jr.: Gridley Adams, Dwayne Orville Andreas, Leon Milton Birkhead, Randy Burke, Abe Burrows, Al Capp, Lucius Du Bignon Clay, Richard Lewis Clutterbuck, Mildred Dilling, Angier Biddle Duke, Joseph Dunninger, Cyrus Eaton, Cy Feuer, Clyde Fisher, Brenda Diana Duff Frazier, Dr. Theodore Seuss Geisel, Celeste Gheen, Edward Forrest Harding, Ned Harrigan, W. Averell Harriman, Tony Hart, Jacob K. Javits, James William Johnson, John Reed Kilpatrick, Thomas Lamb, Jacob Kay Lasser, Abraham Isaac Lastfogel, Douglas Leigh, Joshua Logan, Guy Lombardo, Lesley James McNair, Walter S. Mack, Jr., Ernest H. Martin, Arthur Loeb Mayer, Arthur Simon Meyer, William Mills, John Usher Monro, Stewart Rawlings Mott, David Rockefeller, Eleanor Roosevelt (1948), John Service, Frank Sinatra, Roger L. Stevens, Maurice Frederick Strong, Helen Suzman, John Colquhoun Tysen, Judge Joseph A. Wapner, Sidney James Weinberg, Walter Francis White, John Hay Whitney, Robert Winship Woodruff, John Kirtland Wright, Williams Zeckendorf
By E.J. Kahn, Jr.: *Fighting Divisions: Histories of Each U.S. Army Combat Division in World War II* (wih Henry McLemore) (1945/80);

Peculiar War: Impressions of a Reporter in Korea (1952); *Big Drink: The Story of Coca-Cola* (1960); *The World of Swope* (1965); *Harvard: Through Change and Through Storm* (1969); *Georgia From Rabun Gap to Tybee Light* (1978); *Far-Flung and Footloose: Pieces From* The New Yorker, *1937-1978* (1979); *About* The New Yorker *and Me: A Sentimental Journal* (1979); *Year of Change: More About* The New Yorker *and Me* (1988), others.

James Kaplan: Paul Shaffer

Robert F. Kelley: Richard A. Glendon, Richard J. Glendon

Mary D. Kierstead: Molly Keane, James Houston

Alexander King: Rose O'Neill
By Alexander King: *May This House Be Safe From Tigers* (1960); *I Should Have Kissed Her More* (1961); *The Great Ker-Plunk* (1962); *Is There a Life After Birth?* (1962).

Eugene Kinkead: William Bayard Okie, Jr. (With Russell Maloney), Alexander Petrunkevitch, Rita Ross (with Wolcott Gibbs), Edward T. Townsend, Cynthia Westcott
Eugene Kinkead: *Our Own Baedeker: From the* New Yorker (with Russel Maloney) (1947); *Spider, Egg and Microcosm: Three Men and Three Worlds of Science* (1955); *In Every War But One* (1959/81); *Why They Collaborated* (1960); *A Concrete Look at Nature: Central Park (and other) Glimpses* (1974); *Wildness is All Around Us: Notes of an Urban Naturalist* (1978); *Squirrel Book* (1980); *Central Park: The Birth, Decline and Renewal of a National Treasure* (1990).

John Kirkpatrick: Paul Hodge, Daniel Snyder, Maurice Williams

William Boardman Knox: Cornelius Vanderbilt, Jr.

John Kobler: Lewis J. Brecker, Jacob Buchter, Joseph Cosey
By John Kobler: *The Trial of Ruth Snyder and Judd Gray* (1938); *Some Like it Gory* (1940); *Afternoon in the Attic* (1950); *The Reluctant Surgeon: A Biography of John Hunter* (1960); *Luce: His Time, Life and Fortune* (1968); *Capone* (1971); *Ardent Spirits: The Rise and Fall of Prohibition* (1973); *Damned in Paradise: The Life of John Barrymore* (1977); *Otto the Magnificent: The Life of Otto Kahn* (1989).

Jane Kramer: Henry Blanton, Mario Cecchi, Allen Ginsberg, Robert Cooper Scull
By Jane Kramer: *Off Washington Square: A Reporter Looks at Greenwich Village* (1963); *Allen Ginsberg in America* (1970/97); *Unsettling Europe* (1980); *Europeans* (1988); *The Politics of Memory: Looking for Germany in the New Germany* (1996).

Arthur Krock: Bernard Mannes Baruch (1926), Will H. Hays (1926), A. Charles Schwartz, Al Smith
By Arthur Krock: *In the Nation: 1932-1966* (1966); *Memoirs: Sixty Years on the Firing Line* (1968); *The Consent of the Governed and Other Deceits* (1971); *Myself When Young: Growing Up in the 1890s* (1973).

Daniel Lang: Samuel A. Goudsmit, Martin Gumpert, Susan Cook Russo, Irving Seiden, Jerome B. Wiesner
By Daniel Lang: *Early Tales of the Atomic Age* (1948); *The Man in the Thick Lead Suit* (1954); *From Hiroshima to the Moon* (1959); *A Summer's Duckling* (juv.) (1963); *An Inquiry Into Enoughness* (1965); *Casualties of War* (1969); *Patriotism Without Flags* (1974); *A Backward Look* (1979).

James Lardner: Maurice Braddell

Ring Lardner: Beatrice Kaufman (satire)
By Ring W. Lardner: *Bib Ballads, You Know Me Al* (1915); *Gullible's Travels, Own Your Own Home* (1917); *Treat 'Em Rough* (1918); *The Young Immigrants* (1919); *Symptoms of Being 35, The Big Town* (1921); *How to Write Short Stories* (1924); *What of It?* (1925); *The Love Nest* (1926); *The Story of a Wonder Man, Round Up* (1929). Play: *June Moon* (with George S. Kaufman) (1929).

Andrea Lee: Luciano Bennetton

Margaret K. Leech: Alice Foote MacDougall, Elisabeth Marbury, Anne Morgan
By Margaret Kernochan Leech: *The Back of the Book* (1925); *Tim Wedding* (1926); *Anthony Comstock* (with Heywood Broun) (1927); *The Feathered Nest* (1928); *Reveille in Washington* (1941); *In the Days of McKinley* (1959).

George R. Leighton: Leo M. Cherne

Suzannah Lessard: Eva Zeisel

Newman Levy: Sam Feldman, Deems Taylor
By Newman Levy: *Twelve Hundred a Year* (with Edna Ferber) (1920); *Opera Guyed* (1923); *Gay But Wistful* (1925); *Saturday to Monday* (1930); *Theatre Guyed* (1933).

Sinclair Lewis: Effie Kayshus (pseud.) (satire)
Sinclair Lewis: See biographies by Oliver Harrison (1925); Mark Schorer (1961) and Vincent Sheean (1963).

A.J. Liebling: Terry de la Mesa Allen, Edward Arcaro, George Baker ("Father Divine") (with St. Clair McKelway), Anthony Joseph Dexter Biddle, Jr., Morris Bimstein, General Omar Nelson Bradley, Charles M. Beder, Jr., Philip Cochran, Martin A. Couney, Lew Dufour, Brendane Finucane, Clifford C. Fischer, Maurice-Gustave Gamelin, Augustine J. Grenet, George A, Hamid, Otto Abels Harbach, Roy Wilson Howard, Chich Johnson, Hymie Katz (pseud.), Bluch Landolf, Tim Mara, John Marin, George Catlett Marshall, George Nicholson, "Philadelphia" Jack O'Brien, Ole Olsen, William O'Rourke (pseud.), Joe Rogers, Jacob J. Shubert, Lee Shubert, John R. Stingo (pseud.), John W. Tiebor, John W. Tiebor, Jr., Roland Tiebor, Karl C. Warner, Izzy Yereshevsky
By Abbott Joseph Liebling: *Back Where I Came From* (1938); *The Telephone Booth Indian* (1942); *The Road Back to Paris* (1944); *Mink and Red Herring* (1949); ed. (with E.J. Sheffer) *La Republique du Silence* (1946); *The Republic of Silence* (1947); *The Wayward Pressman* (1947); *Chicago: Second City* (1952); *The Honest Rainmaker* (1953); *The Sweet Science* (1956); *Normandy Revisited* (1958); *The Earl of Louisiana* (1961); *The Press* (1961); *Between Meals* (1962).

Andy Logan: Howard Berkey Bishop, Isaac Fishberg, Vivian Kellems, Valentino Sarra, Wilma Soss

Lois Long: Hattie Carnegie

John McCarten: Earl Russell Browder, Helen Clay Frick, John C. Garland, Frank Hague (1938), Frederick Johnson, H. Kauffman & Sons Saddlery (with Robert Lewis Taylor), Nick Kenny, Clifford Odets

Dwight Macdonald: Roger Nash Baldwin, Alfred H. Barr, Jr., Dorothy Day, Eugene Gilbert, George Hervey Hallett, Jr., Leonor F. Loree, Daniel Persky, William Schlemmer, Richard Weil, Jr.
By Dwight Macdonald: *Henry Wallace: The Man and the Myth* (1948); *The Root in Man* (1953); *The Ford Foundation* (1956); *Against the American Grain: Essays in the Effects of Mass Culture* (1962); *Dwight Macdonald on Movies* (1969); *Politics Past* (1970); *Discriminations: Essays and Afterthoughts* (1938/74); ed., *Parodies, an Anthology From Chaucer to Beerbohm* (1960); *Selected Poems of Edgar Allen Poe* (1966).

W.O. McGeehan: Tex Rickard

Kenneth MacGowan: Samuel A. "Roxy" Rothafel, Joseph Urban, Dr. John B. Watson
By Kenneth MacGowan: *The Theatre of Tomorrow* (1921); *Continental Stagecraft* (1923); *Masks and Demons* (1923); *Footlights Across America* (1929), others.

James Kevin McGuinness: Jack Dempsey
By James Kevin McGuinness: *A Night at the Opera* (1935).

Milton MacKaye: Othmar Hermann Ammann, Joseph E. Corrigan, Edward Corsi, Paul Drennan Cravath, Thomas Darlington, Louis Michael Eilschemius, Joseph D. Goldrick, Frederick William Goudy, William Travers Jerome, Samuel Klein, George McClellan, Robert Moses (1934), Edward Pirce Mulrooney, Arthur Murray, Walter B. Pitkin, James Burton Pond, Franklin Delano Roosevelt (1931), Pauline Morton Sabin, Harold Vanderbilt
By Milton MacKaye: *Dramatic Crimes of 1927: A Study in Mystery and Detection* (1928); *Tin Box Parade: A Handbook for Larceny* (1934).

William Slavens McNutt: Sam Drebin
By William Slavens McNutt: *The Yanks Are Coming* (1918).

John McPhee: Arthur Ashe, Frank Learoyd Boyden, William Warren Bradley, David Brower, Floyd Dominy, Temple Hornaday Fielding, Charles Fraser, Euell Theophilus Gibbons, Clark Graebner, George Hartzog, Thomas P.F. Hoving, Charles Park, Carol Ruckdeschel, Theodore B. Taylor, Robert Twyman
By John McPhee: *A Sense of Where You Are* (1965); *The Pine Barrens* (1968); *The Crofter and the Laird* (1970); *The Survival of the Bark Canoe* (1975); *La Place de la Concorde Suisse* (1984); *Looking For a Ship* (1990); *Annals of the Former World* (1998), many others.

Janet Malcolm: Aaron Green, Ingrid Sischy

Russell Maloney: Paul Draper, Alfred Hitchcock, Leonard Lyons, J.B. Matheus, William Bayard Okie, Jr. (with Eugene Kinkead), Orson Welles, Monty Woolley
By Russell Maloney: *It's Still Maloney; or, Ten Years in the Big City* (1945); *Our Own Baedeker: From the* New Yorker (with Eugene Kinkead) (1947).

Morris Markey: Charles Lindbergh, Hubert Fauntleroy Julian
By Morris Markey: *The Band Plays Dixie* (1927); *That's New York* (1927); *This Country of Yours* (1932); *Manhattan Reporter* (1935); *Well Done!* (1945); *Unhurrying Chase* (1946); *Dr. Jeremiah* (1950).

John Stuart Martin: Mabel Walker Willebrandt

Peter Matthiessen: Cesar Chavez

Ved Mehta: Mohandas K. Gandhi, Amolak Ram Mehta, Shanti Devi Mehta, R.K. Narayan
By Ved Mehta: *Walking the Indian Streets* (1960); *Delinquent Chacha* (1967); *Daddyji* (1972); *New India* (1977); *Mamaji* (1979); *Vedi* (1982); *Ledge Between the Streams* (1984); *Stolen Light* (1989); *Up at Oxford* (1993); *Remembering Mr. Shawn's* New Yorker (1998), others.

Joseph Mitchell: Jane Barnell, Daniel J. Campion, High G. Flood, I. Arthur Ganger, Mazie Phillips Gordon, Joe Gould (1942, 1964), James Jefferson Davis Hall, George H. Hunter, Joe Madden, Louis Morino, Kate Smith, Ellery Franklin Thompson
By Joseph Mitchell: *My Ears Are Bent* (1938); *McSorley's Wonderful*

Saloon (1943); *Old Mr. Flood* (1948); *The Bottom of the Harbor* (1959/94); *Joe Gould's Secret* (1965/96); *Up in the Old Hotel and Other Stories* (1992).

Herbert Mitgang: Gene Robert LaRocque, Helen Wolf
By Herbert Mitgang: *Lincoln As They Saw Him* (1956); *The Return* (1959); *The Man Who Rode the Tiger: The Life and Times of Samuel Seabury* (1963); *Get These Men Out of the Hot Sun* (1972); *The Montauk Fault* (1981); *Working for the Reader* (1970); *Kings in the Counting House* (1983); *Dangerous Dossiers: The Secret War Against America's Authors* (1988); *Words Still Count With Me: A Chronicle of Literary Conversations* (1995). Editor, *The Letters of Carl Sandburg* (1968), *Selected Writings of Abraham Lincoln* (1992).

Alan Moorehead: Agnolo Ambrogini
By Alan Moorehead: *Mediterranean Front* (1942); *Montgomery* (1947); *The Rage of the Vulture* (1949); *Gallipoli* (1956); *Winston Churchill* (1960); *The White Nile* (1961); *The Blue Nile* (1962); *Cooper's Creek* (1963); *The Fatal Impact* (1966), others.

John Chapin Mosher: F. Scott Fitzgerald

Jack Murphy: Archibald Lee Moore

Mark Murphy: George Dudley Tilley, "Patsy" D'Agostino, Richard Olney Hart, Emery Andrew Rovenstein

John Newhouse: Lord Carrington, Roland Dumas, King Hussein of Jordan, David Steel, Margaret Thatcher
By John Newhouse: *Collision in Brussels: The Common Market Crisis of 30 June, 1965* (1967); *Cold Dawn: The Story of SALT* (1973/89); *War and Peace in the Nuclear Age* (1989); *Europe Adrift* (1997).

Hollister Noble: Arthur Bodanzky, Anthony Fokker (with Doreé Smedley), William James Henderson

Harvey O'Higgins: George Creel, Alice Duer Miller
By Harvey O'Higgins: *The Smoke Eaters* (1905); *Don-a-Dreams* (1906); *A Grand Army Man* (1908); *Old Clinkers* (1909); *The Beast and the Jungle* (with Judge Ben B. Lindsey) (1910); *Under the Prophet in Utah*

(wth Frank J. Cannon) (1912); *The Argyle Case* (with Harriet Ford) (1912); *The Dummy* (with Harriet Ford) (1913); *Polygamy* (1914); *Some Distinguished Americans* (1922), others.

J.J. O'Malley: George Gallup, William Colston Leigh (with Barbara Heggie)

Susan Orlean: Kwabena Oppong
By Susan Orlean: *Saturday Night* (1990); *The Orchid Thief* (1998).

Mollie Panter-Downes: Sir Stafford Cripps, Ninnette Da Valois, Robert Anthony Eden, E.M. Forster, Robert Mayer, Algernon Charles Swinburne, Fredrick James Marquis Woolton, 1st Baron
By Mollie Panter-Downes: *At the Pines: Swinburne and Watts-Dunton in Putney* (1971); *London War Notes, 1939-1945* (ed. William Shawn) (1971).

Barry Paris: Lina Basquette
By Barry Paris: *Louise Brooks* (1989); *Tony Curtis: The Autobiography* (with Tony Curtis) (1993); ed., *Stella Adler on Ibsen, Strindberg and Chekov* (1999).

Clare Peeler: Reinald Werrenrath

Creighton Peet: Halsey William Wilson

Brock Pemberton: William Childs (with Foster Ware), Joe Leblang
By Brock Pemberton: *Our Theatre Today* (1936); play, *Our Lady in Waiting* (with Antoinette Perry, based on Margery Sharp's *The Nutmeg Tree*) (1941).

Murdock Pemberton: Richard F. Bach, Walter L. Clark, Harry Kemp, Clinton Peters

David Plante: Steven Runciman

Fred Powledge: Charles Morgan, Jr.
By Fred Powledge: *Black Power/White Persistence: Notes on the New Civil War* (1967); *Model City: A Test of American Liberalism* (1970); *Mud Show: A Circus Season* (1976); *Journeys Through the South* (1979); *Fat of the Land* (1984); *We Shall Overcome: The Heroes of the Civil Rights Movement* (1993); *Pharmacy in the Forest* (1998).

Henry F. Pringle: Roger W. Babson, Harry Laity Bowlby, William E. Cashin, James Bryant Conant, Henry Hastings Curran, John Francis Curry, Lily Damita, Frank Hedley, Herbert Hoover, Miller Huggins, Charles Evans Hughes, John Kenlon, Fiorello La Guardia, Beatrice Lillie, Joseph Vincent McKee, Louis B. Mayer, Franklin Delano Roosevelt (1934), Elihu Root, Charles Emery Rosendahl, Nicholas M. Schenck, Elmer A. Sperry, Henry Lewis Stimson, Norman Thomas, Josef von Sternberg, Robert F. Wagner (1927)
By Henry Fowles Pringle: *Alfred E. Smith: A Critical Study* (1927); *Big Frogs* (1928); *Industrial Explorers* (with Maurice Holland) (1928); *Theodore Roosevelt, A Biography* (1931); *The Life and Times of William Howard Taft* (1939); *Pioneers in Philanthropy: A History of the General Education Board* (with Katharine Douglas) (1944).

Terry Ramsaye: George Eastman
By Terry Ramsaye (1885-1954): *A Million and One Nights* (1926).

Christopher Rand: Constantinos Doxiadis
By Christopher Rand: *Hong Kong* (1952); *A Nostalgia for Camels* (1957); *The Puerto Ricans* (1958); *Grecian Calendar* (1962); *Christmas in Bethlehem* (1963); *Cambridge U.S.A.* (1964); *Mountains and Water* (1965); *Los Angeles* (1967); *The Changing Landscape–Salisbury, Connecticut* (1968).

Herbert Reed: Bobby Jones, Edwin O. Leader, Devereaux Milburn

James Robbins: Charles Francis Adams

Robert Rice: Leonard Bernstein, David Warren Brubeck, Robert Joseph Cousy, Allen Balcolm Dumont, Andrew Gunnar Hagstrom, High K. Johnson, Lawrence Langer, Frank Charles Lauback, Mary Stinson Lord, Elaine May, Mitch Miller, Mike Nichols, William Rabkin, Branch Rickey, Anne Hone Rogers, Mort Sahl, Alexandra Lvovna Tolstoy

Arthur Robinson: Babe (George Herman) Ruth, Pee Wee (Charles Ellsworth) Russell

Joseph Roddy: Glenn Gould

Cameron Rogers: Raymond Ditmars, Paul Manship

Lillian Ross: Ingrid Bergman, Charlie Chaplin (1978), Katharine Cornell, Hume Cronyn, Abraham Ellis, Henry Fonda, Sidney Franklin, Sir John Gielgud, Cedric Hardwicke, William Holden, Akira Kurosawa, Walter Matthau, Zero Mostel, Geraldine Page, Anthony Perkins, Otto Preminger, Michael Redgrave, Jason Robards, Henry Jonas Rosenfeld, Maria Schell, Simone Signoret, Vladimir Sokoloff, Kim Stanley, Maureen Stapleton, Rod Steiger, Eli Wallach, Richard Widmark, Harry Winston
By Lillian Ross: *Picture* (1952); *Portrait of Hemingway* (1961); *Reporting* (1964); *Talk Stories* (1966); *Moments with Chaplin* (1980); *Takes: Stories from Talk of the Town* (1983); *Here But Not Here: A Love Story* (1998).

Virgilia Peterson Ross: Evangeline Booth

Berton Roueché: Frank Emerson Denison, Everett Joshua Edwards, Rev. Edward Thomas Hougen, Louis Haft, Elwood L. Schmidt
By Berton Roueché: *Black Weather* (1945); *Last Enemy* (1956); *The Delectable Mountains* (1959); *What's Left: Reports on a Diminishing America* (1969); *Desert and Plain/The Mountains and the River* (with David Plowden) (1975); *The Medical Detectives* (1980); *Special Places: In Search of Small Town America* (1982).

Richard H. Rovere: Edward Joseph Flynn, Bruno Furst, John Gunther, William F. Howe, Abraham H. Hummel, Peter J. McGuinnes, Newbold Morris, Henry Blackman Sell
By Richard H. Rovere: *Howe & Hummel: Their True and Scandalous History* (1947); *The General and the President* (with A.M. Schlesinger, Jr.) (1951); *Affairs of State: The Eisenhower Years* (1956); *Senator Joe McCarthy* (1959); *The American Establishment* (1962); *The Goldwater Caper* (1965); *Waist Deep in the Big Muddy* (1968); *Arrivals and Departures* (1976).

Helen Drees Ruttencutter: André Previn; The Guarneri Quartet: Arnold Steinhardt, John Dalley, Michael Tree and David Soyer
By Helen Drees Ruttencutter: *Previn* (1985).

G.F.T. Ryall: Hirsch Jacobs, Alfred Gwynne Vanderbilt, Jr., Joseph E. Widener
By George F.T. Ryall: *Beautiful Hialeah* (with Bert Clark Thayer) (1938).

César Saerchinger: Artur Schnabel

Pitts Sanborn: Maria Jeritza
By Pitts Sanborn: *The Metropolitan Book of the Opera* (1937); *Beethoven* (1951).

Winthrop Sargeant: Richard Avedon, Sarah Caldwell, Giuseppe Cipriani, John Crosby, Vittorio De Sica, Eileen Farrell, Enzo Ferrari, William Francis Gibbs, Marilyn Horne, Susanne K. Langer, Rosina Lhevinne, Margaret Mead, Zubin Mehta, Gian Carlo Menotti, Yehudi Menuhin, Sherrill Milnes, Marianna Moore, Pier Luigi Nervi, Birgit Nilsson, Richard Rogers (1961), Glynn Ross, Julius Rudel, Count Guido Chigi Saracini, Beverly Sills, Georg Solti, Edward D. Stone, Teresa Stratas, Joan Sutherland, Daisetz Teitaro Suzuki, Barry Tuckwell, Shirley Verrett, Herbert von Karajan
By Winthrop Sargeant: *Jazz: Hot and Hybrid* (1938); *Genuises, Goddesses and People* (1946); *Listening to Music* (1958); *In Spite of Myself: A Personal Memoir* (1970); *Divas: Impressions of Today's Sopranos* (1973); *The Bhagavad Ghita, an Interlinear Translation* (1979).

Jane Sayre: Daniel Carter Beard

Joel Sayre: John J. Broderick, John Cordes, John "Jack Legs" Diamond, James Joy Johnson, Jim Londos, Chick Meehan
By Joel Sayre: *Persian Gulf Command: Some Travels on the Road to Kazvin* (1945); screenplay for William Faulkner's *The Road to Glory.*

Gilbert Seldes: "Diamond Jim" James Buchanan Brady, George M. Cohan, Emil Coleman, Merian C. Cooper, Katherine Cornell, Donald Desky, Walt Disney, Henry Dreyfuss, John Hays Hammond, Robert Edmond Jones, Gaston Lachaise, Walter Dorwin Teague, Florenz Ziegfeld
By Gilbert Vivian Seldes: *The Seven Lively Arts* (1924); *The Stammering Century* (1928); *The Movies and the Talkies* (1929); *The Wings of the Eagle* (1929); adaptation of *Lysistrata* (1930); *The Years of the Locust* (1933); *Mainland* (1936); *Movies for the Millions* (1937); *Your Money and Your Life* (1938); *Proclaim Liberty* (1942); ed., *The Portable Ring Lardner* (1946); *The Great Audience* (1950); *Writing for Television* (1952); *The Public Arts* (1956), murder mysteries as "Foster Johns". See biography by Michael G. Kammen (1996).

Fred C. Shapiro: Judge Bruce McMarion Wright

Robert Shaplen: Avery Brundage, John Moors Cabot, Robert Whittle Dowling, Arthur Joseph Goldberg, David Newsom, Sirdar Jagjit Singh, Bruce Smith
By Robert Modell Shaplen: *A Corner of the World* (1949); *Free Love and Heavenly Sinners* (1954); *A Forest of Tigers* (1956); *Kreuger: Genius and Swindler* (1960); *The Lost Revolution* (1965); *The Road From War* (rev. 1971); *A Turning Wheel* (1979); *Bitter Victory* (1986).

A.H. Shaw: Albert C. Barnes

Susan Sheehan: Carmen Santana
By Susan Sheehan: *Ten Vietnamese* (1967); *A Welfare Mother* (from *New Yorker* Profile) (1976); *A Prison and a Prisoner* (1978); *Is There No Place on Earth For Me?* (1982); *Kate Quinton's Days* (1984); *A Missing Plane* (1986); *Life For Me Ain't Been No Crystal Stair* (1993).

Robert E. Sherwood: Cecil B. De Mille, Harold Lloyd
By Robert Emmett Sherwood: Plays: *The Road to Rome* (1927); *The Queen's Husband* (1928); *Waterloo Bridge* (1929); *This is New York* (1930); *Reunion in Vienna* (1931); *Acropolis* (1933); *The Petrified Forest* (1934); *Idiot's Delight* (1936); *Abe Lincoln in Illinois* (1938); *There Shall Be No Night* (1940); *The Rugged Path* (1945); *Miss Liberty* (1949). Novel: *The Virtuous Knight* (1931). Biography: *Roosevelt and Hopkins* (1948).

Ik Shuman: John Gillhaus

Robert Alfred Simon: Edward Johnson, Channing Lefebvre, Lawrence Mervil Tibbett
By Robert Alfred Simon: trans. Arthur Schnitzler's *Fraulein Else* (1925); *The New York Wits* (1927).

Lola Jean Simpson: Dr. Alfred Adler

Mark Singer: Goodman Ace, W. Graham Arader III, Sam Cohn, Rubin Levine, Gordon Manning, Errol Morris, Benjamin Shine, Gene Stipe

L.E. Sissman: Dick Cavett
By Louis Edward Sissman: *Dying: An Introduction* (1968); *Scattered Returns* (1969); *Pursuit of Honor* (1971); *Innocent Bystanders* (1975).

Alison Smith: Fritzi Scheff
By Alison Smith: *The Victorian Nude* (1996); *Agnés Varda* (1998).

Helena Huntington Smith: Roy Chapman Andrews, Leopold Auer, Ralph Adams Cram, John Erskine, William Joseph Finn, Edwin Goodman, Jascha Heifetz, Mr. and Mrs. John D. Hertz, Fritz Kreisler, Lewis E. Lawes, Adolphe Menjou, Ignace Padarewski, Emily Post, Charles Ringling, Eleanor Roosevelt (1930), George J. Ryan, Margaret Sanger (1930), Ernestine Schumann-Heink, Elinor Smith, Gloria Swanson, Lillian D. Wald, Helen Newington Wills, Milton C. Work
By Helena Huntington Smith: *We Pointed Them North* (with Edward Charles Abbott) (1939); *A Bride Goes West* (with Nannie T. Alderson) (1942/69).

Earl Sparling: Bill Brown
By Earl Sparling : *Kreuger's Billion Dollar Bubble* (1932).

Henry Anton Steig: Benny Goodman (1937), Ben Stein

James Stevenson: Robert Allen Ackerman, John Carpenter, Max Furman, Edward M. Kennedy (1975, 1979), Bernard Meltzer, Patrick Oliphant, Vince Scully, Gordon Willis

Avery Strakosch: Abraham Rosenbach

Thomas Sugrue: Cardinal Patrick Joseph Hayes
By Thomas Sugrue: *Such is the Kingdom* (1940); *A Catholic Speaks His Mind* (1952), others.

Jo Swerling: Helena Rubenstein, Louis "Frisco" Josephs
By Joseph Swerling: *Guys and Dolls* (libretto, with Abe Burrows) (1950).

Bernard Taper: Charles Abrams, George Balanchine, Pablo Casals

Deems Taylor: Walter Damrosch
By (Joseph) Deems Taylor: *Of Men and Music* (1937); *The Well-Tempered Listener* (1940); *Music to My Ears* (1949), others. Composer: *Processional* (1914); *Portrait of a Lady* (rhapsody for small orch.) (1919); *Fantasy on Two Themes* (1925/43); *The King's Henchman* (opera, book by Edna St. Vincent Millay) (1927) *Peter Ibbetson* (opera) (1931); *Christmas Overture* (1943); *Elegy for Orchestra* (1944); *Restoration* (suite for orch.) (1950); *The Dragon* (1954); others.

Robert Lewis Taylor: Richard S. Aldrich, Paul Dean Arnold, Charles Atlas, Richard Barstow, Pierre Brunet, John Dickson Carr, Bobby (Robert Edwin) Clark, Antoinette and Arthur Concello, Joshua Lionel Cowen, Samuel J. Crumbine, Luis de Florez, Michael Joseph Delehanty, Nate Eagle, Rosalie Barrow Edge, Merle Evans, Joe Falcaro, Robert J. Flaherty, Percy Grainger, Cecil Green, Bryan Hannon, William Fredrick Hoppe, Jacques Andre Istel, H. Kauffman & Sons Saddlery (with John

McCarten), Elisha Keeler, Murray Korman, Lillian (Alize) Leitzel, Bernarr Macfadden, Larry MacPhail, Alfred Meyer, Annie Nathan Meyer, Florence Meyer, Eugene Francis Moran, John Ringling North, Louis Pagliaro, Ernest Henry Peabody, Arthur K. Pope, Erno Rapee (with Barbara Heggie), George Santelli, Artie Shaw, Samuel Slotkin, Frank Stanton, Vilhjalmur Stefansson, John J. Teal, Jr., Pat Valdo, Mickey Walker, Patrick Walsh, Phil Watson
By Robert Lewis Taylor: *Doctor, Lawyer, Merchant, Chief* (1948); *W.C. Fields: His Follies and Fortunes* (1949); *Winston Churchill: An Informal Study of Greatness* (1952/62); *Center Ring: The People of the Circus* (1956); *The Travels of Jaimie McPheeters* (1958); *A Journey to Matecumbe* (1961); *All in Love* (1962); *Two Roads to Guadelupe* (1964); *Vessel of Wrath: The Life and Times of Carry Nation* (1966); *A Roaring in the Wind* (1978).

Mary van Rensselear Thayer: Albert Morris Bagby
By Mary van Rensselear Thayer: *Hui-Lan Koo, an Autobiography* (as told by Madame Wellington Koo) (1943); *Jacqueline Bouvier Kennedy* (1961).

Charles Willis Thompson: William Jennings Bryan
By Charles Willis Thompson: *Woman Voter* (1918); *Presidents I've Known and Two Near-Presidents* (1929); *The Fiery Epoch, 1830-1877* (1931).

James Thurber: Myron T. Herrick, Elliot Vereker (fictional)
James Grover Thurber (1894-1961). Writer, cartoonist, playwright. See biographies by Burton Bernstein (1975), Robert Emmet Long (1988), Neil A. Grauer (1994) and Harrison Kinney (1995).

Calvin Tomkins: Jennifer Bartlett, Romare Bearden, Rosamond Bernier, John M. Brealey, John Cage, Leo castelli, Julia Child, Merce Cunningham, Marcel Duchamp, Richard Buckminster Fuller, Henry Geldzahler, Tatyana Grosman, Eric Hoffer, Pontus Hulten, Philip Johnson, Joe Levine, Richard Lippold, Charles Ludlam, Jnas Mekas, Gerald and Sara Murphy, Michale Murphy, Nam June Paik, Georgia O'Keeffe (1974), Claes Oldenburg, Betty Parsons, John R. Pierce, Robert Rauschenberg, William S. Rubin, Frank Stella, Paul Strand, Jean Tinguely, Robert Wilson

By Calvin Tomkins: *The Bride and the Bachelors* (1965); *Merchants and Masterpieces* (1970); *Living Well is the Best Revenge* (1971); *Off the Wall* (1980); *Post- to Neo-* (1988); *Alex: The Life of Alexander Liberman* (with Dodie Kazanjian) (1993); *Duchamp: A Biography* (1997).

Calvin Trillin: Edna Buchanan
By Calvin Trillin: *An Education in Georgia* (1964); *U.S. Journal* (1971); *American Fried* (1971); *Runestruck* (1977); *Alice, Let's Eat* (1978); *Uncivil Liberties* (1982); *Travels With Alice* (1989); *Deadline Poet* (1994); *Family Man* (1998), others.

George W.S. Trow, Jr.: Ahmet Ertegun, Kal Rudman

J.R. Tunis: Jean Borotra, Henri Cochet, Red (Harold E.) Grange, Betty Nuthall, René Lacoste, Bunny (Elizabeth) Ryan
By John R. Tunis: *Sport for the Fun of It: A Handbook* (1940/50); *Democracy and Sport* (1941); *Million-Miler: The Story of an Air Pilot* (1942); *A Measure of Independence* (1964); *His Enemy, His Friend* (1967); juvenile books *Young Razzle* (1949); *Schoolboy Johnson* (1958) and *Silence Over Dunkerque* (1962).

Ferdinand Tuohy: Jo Davidson, Sacha Guitry, Suzanne Lenglen, Yvonne Printemps
By Ferdinand Tuohy: *The Secret Corps: A Tale of "Intelligence" on All Fronts* (1920); *Occupied, 1918-1930: A Postscript to the Western Front* (1931); *Inside Dope* (1934), *Twelve Lances for Liberty* (1940).

Kenneth Tynan: Louise Brooks, Mel Brooks, Johnny Carson, Sir Ralph Richardson, Tom Stoppard, Nicol Williamson
By Kenneth Tynan: *Alec Guinness* (1953); *Bull Fever* (1955); *Curtains* (1961); *The Sound of Two Hands Clapping* (1975/82); *Show People: Profiles in Entertainment* (1980).

Sanderson Vanderbilt: Arthur Walsh

C. Lester Walker: Hannes Schneider

Foster Ware: William Childs (with Brock Pemberton), Nelson Doubleday, John J. Kiely, Dr. James H. Kimball, Charles Lanier Lawrence, Charles Vincent Paterno

Richard F. Warner: Bruce Barton, George Upton Harvey

Joseph Wechsberg: Franz Allers, Robert Bellet, Rudolf Bing, Willy Brandt, Leo Cesoli, Alexandre Dumaine, Abe Feder, Fritz Frey, Raymond D. Gaston, Hermann Gmeiner, Leopold Godowsky, Michel Guérard, Emil Herrmann, Alexis Lichine, George London, Leopold Ludwig, Raffaele Mattioli, Otto Molden, Maurice Pate, Helmit Qualtinger, Artur Rubinstein, Henri Soulé, Siegmund G. Warburg

By Joseph Wechsberg: *Looking for a Bluebird* (1948); *Homecoming* (1946); *Sweet and Sour* (1948); *The Continental Touch* (1948); *Blue Trout and Black Truffles* (1953); *The Self-Betrayed* (1955); *Avalanche* (1958); *Red Plush and Black Velvet* (1961); *Dining at the Pavilion* (1962); *The Best Things in Life* (1964); *Journey Through the Land of Eloquent Silence* (1964); *The Merchant Bankers* (1966); *Vienna, My Vienna* (1968); *The Voices* (1969); *The First Time Around* (1970); *Prague, the Mystical City* (1971); *The Opera* (1972); *The Glory of the Violin* (1972); *The Waltz Emperors* (1973); *Verdi* (1974); *Dream Towns of Europe* (1976); *In Leningrad* (1977); *Schubert* (1977); *The Vienna I Knew* (1979); *The Lost World of the Great Spas* (1979).

William Weimar: Giuseppe Mario Bellanca, John McEntee Bowman

William Wertenbaker: Maurice Ewing
By William Wertenbaker: *The Floor of the Sea: Maurice Ewing and the Search to Understand the Earth* (1974).

Victor Weybright: Ralph C. Tobin
By Victor Weybright: *Spangled Banner* (1935); *The Americas: South and North* (1940); *Buffalo Bill and the Wild West* (with Henry B. Sell) (1955); *The Making of a Publisher* (1967).

Rogers E.M. Whitaker: Eddie Condon
By Rogers E.M. Whitaker: *All Aboard with E.M. Frimbo, World's Greatest Railroad Buff* (with Anthony Hiss) (1974).

E.B. White: Elinor Wylie (in verse)
Elwyn Brooks White: See biography by Scott Elledge (1984).

William C. White: Peter Bogdanov

Thomas Whiteside: Ted Adams, Henrik Kurt Carlsen, Daniel Fraad, Jr., Fred W. Friendly, Dave Garroway, Ralph Nader, Sylvester L. Weaver, Jr.

Howard Whitman: Jack Kapp

William Whitworth: David Brinkley, Joe Franklin, Bernie Glow, Chet Huntley, Dave Lefkowitz, Roger Miller, Paul Mole, Col. Harland Sanders, Richard M. Scammon, Homer A. Tomlinson

Paul Wilkes: Joseph Greer

Alec Wilkinson: Garland Bunting, John Cronin
By Alec Wilkinson: *Midnights: A Year with the Wellfleet Police* (1982); *Moonshine: A Life in Pursuit of White Liquor* (1985); *Big Sugar: Seasons in the Cane Fields of Florida* (1989).

Edmund Wilson: Edmund Wilson
Edmund Wilson, prolific writer and critic. See autobiographical works *The Twenties* (1975) and *The Thirties* (1980).

Herbert Warren Wind: Karl Friedrich Baedeker, Robert Russell Bennet, John Mason Brown, Wallace Kirkman Harrison, Robert Trent Jones, Hazel Hotchkiss Wightman, P.G. Wodehouse
By Herbert Warren Wind: *The Story of American Golf* (1948; rev. 1956, 1975); *The Modern Fundamentals of Golf* (with Ben Hogan) (1957); *The Greatest Game of All* (with Jack Nicklaus) (1969); *Game, Set and Match* (1979); *Following Through* (1985).

John K. Winkler: Clarence Dillon, Mary Garden, Edward Howland Robinson Green, William Randolph Hearst, Nicholas Longworth, Marie of Roumania, Alexander Pollock Moore, John Pierpont Morgan, John D. Rockefeller, Sr., John D. Rockefeller, Jr., Charles M. Schwab, William Tatem Tilden

By John K. Winkler: *Hearst: An American Phenomenon* (1928); *John D.: A Portrait in Oils* (1929); *Morgan the Magnificent* (1930); *Incredible Carnegie* (1931); *Woodrow Wilson: The Man Who Lives On* (1933); *The First Billion: The Stillmans and the National City Bank* (1934); *The du Pont Dynasty* (1935); *Five and Ten: The Fabulous Life of F.W. Woolworth* (1940); *Tobacco Tycoon: The Story of James Buchanan Duke* (1942); *William Randolph Hearst, A New Appraisal* (1955).

Thyra Samter Winslow: Mae West
By Thyra Samter Winslow: *Picture Frames* (1923); *Show Business* (1926); *People Round the Corner* (1927); *Blueberry Pie* (1932); *My Own, My Native Land* (1939); *Chorus Girl* (1945); *Window Panes* (1946); *The Sex Without Sentiment* (1954).

Robert Wohlforth: James Weldon Johnson

Charles W. Wood: Bishop William Montgomery Brown

George Woodward: Joseph P. Prendiville

W.E. Woodward: Sinclair Lewis (1934)
By William E. Woodward: *Bunk* (1923); *Lottery* (1924); *Bread and Circuses* (1925); *George Washington–The Image and the Man* (1926); *Meet General Grant* (1928); *Money for Tomorrow* (economics) (1932); *Evelyn Prentice* (1933); *A New American History* (1936); *Lafayette* (biography) (1938); *The Way Our People Lived* (1944); *Tom Paine–America's Godfather* (1945); *The Gift of Life* (autobiography) (1947); *Years of Madness* (1951). Collaborator: *Crowded Years,* memoirs of William Gibbs McAdoo (1931).

Alexander Woollcott: Marc Connelly, Noel Coward, Benjamin Ficklin Finney, Jr., Emmanuel Haldeman-Julius, Jack Humphrey, Edwin Leland James, George S. Kaufman, Rudolf Kommer, Charles Gordon MacArthur, Harpo Marx, Lloyd Paul Stryker, Carl Vatell Van Anda, Frank Lloyd Wright, Sam Zolotow
By Alexander Woollcott: *Mrs. Fiske–Her Views on Acting* (1917); *Actors and the Problems of the Stage* (1917); *Shouts and Murmurs* (1923); *Mr. Dickens Goes to the Play* (1923); *Enchanted Aisles* (1924); *The Story of Irving Berlin* (1925); *Going to Pieces* (1928); *Two Gentlemen and a Lady* (1928); *While Rome Burns* (1934); *The*

Woollcott Reader (1935); *Woollcott's Second Reader* (1937). Woollcott performed several times on Broadway, most famously as the loosely biographical Sheridan Whiteside in the comedy *The Man Who Came to Dinner* (1940) by George C. Kaufman and Moss Hart. See biographies by Samuel Hopkins Adams (1945), Edwin Palmer Hoyt (1973) and Howard Teichmann (1976).

BOOKS ABOUT *THE NEW YORKER*

Adler, Renata. *Gone: The Last Days of* The New Yorker. New York: Simon & Schuster, 2000.

Corey, Mary F. *The World Through a Monocle:* The New Yorker *at Midcentury.* Cambridge, Mass.: Harvard University Press, 1999.

Gill, Brendan. *Here at* The New Yorker. New York: Da Capo, 1997 (orig. published 1975).

Grant, Jane C. *Ross,* The New Yorker *and Me.* New York: Reynal, 1968.

Kahn, E.J., Jr. *About* The New Yorker *and Me: A Sentimental Journal.* New York: Putnam, 1979.

____. *Year of Change: More About* The New Yorker *and Me.* New York: Viking: 1988.

Kunkel, Thomas. *Genius in Disguise: Harold Ross of* The New Yorker. New York: Random House, 1995.

____, ed. *Letters From the Editor:* The New Yorker's *Harold Ross.* New York: Modern Library, 2000.

Mehta, Ved. *Remembering Mr. Shawn's New Yorker: The Invisible Art of Editing.* Woodstock, N.Y.: Overlook Press, 1998.

Remnick, David, ed.. *Profiles from* The New Yorker. New York: Random House, 2000.

Ross, Lillian. *Here But Not Here: A Love Story.* New York: Random House, 1998.

Thurber, James. *The Years with Ross.* New York: Penguin, 1984 (orig. published 1959).

Yagoda, Ben. *About Town:* The New Yorker *and the World It Made.* New York: Scribner, 2000.